Logo

MIT Logo for the Apple
(Terrapin/Krell)

Benjamin/Cummings Series in Structured Programming

R. Billstein, S. Libeskind, J. Lott
MIT Logo for the Apple (1985)

R. Billstein, S. Libeskind, J. Lott
Apple Logo (1985)

G. Booch
Software Engineering with Ada (1983)

D.M. Etter
Structured FORTRAN 77 for Engineers and Scientists (1983)

D.M. Etter
Problem Solving with Structured FORTRAN 77 (1984)

D.M. Etter
WATFIV: Structured Programming and Problem Solving (1985)

P. Helman, R. Veroff
Intermediate Problem Solving and Data Structures (1985)

A. Kelley, I. Pohl
A Book on C (1984)

M. Kittner, B. Northcutt
BASIC: A Structured Approach (1985)

W. Savitch
Pascal Programming: An Introduction to the Art and Science of Programming (1984)

For more information, call toll-free: (800) 227-1936 (USA),
(800) 982-6140 (CA), or write to the publisher.

Logo

MIT Logo for the Apple (Terrapin/Krell)

Rick Billstein
Shlomo Libeskind
Johnny W. Lott

University of Montana
Missoula, Montana

The Benjamin/Cummings Publishing Company, Inc.
Menlo Park, California • Reading, Massachusetts • Don Mills, Ontario
Wokingham, U.K. • Amsterdam • Sydney • Singapore
Tokyo • Mexico City • Bogota • Santiago • San Juan

To Esther, Jane, Molly, and Karly   R.W.B.
To Ran and Nureet   S.L.
To Warren, Ouidamai, Carolyn, and John   J.W.L.

Sponsoring Editor: Alan Apt
Production Editor: Wendy Earl
Copy Editors: Lisa Yount and Harry Henderson
Interior and Cover Design: Michael Rogondino
Production Design: Victoria Philp
Technical Art: Linda Harris-Sweezy
Composition: Graphic Typesetting Service

Library of Congress Cataloging in Publication Data
Billstein, Rick.
   Logo: MIT Logo for the Apple (Terrapin/Krell)
1. LOGO (Computer program language) 2. Apple computer
—Programming.   I. Libeskind, Shlomo. II. Lott,
Johnny W., 1944-.   III. Title.
QA76.73.L63B55 1985   001.64'24   84-24229
ISBN 0-8053-0860-1

ABCDEFGHIJ-AL-898765

The Benjamin/Cummings Publishing Company, Inc.
2727 Sand Hill Road
Menlo Park, California 94025

Preface

The Logo language has been greeted with a great deal of enthusiasm because of its ease of use and potential as a powerful introductory programming language. There have been a large number of Logo books written with the novice in mind. We wrote this book not only to teach novices how to program in Logo but also to offer exciting advanced applications of Logo to intermediate and advanced Logo programmers. Our primary goals have been:

1. To present an introduction to Logo that is enjoyable and accessible for readers without previous background in computers, yet comprehensive enough to include problems and topics for readers who want to learn and use more advanced features of the language.

2. To teach problem solving techniques as an integral part of the text.

3. To provide unique, optional mathematical applications of Logo for interested readers while keeping the book accessible to readers with little mathematical background.

4. To encourage readers to investigate, try new ideas, and learn from them.

5. To help readers experience the joy of exploration and discovery in Logo.

Special Features

New Vocabulary/Reference To make the book easy to use when readers are programming, each chapter is preceded by a single page listing the new terms, commands, and keys introduced in that chapter, along with a page reference for each. In addition, each new term is highlighted in boldface type and also appears in the margin for easy reference when it is first defined in the text.

Mathematical Aside Mathematical derivations or explanations are boxed under this heading. They may be studied by the interested reader, or they may be skipped. This should be of keen interest to teachers or students who wish to use Logo to develop creative solutions to mathematical problems.

Summary of Commands Each section ends with a boxed summary of Logo commands introduced in that section, including a brief explanation of the commands and their use.

Problem Sets The end of each section includes a problem set with a variety of problems for practice and exploration. Stars (☆) indicate challenging problems.

Chapter Problem Sets Each chapter ends with a problem set based on the material presented in the whole chapter.

Glossary Includes an alphabetical list of Logo commands with definitions and examples of their use. Also includes a summary of common error messages.

Bibliography Includes a list of related textbooks and articles on Logo.

Games and Answers Disk The text comes with a disk that contains six games written in Logo. No previous knowledge of Logo is required to play these games. The games are intended to be entertaining and also to demonstrate some of the powerful properties of Logo. The disk also contains answers to most odd-numbered problems.

Appendix Includes documentation for the Games and Answers disk. Additional projects, modifications of the games, and new games are suggested in the Appendix.

The Instructor's Guide Includes solutions to even-numbered as well as odd-numbered problems.

Problem Solving Each chapter begins with a preliminary problem that poses a question students can answer after mastering the material in the chapter. The last section in each chapter gives a solution to the preliminary problem, using the following four steps based on George Polya's work in mathematical problem solving:

Understanding the Problem
Devising a Plan
Carrying Out the Plan
Looking Back

In *Understanding the Problem* we restate the problem as clearly as possible. We ask ourselves such questions as: What is the goal; what information do we obtain from the problem; what information, if any, is needed but is missing.

In *Devising a Plan* we use a variety of strategies, including the following: Examine related problems and determine whether the same techniques can be applied to this one; examine a simpler case of the problem to gain insight into the solution of the original problem; use trial and error; identify any necessary subgoals.

In *Carrying Out the Plan* we combine the steps developed in Devising a Plan into a computer procedure.

In *Looking Back* we check our work; explore whether there are different or more efficient techniques for solving the problem; and look for related or more general questions that could be explored.

Other problems in the text are introduced under the heading "Problem." They also are solved using the Polya approach, although the four subheadings are omitted.

We have tried to introduce most of the material in the text in the problem-solving spirit. As much as possible we tried to motivate each step in writing a procedure so that the reader is aware of the purpose of each step and why the step brings us closer to the goal.

Content

We have written the book so that the material could be used by students with diverse backgrounds and needs. We have included enough topics to allow instructors to adapt the text to a variety of audiences and course lengths. Section 6-5, preceded by an asterisk (*), is optional and can be omitted without loss of continuity. The chapters cover the following topics:

Chapter 0   History and Philosophy. Discusses the origins of Logo, its aims and features.

Chapter 1   Logo: A Beginning. Introduces the basic Logo commands and keys, the turtle, and basic arithmetic operations.

Chapter 2   Teaching the Turtle. Introduces the edit mode and shows how to teach the computer new words called procedures that it can understand and act upon.

Chapter 3   Procedures with Variables. Introduces the concept of a variable or variables in a procedure.

Chapter 4   Recursive Procedures. Introduces recursion, one of Logo's most interesting and powerful features.

Chapter 5   The Coordinated Turtle. Introduces commands for using the turtle with coordinates. The chapter discusses procedures to do some geometrical constructions and tessellations.

Chapter 6   Using Arithmetic Operations in Procedures. Introduces additional arithmetic commands and uses them to solve both arithmetic and geometric problems.

Chapter 7   Application of Turtle Graphics. Deals with experiments in which the turtle simulates simple animal-like behavior; examines procedures for writing games and using the Logo Shape Editor.

Chapter 8   An Introduction to List Processing. Introduces commands for manipulating words and sentences and applies them to different problems.

Special Acknowledgment

We wish to acknowledge the work of Ran Libeskind-Hadas on this text. He had the primary role in the writing of Chapter 7 and the preparation of the games and answers disk.

Acknowledgments

We would like to thank the students we have taught over the past several years for their patience, suggestions, and enthusiasm as we have class-tested this text. Our sincere thanks also go to our editor, Alan Apt, whose encouragement, dedication, and ability to make decisive judgments helped us bring the book to its present form. We also appreciate the help we received from Alan Apt's assistant, Mary Ann Telatnik. Finally, we would like to thank the staff at Benjamin/Cummings—in particular, Wendy Earl—for their hard work in preparing this book.

Rick Billstein
Shlomo Libeskind
Johnny W. Lott

Missoula, Montana

Contents

Chapter 0   History and Philosophy   1

Chapter 1   Logo: A Beginning   7

Preliminary Problem   8

Introduction   9
1-1   The Nodraw Mode   10
         Starting Logo   10
         Stopping Logo   10
         Entering the Nodraw Mode   11
         Introducing the PRINT Command   11
         Problem Set 1-1   14

1-2   Meet the Turtle   15
         Entering the Draw Mode   15
         Format for Turtle Commands   16
         Turtle Heading   18
         Problem 1-1   19
         Clearing the Screen and Homing the Turtle   20
         Using the SPLITSCREEN, FULLSCREEN, and TEXTSCREEN
              Commands   20
         The Wrap and Nowrap Modes   21
         Creating Drawings with the Turtle   21
         Introducing the REPEAT Command   23
         Stopping Execution   23
         Problem 1-2   24
         Problem Set 1-2   26
         Games Disk Activity   30

1-3   Arithmetic Operations   30
         Problem Set 1-3   31

Solution to the Preliminary Problem   32

Chapter 1 Problem Set   35

Chapter 2   Teaching the Turtle   37

Preliminary Problem   38

Introduction   39

2-1   The Edit Mode   39
          Entering the Edit Mode   40
          The END Command   43
          Long Command Lines   43
          Problem 2-1   44
          Editing Procedures   44
          Drawing An Equilateral Triangle   46
          Problem Set 2-1   48

2-2   More on the Editor and Workspace Management   51
          Defining Several Procedures   51
          Editing Several Procedures   52
          Examining the Workspace   53
          Eliminating Procedures   54
          Problem Set 2-2   57

2-3   Using Procedures as Building Blocks   58
          Breaking Projects Down into Steps   58
          Problem 2-2   63
          Error Messages   65
          Problem Set 2-3   68

2-4   Creating Files on a Disk   70
          Caring for Your Disk   71
          Cataloging the Disk   71
          Saving Files on Disk   72
          Reading Files from the Disk   73
          Adding Procedures to a File   74
          Saving and Reading Pictures on a Disk   74
          Erasing Files and Pictures   75
          Problem Set 2-4   76

Solution to the Preliminary Problem   77

Chapter 2 Problem Set   82

Chapter 3   Procedures with Variables   85

Preliminary Problem   86

Introduction   87

3-1   Procedures with Variables 87
Introducing a Variable 87
Using Variables with Procedures Calling Procedures 90
Using Arithmetic with Variables 91
Problem 3-1 92
Procedures with Several Variables 93
Local Variables 94
Debugging Commands: TRACE and NOTRACE 96
Debugging Commands: PAUSE, CONTINUE, and CTRL-Z 98
Problem Set 3-1 100

3-2   The Turtle Takes a Trip 102
Problem 3-2 104
Procedures for Drawing Polygons 105
Problem 3-3 107
Problem Set 3-2 108

3-3   Procedures for Circles and Arcs 109
Logo Circles 109
Drawing Circles Faster 110
Drawing Arcs 111
Problem 3-4 112
Drawing a Circle with a Given Radius 113
Problem Set 3-3 114

3-4   Programming with Color 117
Erasing Drawings 118
The RANDOM Command 118
Problem Set 3-4 121

Solution to the Preliminary Problem 122

Chapter 3 Problem Set 127

Chapter 4   Recursive Procedures 129

Preliminary Problem 130

Introduction 131

4-1   POLY and Other Recursive Procedures 131
Tail-end Recursion 131
The POLY Procedure 132
POLYSPI: A Variation of the POLY Procedure 134
The IF and STOP Commands 135

Problem 4-1   137
Problem Set 4-1   140

4-2   Other Ways to Stop Recursion   143
Stopping POLY When the Turtle's Initial Heading Is Not
Known   145
The POLYROLL Procedure   147
Logo Words, the MAKE Statement, and Global
Variables   149
Problem Set 4-2   152

4-3   Further Variations on the POLY Procedure   154
Problem Set 4.3   158

4-4   Embedded Recursion   158
Other Examples of Embedded Recursion   164
Problem Set 4-4   166

Solution to the Preliminary Problem   170

Chapter 4 Problem Set   172

Chapter 5   The Coordinated Turtle   177

Preliminary Problem   178
Introduction   179

5-1   Coordinating the Turtle   179
Problem 5-1   182
Using SETXY to Draw Line Segments   184
Finding the Length of a Line Segment   184
Using Coordinates with Circle Procedures   190
Problem 5-2   191
Problem 5-3   192
Problem Set 5-1   196

5-2   Constructing the Triangles with the Turtle   196
Constructing a Triangle Using SAS   197
Constructing a Triangle Using ASA   199
Writing a Continuous Checking Procedure   200
Constructing a Triangle Using SSS   203
Problem Set 5-2   208

5-3   Strips and Tessellations   210
Tessellating with Squares   219
Tessellating with Triangles   219

Tessellating with Hexagons 223
Problem Set 5-3 225

Solution to the Preliminary Problem 227

Chapter 5 Problem Set 231

Chapter 6   Using Arithmetic Operations in Procedures 233

Preliminary Problem 234

Introduction 235

6-1   Arithmetic Operations Revisited 235
Operations on Real Numbers 236
Problem 6-1 238
Problem Set 6-1 240

6-2   Arithmetic Procedures 241
Problem 6-2 243
Problem 6-3 247
Problem Set 6-2 250

6-3   More Recursive Procedures Involving Arithmetic 252
Arithmetic and Geometric Sequences 254
Problem 6-4 264
The Fibonacci Sequence 255
Problem 6-5 256
Determining Whether a Number Is Prime 257
Finding the LCM of Two Positive Integers 260
Problem Set 6-3 261

6-4   Random Numbers 263
Coin Tossing Simulation 264
The Use of the RANDOM Primitive in Turtle Graphics 266
Problem Set 6-4 268

*6-5   Mathematics of the POLY Procedure 270
Problem 6-6 271
Finding the Number of Different POLY Figures with a
    Given Number of Sides 273
Problem 6-7 273
Problem Set 6-5 276

Solution to the Preliminary Problem 278

Chapter 6 Problem Set 280

Chapter 7 Applications of Turtle Graphics 285

Preliminary Problem 286

Introduction 287

7-1   Radio Transmitter Simulation 287
      Developing an Algorithm 288
      Using the DISTANCE Procedure 289
      Incorporating the Algorithm 290
      SEARCH Procedure Outline 290
      Debugging the SEARCH Algorithm 291
      Improving the SEARCH Algorithm 292
      Problem Set 7-1 293

7-2   Fox-and-Hare Simulation 294
      Developing the CHASE Algorithm 294
      Developing the CHASE Procedure 295
      Further Explorations 297
      Problem Set 7-2 298

7-3   Four-Bugs Simulation 299
      Developing the INTERACT Procedure 300
      Problem Set 7-3 303

7-4   Animation 303
      Developing the READKEY Procedure 305
      Stopping the ANIMATE Procedure 307
      Controlling the Turtle in ANIMATE 308
      Modifying the CHECK Procedure 308
      Track Games 309
      Problem Set 7-4 313

7-5   Creating a Game 313
      Problem Set 7-5 316

7-6   The Turtle Takes on New Shapes 317
      Using the SHAPE Editor 317
      Using SAVESHAPES 318
      Using SETSHAPE 319
      Using SIZE 319
      Problem Set 7-6 321

Solution to the Preliminary Problem 322

Chapter 7 Problem Set 327

Chapter 8   An Introduction to List Processing   329

Preliminary Problem   330

Introduction   331

8-1   Words and Numbers   331
      Operating on Words and Numbers   333
      Problem 8-1   336
      Problem 8-2   337
      Creating Palindromes   338
      Problem Set 8-1   341

8-2   Lists   344
      Writing a Multiplication Procedure   348
      Problem 8-3   351
      Problem 8-4   353
      Problem Set 8-2   354

8-3   Applications in List Processing   358
      Picking a Word from a List   359
      Picking a Word at Random from a List   360
      Constructing Sentences   361
      The Fibonacci Sequence   363
      Problem Set 8-3   365

Solution to the Preliminary Problem   366

Chapter 8 Problem Set   372

Appendix A: Games and Answers Disk Appendix   374

Glossary   384
      Logo Commands   384
      Editing Commands   394
      Non-Editing Control Characters   395
      Shape Editor Commands   396
      Error Messages   396

Select Bibliography   401

Index   410

Index of Procedures   413

0

History and Philosophy

The computer language Logo was developed by the Logo Group of the Massachusetts Institute of Technology (MIT) under the direction of Seymour Papert, author of *Mindstorms: Children, Computers, and Powerful Ideas*. The name **Logo** is derived from the Greek word for "thought." [The developers of Logo were influenced by the field of artificial intelligence, the computer language LISP, and the theories of Jean Piaget.] Logo was designed to permit learning by discovery in much the same way that children normally find out about the world around them. [Logo is intended to provide an environment in which learners progress through the developmental stages of learning by exploration.]

Logo is often described as a language for children. But it is more than that: It is a language that can serve people at all ages and levels of skill. In this respect, Logo is like chess. An elementary school student can learn the basic moves of chess, but the masters are still striving to learn more about the game. The same is true with Logo. Its designers refer to it as a language with "no threshold and no ceiling." For example, Logo has been used both to teach elementary school children and to teach Newton's laws of motion to undergraduate students at MIT.

The Logo Group first implemented Logo on a powerful and expensive computer. Only the introduction of inexpensive microcomputers with considerable memory made it possible for Logo to be available to the general public. Implementations of Logo for Texas Instrument and Apple computers were the first to be developed. Implementations

Logo

for many other computers are now on the market as well. These implementations are being periodically upgraded, and Logo is becoming more powerful as more memory capacity becomes available in microcomputers.

primitives

Logo makes it possible for beginners to learn to program in a relatively short period of time. Users can play, explore, and learn quickly because Logo starts out with a set of words called **primitives** that are easy to understand and that can be used for experimentation. For example, the primitive FORWARD along with an input of 50 tells the Logo turtle to move forward 50 units in the direction it is facing.

In Logo, the learner can write a set of instructions called a procedure, name it, and use it to build other procedures. [Programming in Logo can be thought of as teaching the computer new concepts based on what it already knows—that is, using known procedures to write new procedures.] In this way, the <u>user becomes a teacher and learns by teaching the computer to perform various tasks</u>. Problems that at first appear beyond the ability of the user can be broken down into "mind-sized bites," and these in turn can be worked on and then reassembled to solve the original problem.

In an ideal Logo environment, much of the programming is not taught as such; rather, it is learned through a series of activities. Students can choose many of their own problems and decide how to solve them based on their experience in generating and solving other problems. They teach the computer to perform a specific task and get immediate feedback. (In a Logo environment there are no mistakes in the traditional sense, only **bugs** that occur when something does not work as the user expected.) The process of finding and correcting bugs is often referred to as **debugging.** Learning occurs when a program is debugged as well as when it is written.

bugs

debugging

turtle

The best-known feature of Logo is "turtle graphics." The display creature in turtle graphics is a triangular figure known as the **turtle.** Papert refers to the turtle as "an object to think with." The turtle resides on the computer screen in the draw mode of Logo. Harold Abelson and Andrea diSessa in their text, *Turtle Geometry*, report that the tradition of calling the display creature a turtle can be traced to work of Grey Walter, a neurophysiologist who experimented in Britain in the 1960s with tiny robot-like creatures that he called "tortoises." These creatures inspired the first turtle designed at MIT, a computer-controlled robot that moved around the floor in response to the commands **FORWARD** and **RIGHT**. Work with computer graphics soon followed, and the screen "creature" inherited the turtle terminology. The computer turtle can be moved forward and backward and turned left and right; the user can have the turtle leave tracks on the screen when it moves, or the turtle can be told to move without leaving tracks.

The information needed to control the turtle is already present in the users' knowledge of how to move their own bodies forward and backward and how to turn left and right. (Programming the turtle thus becomes an extension of something that the programmers already know how to do.) Users may find themselves twisting their bodies in their chairs in an effort to identify with the turtle as they work through a program.

Mathematics can be studied through the use of turtle graphics. An approach to geometry using turtle graphics is referred to as "turtle geometry." In their book, Abelson and diSessa claim that "The most important thing to remember about turtle geometry is that it is mathematics designed for exploration, not just for presenting theorems and proofs." Aspects of mathematics that can be studied using Logo include positive and negative numbers, the concept of variables, linear and angular measurement, symmetry and similarity, coordinate systems, the ideas involved in transformations, and topics about number theory.]

In this book we concentrate mainly on turtle graphics, although we also pay some attention to the other capabilities of Logo. It has been our experience that after learners become acquainted with turtle graphics and feel somewhat comfortable with it, they want to learn more about the other capabilities of Logo.

What Can You Expect with Logo?

Logo Is Procedural

A Logo program is not necessarily written as one large unit. Rather, it can be divided into smaller pieces, and a separate procedure can be written for each piece. A **procedure** is a group of one or more instructions to the computer that the computer can store to be used

procedure

at a later time. Logo users start with a vocabulary of primitives and use them to develop new Logo vocabulary and procedures.

Logo Is Interactive

A Logo procedure can be carried out immediately by simply typing the name of the procedure with any necessary inputs. It is easy to change or correct a procedure in Logo because the editing process is built into the language.

Logo Is Recursive

In a Logo program, one procedure can use another procedure as a subprocedure. This is very useful because it allows an involved problem to be described in simple terms. A procedure can also call upon itself as a subprocedure. When a procedure calls itself, the process is called **recursion.**

recursion

Logo Has Graphics

Turtle graphics allows learners to order a turtle to move forward or backward and turn left or right. As stated previously, the turtle can leave a trace (a line), or it can move without leaving a trace. With simple commands, the user can "teach" the turtle to draw very complex drawings. These drawings can be created with or without reference to any coordinate system. Turtle graphics can be used as an introduction to structured programming and also as an aid to teaching mathematical concepts.

Logo Has List Processing

Logo provides operations for manipulating character strings that Logo calls "words." Logo also has the ability to combine data into structures called "lists." These lists can be used to create very complex data structures.

To obtain the best results with Logo, approach it with an adventurous, playful, and discovery-oriented spirit. Do not be afraid to try things on your own. An important part of Logo is debugging. Learn to enjoy your bugs! The chances are that if your programs do not work the way you want them to, they may do something interesting anyway. This in turn can lead to further interesting projects—perhaps even more interesting than the one you started with. [Learning Logo is really just discovering, exploring, and extending microworlds. A **microworld** is any learning environment in which the learner is interested and in which important concepts can be learned.]

microworld

New Vocabulary in Chapter 1

Terms	Primitives	Keys
software p. 10	GOODBYE p. 10	RETURN p. 12
memory p. 10	PRINT (PR) p. 11	[1][p. 12
booting p. 11	NODRAW (ND) p. 14	[2]] p. 12
turtle graphics p. 11	DRAW p. 15	SHIFT p. 12
nodraw mode p. 11	FORWARD (FD) p. 16	ESC p. 13
cursor p. 11	BACK (BK) p. 16	→ p. 13
prompt p. 11	RIGHT (RT) p. 16	← p. 13
input p. 12	LEFT (LT) p. 16	[3]REPT p. 13
crash p. 15	PENUP (PU) p. 16	CTRL p. 13
draw mode p. 15	PENDOWN (PD) p. 16	CTRL-D p. 13
turtle p. 15	HIDETURTLE (HT) p. 16	RESET p. 15
home p. 15	SHOWTURTLE (ST) p. 16	CTRL-Y p. 15
position p. 15	HEADING p. 18	CTRL-P p. 23
heading p. 15	CLEARSCREEN (CS) p. 20	CTRL-G p. 24
splitscreen mode p. 15	HOME p. 20	+ p. 30
	FULLSCREEN (CTRL-F) p. 20	− p. 30
	SPLITSCREEN (CTRL-S) p. 20	* p. 30
	TEXTSCREEN (CTRL-T) p. 20	/ p. 30
	NOWRAP p. 21	
	WRAP p. 21	
	REPEAT p. 23	

[1]On an Apple II+, this is obtained by holding down the SHIFT key and pressing the M key.
[2]On an Apple II+, this is obtained by holding down the SHIFT key and pressing the N key.
[3]On an Apple IIe or Apple IIc, this key is not present.

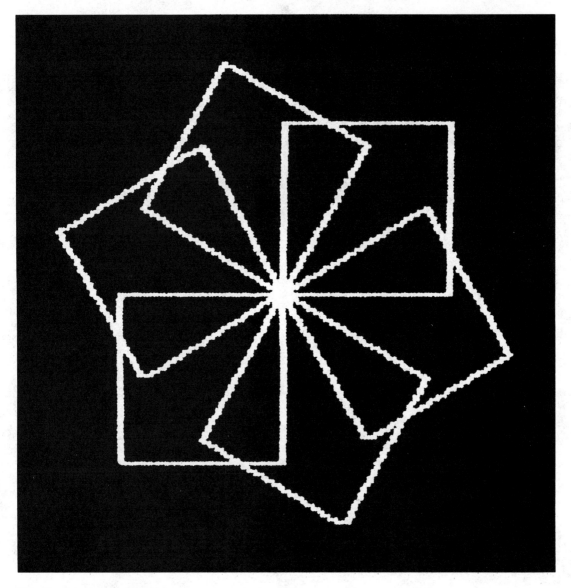

Preliminary Problem

Use the turtle to draw a figure similar to the one shown above.

1

Logo: A Beginning

Introduction

In Chapter 1 the basic Logo commands will be introduced. By the end of the chapter, you should be able to produce drawings similar to the one shown in the Preliminary Problem. Keep this figure in mind as you work through the chapter, and stop from time to time and try to discover a technique for creating this shape. A solution and discussion using a four-step problem-solving format will be given at the end of the chapter.

Each chapter will be introduced by a Preliminary Problem that you will be asked to consider as you work through the chapter. Keep in mind that the only way to become a good problem solver is to try numerous problems. Problem-solving is not a spectator sport. As you work through the material, you should have a computer available if at all possible.

1-1 The Nodraw Mode

Starting Logo

software

memory

Microcomputers are multipurpose devices designed to serve various needs. Present microcomputers have limited capacity to store information. Consequently, it would be impossible for a microcomputer to store all available software in its limited memory. **Software** includes programs that cause computers to perform certain operations. The space in which the computer stores its data is **memory**.

Software for most modern microcomputers is stored on disks and can be transferred into the computer's memory via a device called a disk drive. To load MIT Logo (Terrapin or Krell versions) into the computer's memory, we insert the Logo disk into the disk drive by opening the door on the drive, picking up the disk so that the label is face up and turned away from us, sliding the disk into the slot in the disk drive, and closing the door. The disk drive is now ready to load Logo into the computer. Next, we turn on the computer and the monitor. A red light on the disk drive is lit when the computer is turned on. This tells us that Logo is being loaded. After a short time, a message will appear on the monitor screen to tell us that Logo is ready to be used. We can now remove the disk from the disk drive, return it to its jacket, and put it in a safe place. It is important that you take special care of this disk because it is an uncopyable master disk. (At present, on the Apple IIe or Apple IIc, the CAPS LOCK key must be depressed to make Logo run correctly.)

Stopping Logo

GOODBYE

Logo can be stopped by turning off the computer. (You should also remember to turn off the monitor.) Once the computer is turned off, it will be necessary to go through the setting-up steps described above in order to run Logo again. If someone else wishes to use the computer, do not turn off the power. Instead, type **GOODBYE** and press the

RETURN key. This will clear the computer's memory and have the same effect as **booting** (starting) Logo again.

booting

Entering the Nodraw Mode

Before starting work with **turtle graphics** (drawing on the screen with the turtle), we present a short section whose main purpose is to acquaint you with the computer keyboard and the functions of several special keys. The computer keyboard works very much like an electric typewriter. It provides one way to communicate with the computer.

turtle graphics

The mode that the computer is in immediately after Logo is loaded is called the **nodraw mode.** After a greeting, a question mark and a flashing, rectangular **cursor** will appear. The question mark, called a **prompt,** indicates that Logo is awaiting instructions. The cursor appears when Logo wants us to type something, and it shows us where the next character typed will appear.

nodraw mode
cursor
prompt

Introducing the PRINT Command

To get acquainted with the keyboard and the nodraw mode, we learn to make the computer print the word HELLO. We have to be very careful when we give the computer commands, because it does not "think" the way people do. Instructions have to be given in a form that the computer can understand. With a little practice we are able to determine how the computer will react to various keystrokes. Remember that the computer is a machine and does what we tell it to do, not necessarily what we want it to do.

In order to have the computer print the word HELLO, we use the **PRINT (PR)** command. In Logo, many commands have abbreviations that may be used in place of the whole command names. Type the

PRINT (PR)

RETURN

lines below and press the **RETURN** key after each line. The RETURN key must be used each time we want the computer to respond to what we have typed. We can think of the RETURN key as the "do it" key. In the remainder of this text, we will omit most references to the RETURN key and assume that you will press it each time you want the computer to act.

(a) PRINT "HELLO

(b) PR "HELLO

(c) PRINT "HELLO"

(d) PRINT   "HELLO

(e) PRINT "   HELLO

(f) PRINT"HELLO

(g) PRINTHELLO

(h) PRINT HELLO

(i) PRINT "HELLO THERE

There are several important things to remember about using the PRINT command. (Do not worry about the error messages that appear from time to time; they will be discussed later.) Logo always needs a space between the PRINT command and its **input,** that is, the word or number following the command. This is true for all Logo commands. However, there is no space between the quote marks and the word to be printed, and the pair of quote marks is used only on the left side.

input

In line (i) you saw that Logo printed the word HELLO and then returned an error message. Logo does not like the space between the words. One way to print messages with spaces between the words is to put these words in the form of a "list." For now, all this means is that we enclose the message to be printed in brackets, as shown below. (Lists will be discussed in Chapter 8.)

PR [HELLO THERE]

[and]
SHIFT

(On the Apple II+ there are no bracket keys ([and]). To obtain the left bracket, press the N key while holding the **SHIFT** key down; for the right bracket, press the M key while holding the SHIFT key down.)

Before practicing with the **PRINT** command, we introduce some special keys. These keys may or may not be present on your computer, depending on the model. Experiment with these keys, if you have them, until you feel confident about their functions.

Special Keys

[1]ESC	This is called the ESCAPE key. It causes the character immediately to the left of the cursor to be rubbed out and then moves the cursor one space to the left.
→ or ←	These keys move the cursor one space right or left, respectively, without erasing any characters.
[2]REPT	This is called the REPEAT key. Holding the REPT key down and pressing any other key causes the character generated by the other key to be transmitted as long as the two keys are held down.
CONTROL (CTRL)	This is called the CONTROL key. Holding the CTRL key down while pressing another key allows entry of control characters; for example, see CTRL-D below.
CTRL-D	To produce this control character, hold the CTRL key down and press the D key. CTRL-D deletes the character over which the cursor is flashing.

---

[1]On the Apple IIe or Apple IIc with version 2.0 Terrapin Logo, the DELETE key acts like the ESC key.

[2]The Apple IIe and Apple IIc do not have a REPT key. Instead, they have an automatic repeat feature that is activated by holding down the key to be repeated.

Experiment with the following exercises to become familiar with the keyboard, to better understand how the **PRINT** command works, and to practice correcting typing errors. Notice that when a character is typed, it is inserted into the line at the cursor position and the cursor moves one place to the right. Similarly, a blank space can be inserted by moving the cursor to the desired position and pressing the space bar.

NODRAW (ND)

Any time the screen becomes too cluttered, type NODRAW (ND) to clear the screen. The **NODRAW (ND)** primitive gives a clear page for text and moves the cursor to the upper left corner of the screen.

Summary of Commands

GOODBYE	Takes no input. Clears the memory and restarts Logo.
PRINT (PR)	Takes a variable number of inputs (default is 1) and prints them on the screen separated by spaces and moves the cursor to the next line. PRINT (PR) can take a list as input.
NODRAW (ND)	Gives a clear page for text and moves the cursor to the upper left corner.

Problem Set 1-1

1. Explore what happens when each of the following is entered into the computer. Make a guess before trying each one. Remember to press RETURN after typing each line.

    (a) PRINT "TURTLE
    (b) PRINT " TURTLE
    (c) PRINT"TURTLE
    (d) PR "TURTLE"
    (e) PRINT "TURTLE POWER
    (f) PR "TURTLE.POWER
    (g) PR   "TURTLE
    (h) PR [THIS IS A LIST]
    (i) PR [ ]
    (j) PR "
    (k) PRINT "2+3
    (l) PRINT 2+3
    (m) PR [LEAVE   SOME   SPACES]

2. Type the word NON. Now use the arrow keys to place the cursor directly on top of the O. Now type O on the keyboard. What is the result? Now press the space bar. What is the result? Press the space bar three more times. Now use the ESC key to make the display read NON again.

3. Type the following line *without* pressing the RETURN key:

   ON A MISTY, MOISTY MORNING

   Now, using the keys introduced in this section, change the line to the form given in each of the following lines.

   (a) ON A MUSTY, MOISTY MORNING.
   (b) ON A MOISTY, MISTY MORNING.
   (c) ON A MISTY MORNING.
   (d) MONDAY WAS A MISTY MORNING.

4. Have the computer print your name on the screen.

5. Press **RESET** or **CTRL-RESET** to experience a "**crash.**" You will know the system has crashed if a variety of unexpected symbols and numbers appear on the screen. Will the computer respond to commands when it is crashed? Try to recover from the crash by pressing **CTRL-Y** and then RETURN. If a recovery is not possible, Logo must be rebooted.

RESET
crash

CTRL-Y

1-2 Meet the Turtle

Entering the Draw Mode

To enter the **draw mode** of Logo, type **DRAW** and press RETURN. The triangular pointer called the **turtle** appears in the middle of the screen. We refer to this position of the turtle as **home**. Wherever the turtle is on the screen, it always has **position**—that is, location on the screen—and heading. **Heading** refers to the direction that the turtle is pointing. The most important commands in the draw mode are commands that affect either the turtle's position or the turtle's heading.

draw mode
DRAW
turtle
home
position
heading

The mode that the turtle is in after the DRAW command is entered is called the **splitscreen mode.** In the splitscreen mode the prompt and the cursor are located towards the bottom of the screen. Logo saves the top part of the screen for graphics. The bottom four lines are reserved for text, that is, for typing commands and for all the computer's responses.

splitscreen mode

FORWARD (FD)
BACK (BK)
RIGHT (RT)
LEFT (LT)

Basic primitives to which the turtle responds are **FORWARD (FD)** and **BACK (BK)**, which change the turtle's position, and **RIGHT (RT)** and **LEFT (LT)**, which change the turtle's heading. As with the PRINT command, Logo allows shortened versions of the commands; the shortened versions are given in parentheses following each command. Each of these commands requires a numeric input to tell the turtle how far to move or how much to turn. Input in this case just means a number (which could be a decimal) following the command.

As the turtle moves, it can leave a track. Young students may think of this as the turtle dragging its tail in the sand. A series of commands, along with the computer's responses, is shown in Figure 1-1. Each frame continues from the previous frame. Type each of the lines under the frames to investigate how these commands work. Then try several other experiments using the commands before reading on. All the commands introduced in Figure 1-1 are discussed following the figure.

When we explore these commands, we find that when we type FORWARD 100 or FD 100 (notice the spacing), we are telling the turtle to move forward 100 units (turtle steps) in the direction it is facing. We also notice that the commands RIGHT and LEFT along with an input can change the turtle's heading (direction). The inputs for RIGHT and LEFT are in degrees. For example, RT 90 turns the turtle to the right 90 degrees from the direction it was facing. At this point we should be able to create simple figures such as a square. Before reading further, try to draw a square with a side of length 50 turtle steps.

PENUP (PU)
PENDOWN (PD)

HIDETURTLE (HT)
SHOWTURTLE (ST)

When the draw mode is entered, the turtle leaves a track as it moves from point to point. Sometimes in creating a figure we may want to move the turtle without leaving a track. This can be accomplished by using the command **PENUP (PU).** To make a turtle leave a track as it did originally, we use the command **PENDOWN (PD).** The exploration in Figure 1-1 also showed that it is possible to hide the turtle by typing **HIDETURTLE (HT).** To make the turtle reappear, type **SHOWTURTLE (ST).** Notice that typing DRAW sends the turtle home, sets it facing north, and clears the screen.

Format for Turtle Commands

Instructions to the computer must be given in a specific format. To investigate how Logo reacts to various inputs and formats, type each

Figure 1-1

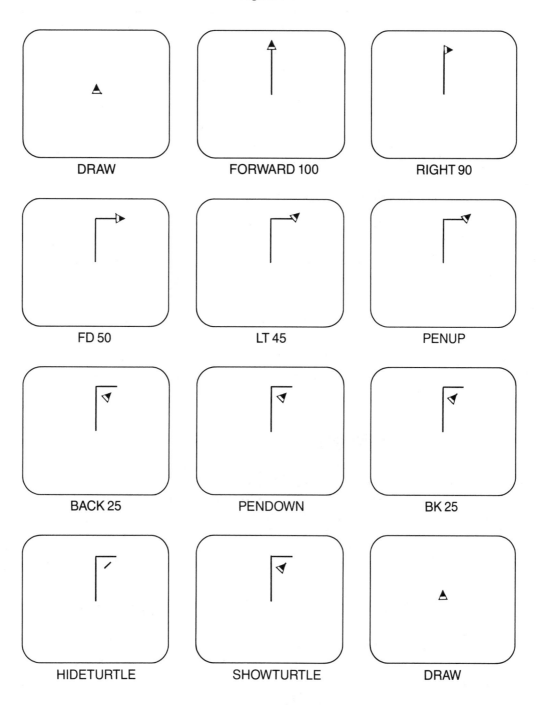

of the following lines and record the results. Then try similar investigations with the other three basic primitives.

(a) FD   50

(b) FD50

(c) FD "50

(d) FD

(e) FOWARD 50

(f) FO 50

(g) FD − 50

(h) FD 100 − 50

So far, we have executed only a single command at a time. What happens if we type multiple commands on a single line and then press the RETURN key? Try it and see. For example, type the following and press RETURN.

DRAW FD 100 RT 90 FD 50

Type other lines with multiple commands to see how the turtle reacts.

Turtle Heading

HEADING

After **DRAW** is typed, the turtle is in its initial position: it faces straight up (north on Figure 1-2) and is said to have heading 0. As the turtle turns to the right or left, its heading changes according to the compass pictured in Figure 1-2. For example, if the turtle is initially facing north and then is turned right 45 degrees, it will have a new heading of 45. If we turn it right 45 degrees again, it will have a heading of 90. Any time we want to know the turtle's heading, we type **HEADING**, and the turtle's heading is displayed.

To explore the **HEADING** command, type **DRAW** and then **LT 45**. What should the heading be? Type **HEADING** to see if you were correct. Next, type **DRAW** and then **LT − 45**. Now what is the heading? Check your answer.

Figure 1-2

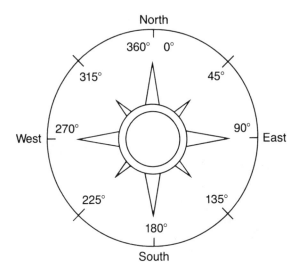

Problem 1-1

Determine the turtle's heading after each of the following lines is executed.

(a) DRAW FD 50 RT 100 FD 20 LT 30 FD 30 RT 10

(b) DRAW RT 60 FD 50 RT −60 FD 50

Solution

(a) One way to compute the heading is to ignore the commands involving position. The initial heading is 0 because the **DRAW** command sets the heading to 0. The **RT 100** changes the heading to 100, the **LT 30** command changes the heading to 70, and the **RT 10** command gives a final heading of 80. This can be verified by executing the line and then using the **HEADING** command.

(b) The initial heading is 0. **RT 60** changes the heading to 60. **RT −60** then turns the turtle in a counterclockwise direction, giving a final heading of 0. The **HEADING** command can again be used to verify the result. Notice that **RT −60** is equivalent to **LT 60**.

Clearing the Screen and Homing the Turtle

We have seen that the DRAW command clears the screen and brings the turtle to the home position with heading 0. An alternate way to clear the graphics screen is to type CLEARSCREEN (CS). Place some figures on the screen and type CLEARSCREEN. How does the result compare with that obtained by typing DRAW?

CLEARSCREEN (CS)

HOME

We see that the command **CLEARSCREEN (CS)** clears the screen but does not affect the turtle's position or heading. The command **HOME** returns the turtle to the center of the screen and sets its heading to 0. How does the result obtained by typing HOME and then CLEAR-SCREEN compare with the result obtained by typing DRAW? If the order of typing CLEARSCREEN and HOME is reversed, does it affect the result? Place the turtle in various locations on the screen and practice using these commands.

Using the SPLITSCREEN, FULLSCREEN, and TEXTSCREEN Commands

For the next exploration, type DRAW and then type BK 110. Does the turtle disappear? Why? The turtle is not visible because it is hidden under the bottom four lines, which are reserved for text in the split-screen mode. To remove the bottom four lines of text from the screen and have the whole screen available for drawing, we either type the command **FULLSCREEN** and press RETURN or type CTRL-F. (Recall that "type CTRL-F" means to press the F key while holding down the CTRL key.) Any typing that is now done will not be visible. To return to the splitscreen mode, we can either type the command **SPLITSCREEN** or type CTRL-S.

FULLSCREEN (CTRL-F)

SPLITSCREEN (CTRL-S)

Remark: Commands such as FULLSCREEN and SPLITSCREEN can be used in programs or typed at the prompt. Control characters cannot be used as lines in programs.

TEXTSCREEN (CTRL-T)

If a set of directions in the draw mode is longer than four lines, not all the lines will be visible in the splitscreen mode. To examine previous lines, we type either the command **TEXTSCREEN** or CTRL-T. The TEXTSCREEN command in the draw mode gives a full text screen. We can return to the splitscreen mode by typing either the command SPLITSCREEN or CTRL-S. Experiment using these commands.

The Wrap and Nowrap Modes

In the experiment above, we started the turtle in the home position and typed BK 110, and the turtle disappeared behind the bottom four lines reserved for text. Now type DRAW FD 140 and press RETURN. What happens to the turtle?

If we type FULLSCREEN (CTRL-F), we again find the turtle at the bottom of the screen. How did it get there? When the turtle moves more steps than are visible on the screen, it either disappears or "wraps around" the screen and returns on the other side. For example, if the turtle is at home with heading 0 and we enter FORWARD 200, the turtle reappears at the bottom of the screen and continues forward. Likewise, if the turtle leaves the screen on the right side, it reappears on the left side. For example, try DRAW RT 90 FD 300. What do you think will happen if we start the turtle at home with heading 0 and then turn RT 30 and move FD 2000? Try it. Why did the tracks not wrap around on themselves as in the other experiments?

If we do not want the turtle to wrap around, we can use the NOWRAP command. To see how NOWRAP works, type NOWRAP and then DRAW FD 200. The command **NOWRAP** causes Logo to give an error message any time the turtle attempts to cross over the boundaries of the screen. To restore the turtle to the original wraparound behavior, we type **WRAP** and then press RETURN.

NOWRAP

WRAP

Creating Drawings with the Turtle

The commands introduced above can be used to draw various figures. Consider how you might start in the home position with heading 0 and have the turtle draw the plus sign shown in Figure 1-3.

Figure 1-3

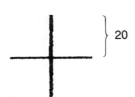

} 20

To complete this drawing, we use the strategy of "playing turtle" and think how we might walk out an outline of the figure. One possibility is to walk forward 20 steps, back up 20 steps, turn right 90 degrees and then walk forward 20 steps, back up 20 steps, turn right 90 degrees again, and continue in this manner until the drawing is complete. The sequence of commands needed to make the turtle do this is summarized in Figure 1-4, along with a drawing of the figure it produces.

DRAW
FD 20 BK 20
RT 90
FD 20 BK 20
RT 90
FD 20 BK 20
RT 90
FD 20

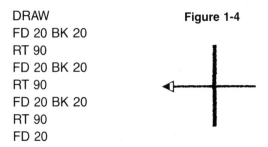

Figure 1-4

Remark: We start the set of instructions with the **DRAW** command in order to clear previous drawings and to bring the turtle to the home position with heading 0. If the screen and the turtle already meet these conditions, the **DRAW** command is not necessary.

When the drawing in Figure 1-4 was created, the turtle's initial position was at home and its initial heading was 0. When finished, the turtle is in a position 20 units directly west of home with a heading of 270. It is often convenient when doing complicated drawings to have the turtle return to its initial position and heading. In Figure 1-4, this can be accomplished by backing the turtle 20 steps and turning right 90 degrees, or adding the commands **BK 20 RT 90** to our list. The figure produced with these changes is shown below in Figure 1-5.

DRAW
FD 20 BK 20
RT 90
FD 20 BK 20
RT 90
FD 20 BK 20
RT 90
FD 20 BK 20
RT 90

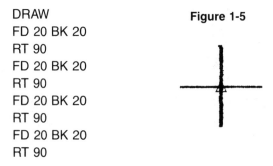

Figure 1-5

Notice that Figure 1-5 could be obtained by executing the line FD 20 BK 20 RT 90 four times. A helpful command that saves retyping a line in the draw or nodraw mode is CTRL-P (P stands for "previous"). For example, type

CTRL-P

FD 20 BK 20 RT 90

and press the RETURN key. Now press CTRL-P. The previous line is retyped and can be executed again by pressing RETURN. Do you see how to finish drawing the plus sign using CTRL-P? (Note, however, that CTRL-P is nullified in some versions of Logo if a REPEAT, READ, or SAVE command is used in the typed line. These commands will be discussed later.)

Introducing the REPEAT Command

The REPEAT command in Logo allows us to execute a set of instructions a given number of times. The **REPEAT** command takes a number and a list of instructions as inputs, and executes the instructions in the list the designated number of times. Using the REPEAT command, the sequence of commands to draw the plus sign in Figure 1-5 could be written in one line, as shown below. (Remember that on an Apple II + the left and right brackets are obtained by SHIFT-N and SHIFT-M, respectively.)

REPEAT

REPEAT 4[FD 20 BK 20 RT 90]

Remark: Spaces may be inserted between the number of repeats and the list of instructions.

The plus sign can also be drawn in different ways. Design another set of instructions for drawing the figure. Can you do it by repeating a list of commands twice? Can you do it without using the BK command?

REPEAT commands can be nested; that is, they can be contained within other REPEAT commands. For example, what result do you think would occur if the line given below were executed?

REPEAT 3[REPEAT 4[FD 20 BK 20 RT 90] RT 30]

Stopping Execution

When a program is being run and a bug is found, it is often convenient to halt the program rather than wait for it to be completed. This can be done by typing CTRL-G. **CTRL-G** causes Logo to stop whatever it was doing and wait for a new command. The message

STOPPED!

appears on the screen. For example, if you type REPEAT 1000[FD 2], you can halt this command's execution by pressing CTRL-G.

Warning: Make sure you use CTRL-G to stop execution rather than RESET or CTRL-RESET; otherwise you may crash the Logo system, that is, cause Logo to shut down so it will not accept Logo commands.

Problem 1-2

Write a set of instructions to draw the following figure. Assume that each square has a side of length 30 units.

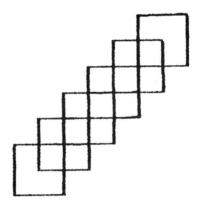

Solution

If the turtle starts at home with heading 0, the figure can be obtained by drawing a square, picking up the pen, moving the turtle to an appropriate new position and heading to draw the next square, putting the pen down, and repeating this process the desired number of times. A square can be drawn by executing REPEAT 4[FD 30 RT 90].

The turtle can be moved to the new drawing position in a variety of ways. One way is given below.

PU FD 15 RT 90 FD 15 LT 90 PD

Because six squares are required, we can write the set of directions as follows:

REPEAT 6[REPEAT 4[FD 30 RT 90] PU FD 15 RT 90 FD 15 LT 90 PD]

Summary of Commands

DRAW	Needs no input. It sends the turtle home and clears the graphics screen.
NODRAW (ND)	Needs no input. It exits the graphics mode, clears the screen, and places the cursor in the upper left corner.
FORWARD (FD)	Takes one input. It moves the turtle forward (in the direction the turtle is facing) the number of turtle units that are input. For example, FD 20 moves the turtle forward 20 units.
BACK (BK)	Takes one input. It moves the turtle backward the number of turtle units that are input. For example, BK 40 moves the turtle backward 40 units.
RIGHT (RT)	Takes one input. It turns the turtle right from its present heading the number of degrees that are input. For example, RT 90 turns the turtle right 90 degrees.
LEFT (LT)	Takes one input. It turns the turtle left from its present heading the number of degrees that are input. For example, LT 90 turns the turtle left 90 degrees.
PENUP (PU)	Needs no input. In the graphics mode, it enables the turtle to move without leaving a track.
PENDOWN (PD)	Needs no input. In the graphics mode, it causes the turtle to leave a track.
HIDETURTLE (HT)	Needs no input. It causes the turtle to disappear.
SHOWTURTLE (ST)	Needs no input. It causes the turtle to reappear.
HEADING	Needs no input. In the draw mode, it outputs the turtle's heading.

Continued

CLEARSCREEN (CS)	Needs no input. It clears the graphics screen without moving the turtle.
HOME	Needs no input. It returns the turtle to the center of the screen and sets its heading to 0. If the pen is down, it leaves a track from the turtle's initial location to the home position.
FULLSCREEN (CTRL-F)	Needs no input. In the draw mode, it gives a full graphics screen.
SPLITSCREEN (CTRL-S)	Needs no input. In the draw mode, it gives a mixed graphics and text display.
TEXTSCREEN (CTRL-T)	Needs no input. In the draw mode, it gives a full text screen.
NOWRAP	Needs no input. It causes Logo to give an error message any time the turtle attempts to cross the boundaries of the screen.
WRAP	Needs no input. It causes the turtle to "wrap around" the screen when commands take the turtle off the screen.
CTRL-P	Needs no input. In the draw or nodraw mode, it causes the previously typed line to be retyped. Type RETURN to execute the line.
REPEAT	Takes a number and a list as input. It executes the instructions in the list the designated number of times.
CTRL-G	Causes Logo to stop whatever it was doing and wait for a new command.

Problem Set 1-2

1. Draw each of the following shapes. Type **DRAW** after completing each part.

   (a)   (b)   (c)

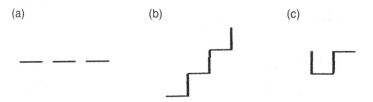

(d)   (e)   (f)

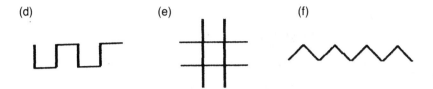

2. Predict what happens when each of the following lines is exe-
    cuted. Check your answers using the computer. Type DRAW after
    each line.

    (a) BK   50
    (b) FR 50
    (c) RT "50
    (d) BK40
    (e) FD 50 BK 25
    (f) BK 30 + 40
    (g) BK − 100
    (h) BK 32.89
    (i) RIGHT 180
    (j) LT 360
    (k) RIGHT 390 HEADING
    (l) FD 50 RT 90 FD 50 RT 90
    (m) RT 180 − 90
    (n) FD 20*2 (What do you think the * does?)
    (o) BK 90/3 (What do you think the / does?)
    (p) FD 50 HT RT 90 FD 25 ST
    (q) FD 50 PU RT 90 FD 50 RT 90 PD FD 50 HT
    (r) RT 10 FD 1000

3. Predict the result if the following lines are executed. Compare
    your sketch with the figure drawn by the computer.

    DRAW
    FD 50 RT 135
    FD 40 LT 90
    FD 40 RT 135
    FD 50
    HT

4. (a) What happens if you type the line below followed by RETURN?

   FD 50 RT 90 FD 50 FT 90

   (b) What happens if you now type CTRL-P followed by RETURN?

   (c) What happens if you type CTRL-P twice before pressing RETURN? Why does this occur?

5. Determine the dimensions of the screen in turtle steps.

6. Make the turtle draw each of the following:

   (a) a square
   (b) a rectangle
   (c) a triangle
   (d) a capital letter **A**

7. Sketch what you think will happen when each of the following lines is executed. Compare your sketches with the results actually obtained when each line is executed. Type **DRAW** before executing each line.

   (a) REPEAT 3[FD 20 RT 60]
   (b) REPEAT 3[LT 30]
   (c) REPEAT 5[FD 30 RT 72]
   (d) REPEAT 6[FD 40 RT 60]
   (e) REPEAT 4[FD 8 PU FD 8 PD]
   (f) REPEAT 36[FD 10 RT 10]

8. Write a set of instructions to draw each of the following figures. Use the computer to check your instructions.

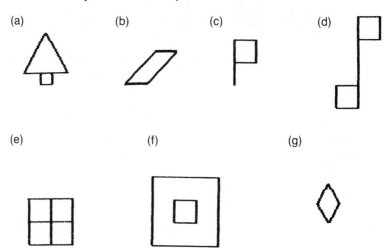

(a)   (b)   (c)   (d)

(e)   (f)   (g)

(h)   (i)   (j)

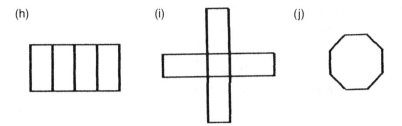

9.   Design three figures of your own that make use of the **REPEAT** command.

10. Write a set of directions to draw your initials in block letters. Are some letters in the alphabet harder to draw than others? Why or why not?

11. Draw a shape in which the turtle does not return to its original starting position. Use the **REPEAT** command to draw the shape five times. Use this idea to create different shapes.

12. In this section, the only commands that need inputs are **FORWARD (FD)**, **BACK (BK)**, **LEFT (LT)**, and **RIGHT (RT)**. Investigate what happens if an input is used with other commands, such as **DRAW 50** or **CLEARSCREEN 50**. Is the desired result still obtained? How does the result differ from that obtained by using the command without an input?

13. Use something that will stick to the screen to mark a spot on the screen. Practice the **FORWARD, BACK, RIGHT,** and **LEFT** commands by maneuvering the turtle around the screen until it reaches the mark.

14. Draw a maze on a piece of plastic and tape the plastic to the screen. Maneuver the turtle through the maze using the basic turtle commands. Could you have the turtle draw the maze and then move the turtle through it?

15. (a) Enter the nodraw mode by typing **ND** and pressing RETURN. Type the following, press RETURN, and record your results.

     FD 50 RT 90 FD 50

     (b) Type CTRL-T and then type the following line.

     FD 50 LT 90 FD 50
     Now press RETURN and record your results. How does this result compare with the result in part (a)? Now type CTRL-S. What happens?

16. Investigate what happens if a decimal is used as part of the input for the REPEAT command. Try each of the following:

    (a) REPEAT 3.2[FD 50 RT 90]
    (b) REPEAT 3.5[FD 50 RT 90]
    (c) REPEAT 3.8[FD 50 RT 90]

Games Disk Activity

There are games on the games disk that will help reinforce the concepts of distance and direction introduced in this chpater. Turn to the appendix to find out how to load the games disk, then try DART-GAME and GOLF.

1-3 Arithmetic Operations

Several arithmetic operations have already been introduced. The basic operations and examples of each are summarized in Table 1-1.

Table 1-1 Basic Arithmetic Operations

Operation	Logo Symbol	Logo Example
Addition	+	2 + 3
Subtraction	−	5 − 4
Multiplication	*	7*8
Division	/	9/3

When more than one arithmetic operation is used, operations in parentheses are done first. Then multiplications and divisions are performed in the given order (left to right). Finally, additions and subtractions are performed in the given order (left to right). For example, if we type 1 + 13*13 and press RETURN, the computer prints

RESULT: 170

If the command **PRINT** is used before the computation is performed, the format for the answer changes. For example, if we execute the line

PRINT 1 + 13*13

the answer 170 alone appears. The **PRINT** command is used with arithmetic operations in order to obtain the output in the form of a numeral without the word **RESULT** preceding it. The reasons for this are discussed in Chapter 6, along with other topics involving arithmetic operations.

Logo allows us to have decimal inputs or negative inputs with numeric operations. For example, if we type

PR 13.57*(−3)

the answer −40.71 appears.

Remark: Negative numbers involved in computations are often placed in parentheses if there is any danger that the negative sign might be misinterpreted.

Problem Set 1-3

1. Predict what will happen in each of the following cases. Use the computer to check your answers.

a.	PR 13 − 9	b.	PR 13 − 9 + 5*3
c.	PR14*2	d.	PR "3 + 2
e.	PR 18/2 + 6/2	f.	PR 3*3*3*3
g.	PR 10 − 7*8	h.	PR (10 − 7)*8
i.	PR (8 − 9)*6/3	j.	PR 28.44/3.6
k.	PR 3 +	l.	PR − (−5)
m.	PR 5 − 6*7/2 + 8	n.	PR 5 − 6*(4 + 7)
o.	PR 5 − 6(4 + 7)		

2. Write a PRINT statement to compute and print out the values of each of the following.

   (a) $9 - 6 \times 7 + (8 - 2)$

   (b) $(3 \times 7) - (5 - 2)$

   (c) $(5.57) \times (6.3 - 7)$

   (d) $5 \times 5 \times 5$

3. Predict the results of each of the following. Check your predictions using the computer.

   (a) DRAW FD 2*40 BK 80

   (b) DRAW FD 80/2 RT 90 FD 20 + 20 HOME RT − 90 FD 2*(5 + 15)

   (c) DRAW RT 3*120

4. How many places does Logo carry out nonterminating (nonending) decimals? Investigate this by computing 1/3.

5. How does Logo handle divisions involving zero? To find out, try each of the following:

   (a) 0/3   (b) 3/0   (c) 0/0

Solution to the Preliminary Problem

Understanding the Problem

The problem is to reproduce a drawing similar to the one in Figure 1-6. It appears that this figure is made up of squares of the same size, all having a common vertex (corner). The only difference in the squares is their orientation. Because we are not given a specific length for a side of the square, we may choose any length—for example, 50.

Figure 1-6

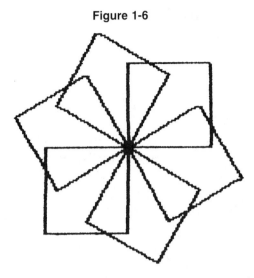

Devising a Plan

Assuming that we know how to draw a square of size 50, and assuming we start at home with heading 0, how can the six squares in Figure 1-6 be drawn? If we draw a square, as in Figure 1-7(a), the turtle returns to its original position and heading after the square is drawn. After the square is completed, we need to turn the turtle right by some angle to draw the next square. This is shown in Figure 1-7(b).

If the turtle continues this process until six squares have been drawn, the required figure will be obtained. To assure that we obtain the required drawing, we need to determine the amount of the turtle turn after each time a square is drawn. If we "play turtle," starting with an initial heading of 0 and make six turns of equal measure so that

Figure 1-7

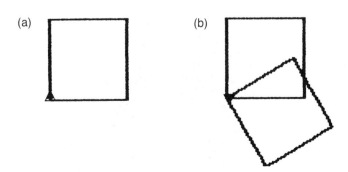

(a) (b)

we again return to our initial heading, we notice that we have turned in a complete circle. Because the total turning of the turtle amounts to a complete circle (360 degrees), the amount of turning for each of the six angles is 360/6 or 60 degrees.

Carrying Out the Plan

To draw the desired figure, we need to draw a square, turn the turtle 60 degrees to the right, and repeat the process. We can use a REPEAT command to obtain the program given below.

REPEAT 6[REPEAT 4[FD 50 RT 90]RT 60]

Looking Back

In this step of problem-solving, we usually check our work, explore whether there are different or more efficient techniques for working the problem, and determine whether there are other related or more general problems for which the same techniques will work. Different techniques for working this type of problem are developed in later chapters. For now, you might consider the following related problems.

1. Is the shape created above changed if the 6 is replaced by 8? What if it is changed to 4? Why?

2. Using the techniques given in this problem, create a shape that uses a hexagon (six-sided figure) rather than a square for its basic shape. Next, create new shapes using figures other than squares or hexagons.

3. Create a shape similar to the one in the Preliminary Problem in which a square is drawn 18 times, as shown below.

4. Enter various values in the blanks below to generate different figures. Sketch the result of each instruction before running it on the computer.

    REPEAT__[REPEAT 4[FD 50 RT 90] RT 360/__]

Chapter 1 Problem Set

1. Use a PRINT command to print each of the following:
    (a) AS THE TURTLE TURNS
    (b) TURTLERIFIC

2. Have the turtle draw each of the following figures.

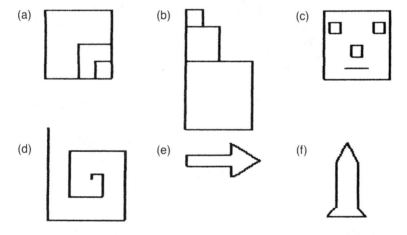

3. Use the primitives introduced in this chapter to draw a house. Sketch your figure on paper and record your commands before entering them on the computer.

4. Sketch the results of each of the following sets of commands. Use the computer to check your sketches. Clear the screen after each part.

    (a) RT 60 FD 70 HOME
    (b) RT 60 FD 70 RT 120 HOME
    (c) RT 60 FD 40 RT 120 FD 40 RT 120, press RETURN and then press CTRL-P and RETURN

5. Sketch the final result when each of the following series of commands is executed.

   (a) DRAW
       REPEAT 2[FD 30 RT 90 FD 15 RT 90]
       LT 90
       PU FD 40 PD
       REPEAT 2[FD 30 RT 90 FD 15 RT 90]
       HT

   (b) DRAW
       REPEAT 4[FD 50 RT 90]
       FD 50 RT 30
       REPEAT 3[FD 50 RT 120]
       HT

6. Choose a three-letter word and have the turtle draw this word in block letters on the screen.

7. By moving the turtle, find approximately how many turtle steps there are from the lower left-hand corner of the full screen to the upper right-hand corner.

8. Use the **REPEAT** command to draw each of the following:

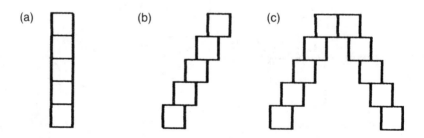

(a)   (b)   (c)

☆9. Have the computer draw a five-pointed star similar to the one shown below. Give each side of the star a length of 50.

2

New Vocabulary in Chapter 2

Terms	Primitives	Keys
procedure p. 39	TO p. 40	CTRL-C p. 41
edit mode p. 40	END p. 41	CTRL-A p. 45
editor p. 40	EDIT (ED) p. 45	CTRL-E p. 45
workspace p. 41	EDIT ALL (ED ALL) p. 52	CTRL-K p. 45
equilateral triangle p. 46	PRINTOUT (PO) p. 53	CTRL-N p. 45
top-down programming p. 62	PRINTOUT TITLES (POTS) p. 53	CTRL-O p. 45
level number p. 66	PRINTOUT ALL	CTRL-P p. 45
permanent memory p. 70	(PO ALL) p. 54	CTRL-F p. 53
initialize p. 70	ERASE (ER) p. 54	CTRL-B p. 53
file p. 71	ERASE ALL (ER ALL) p. 55	CTRL-L p. 53
backup copy p. 74	CATALOG p. 71	CTRL-W p. 54
	SAVE p. 73	
	READ p. 73	
	SAVEPICT p. 75	
	READPICT p. 75	
	ERASEFILE p. 75	
	ERASEPICT p. 75	

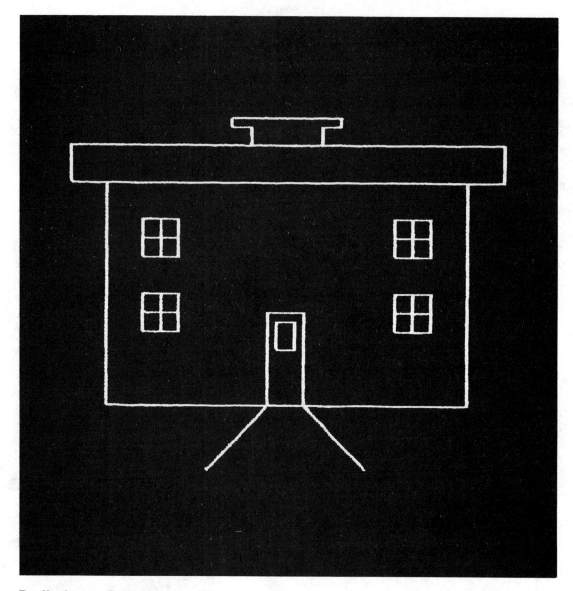

Preliminary Problem

Use the turtle to draw a figure similar to the one shown above. Save your drawing on disk under the name HOUSE.

2

Teaching the Turtle

Introduction

In Chapter 2, we learn how to use the edit mode and teach the computer new words that it can understand and act upon. We learn how to manage the computer's working memory or workspace and how to store our work in permanent memory on disk. A major portion of the chapter is devoted to discussing ways to approach a project such as the one described in the Preliminary Problem. Several steps that may be helpful in creating such projects are given.

2-1 The Edit Mode

In the previous chapter we discussed ways to draw figures. However, once the screen was cleared, the figure was lost; to obtain the figure again, we had to retype the instructions. Fortunately with Logo we can teach the computer a sequence of commands that can be stored in memory and used later as many times as desired. A series of instructions that has been given a name so that the computer can recall the instructions when the name is typed is called a **procedure.** In Logo, defining or creating a procedure is the same thing as writing a pro-

procedure

gram. Procedures can be defined using primitives such as those intro-duced in Chapter 1 or using previously defined procedures.

Entering the Edit Mode

edit mode
editor
TO

We create procedures in the **edit mode.** To enter the edit mode, or the **editor,** we type **TO** followed by the name of the procedure we have chosen, and then press the RETURN key. The primitive **TO** warns the computer that what follows is the name of a new procedure. Unless it sees **TO** before a name, the computer will check its memory to see if the name is a primitive or a previously defined procedure.

In the edit mode, typed lines are not immediately executed as they are in the draw mode. For example, suppose we want the computer to draw the plus sign designed in Chapter 1 each time we type the word PLUS. To create the procedure PLUS, we type **TO PLUS** and press the RETURN key. The computer then enters the edit mode, and the screen appears as shown in Figure 2-1.

Figure 2-1

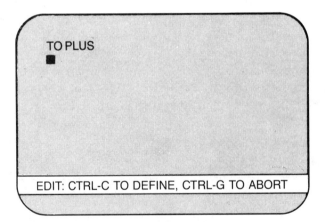

Normally, the name we choose for a procedure should remind us of what the instructions are to accomplish. For example, a procedure that draws a square might be called SQUARE. The name for a pro-cedure cannot be all numerals; it cannot be the name of a primitive such as FORWARD; and it cannot be made up of two words, such as SQUARE PIECE. If we want two words in our procedure title, we may place a period between the two words, as in SQUARE.PIECE. Then the computer will think of the title as one word.

Steps for defining the **PLUS** procedure are given below.

Step	Example	
1. Type **TO** followed by the procedure name.	TO PLUS	
2. Type the body of the procedure (program).	REPEAT 4[FD 20 BK 20 RT 90]	
3. Type **END** (on its own line) to indicate that the procedure is complete.	END	**END**
4. Press **CTRL-C** to send the procedure to the computer's memory. The computer will then exit the edit mode and enter the nodraw mode.		**CTRL-C**

Once the edit mode has been exited with CTRL-C, the computer has "learned" the procedure by entering it in memory. Logo then enters the nodraw mode and responds with the message

PLUS DEFINED

If we change our minds and decide not to finish defining the procedure we are working on, we can abort the procedure while in the edit mode by typing CTRL-G instead of CTRL-C.

Remark: In the remainder of this text we will use the expression "type CTRL-C" to mean "hold the CTRL key down and then press the c key." This terminology will also be used with other control characters. It is important that you understand that when you see CTRL-, you should press the CTRL key rather than typing the word "CTRL."

The **PLUS** procedure is now in the computer's memory. We say that it is part of the computer's **workspace** or working memory. The workspace is made up of all currently defined procedures and variables. (Variables will be discussed in Chapter 3.) Typing the name of

workspace

the procedure and pressing the RETURN key causes the computer to execute the instructions in the procedure. For example, if we type PLUS and press RETURN, a drawing like that in Figure 2-2 will appear.

Figure 2-2

Warning: Many beginners forget to exit the editor with CTRL-C before attempting to execute a new procedure. Make sure you are outside the edit mode before asking Logo to act on your procedure.

Once a procedure such as PLUS has been defined, it can be used in other procedures. For example, we can use the PLUS procedure to make the design in Figure 2-3 by clearing the screen, typing PLUS RT 45 PLUS, and pressing the RETURN key.

Figure 2-3

We can use PLUS to make other designs as well. For example, consider the results of each of the following. Type DRAW before executing each line.

REPEAT 5[PLUS RT 20]
REPEAT 10[PLUS RT 20]

The END Command

For the next investigation, enter the edit mode and write the following procedure. Do *not* put an END statement on your procedure.

TO DOTTED
REPEAT 10[FD 3 PU FD 3 PD]

Exit the edit mode with CTRL-C. Will Logo now carry out the procedure if you type its name and press RETURN? Now reenter the edit mode by typing **TO DOTTED** and examine the procedure. Is the procedure exactly as you left it?

If a procedure being defined in the editor does not have END as a last line, Logo assumes that you forgot to type it and adds it automatically. However, it is a good habit to end all procedures with the END statement. As we shall see later, a second procedure being entered in the edit mode could be merged with an earlier procedure if the END statement of the first procedure is missing.

Long Command Lines

Lines in Logo procedures can be 255 characters long. However, a single line on the computer screen is only 40 characters long. When a line longer than 40 characters is typed in the editor, Logo places an exclamation point when the right edge of the screen is reached, but it considers the instructions to continue until RETURN is pressed. The exclamation point is only a visual marker and does not affect the instruction at all. An example of the exclamation point is shown in the command line below.

PU LT 90 FD 120 RT 135 FD 25 RT 45 FD 8!
0 LT 90 PD

Enter the edit mode and type a line with more than 40 characters to see how this works.

Problem 2-1

(a) Write a procedure called **SQUARE** that draws a square of size 50 as shown in Figure 2-4(a).

(b) Use the procedure designed in part (a) to write a procedure to draw the figure in Figure 2-4(b).

Figure 2-4

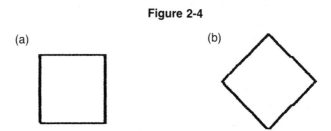

(a)   (b)

Solution

(a) We know how to write a procedure for drawing a square from our work with the **REPEAT** command in Chapter 1. A **SQUARE** procedure for drawing a square of size 50 is given below.

```
TO SQUARE
REPEAT 4[FD 50 RT 90]
END
```

(b) The figure in 2-4(b) is just the square figure drawn with an initial heading of 45. In Logo, once a procedure has been defined, it is possible to use it in another procedure. Thus, the diamond procedure may be written as follows.

```
TO DIAMOND
RT 45 SQUARE
END
```

Editing Procedures

Suppose we would rather draw a plus sign of size 50 than one of size 20 as in Figure 2-2. How can we change the **PLUS** procedure to accomplish this?

We return to the edit mode to make the necessary changes by typing one of the following:

TO PLUS   or   EDIT PLUS   or   ED PLUS

After we type one of these instructions and press the RETURN key, the PLUS procedure will be displayed. If we type only **EDIT (ED),** the computer will display the most recently edited procedure.

EDIT (ED)

In order to change or correct a procedure that has already been defined, we must add and delete characters. This can be done by moving the cursor around in the edit mode. In addition to the special keys introduced in Chapter 1, we may need some or all of the editing features listed below.

Summary of Special Keys

CTRL-A	Moves the cursor to the beginning of the current line.
CTRL-E	Moves the cursor to the end of the current line (E stands for "end").
[1]CTRL-K	Deletes all the characters on the current line beneath and to the right of the cursor (K stands for "kill").
CTRL-N	Moves the cursor down one line (N stands for "next").
CTRL-O	Opens a new line at the position of the cursor (O stands for "open").
CTRL-P	Moves the cursor up one line (P stands for "previous").

---

[1]In Terrapin Logo version 2.0, CTRL-X is used in place of CTRL-K. CTRL-Y allows the most recently deleted line to be "yanked back" into the editor.

Remark: In Terrapin Logo version 2.0, all four arrow keys on the Apple IIe or Apple IIc may be used in the editor to move the cursor.

After you type **TO PLUS** and press the RETURN key, the original PLUS procedure will be displayed, as shown below.

```
TO PLUS
REPEAT 4[FD 20 BK 20 RT 90]
END
```

To change the size of the plus sign, we must change each 20 in the procedure to 50. We can do this by using CTRL-N to move the cursor down one line and then using the right arrow key to move the cursor to the right until the cursor is directly over the 2 in FD 20. We can use CTRL-D to delete the 2 and then type a 5 to replace it. We can replace BK 20 with BK 50 in a similar way. Note that there are other ways to accomplish these changes.

To add the line PU FD 50 PD after the title line in the PLUS procedure, we would place the cursor before the line REPEAT 4[FD 50 BK 50 RT 90] and then press CTRL-O to open a line and then type PU FD 50 PD. To redefine the PLUS procedure, we type CTRL-C.

Drawing an Equilateral Triangle

equilateral triangle

We can use Logo to draw various geometrical figures. We have already looked at a procedure for drawing a square. Now let's work out a procedure for drawing an equilateral triangle with sides of measure 50 units each. An **equilateral triangle** has all sides with the same measure and all angles with the same measure. Try writing a procedure called TRIANGLE to draw such a triangle before reading on.

It is often helpful to sketch a figure before trying to write a procedure to draw it. To discover the measure of the angle that the turtle must turn at each vertex, we consider the sketch given in Figure 2-5.

Figure 2-5

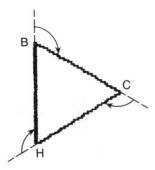

The turtle must be turned through three angles of equal measure to draw the equilateral triangle. Because the turtle returns to its initial heading after the three turns, its total turning amounts to a complete circle or 360 degrees. Thus, the amount of turning for each angle must be 360/3 or 120 degrees.

In Figure 2-5, suppose the turtle starts at home, H, and moves forward 50 units to point B. This can be accomplished by typing **FD 50**. At point B, the turtle has heading 0. In order to walk on the line segment connecting points B and C, the turtle must turn 120 degrees to the right. Thus, the next command should be **RT 120**. Because the triangle has three sides of equal length and three angles of equal measure, the turtle must repeat the sequence **FD 50 RT 120** three times. The **TRIANGLE** procedure is given below.

```
TO TRIANGLE
REPEAT 3[FD 50 RT 120]
END
```

Many people may obtain incorrect drawings when they try to work out this procedure. For example, they may think the measure of the turn angle should be 60 degrees instead of 120 degrees because the measure of an interior angle of the triangle is 60 degrees. An alternate way to find the measure of each turning angle is to recall that each interior angle must have the same measure and that the sum of the measures of the interior angles is 180 degrees. Thus, each interior angle must have measure 180/3 or 60 degrees. This implies that the turning angle is 180 − 60 or 120 degrees.

Many people think of triangles only in "textbook position"—that is, with one of the bases horizontal. The textbook position for the equilateral triangle is shown in Figure 2-6. Edit your **TRIANGLE** procedure to make it draw a triangle in this position.

Figure 2-6

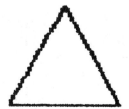

Problem Set 2-1

---

1. Write a procedure called TRI that draws an equilateral triangle with sides of length 50 and one of the bases horizontal, as in Figure 2-6.

2. Write procedures to draw each of the shapes shown below.

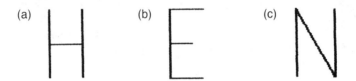

   (a)   (b)   (c)

3. Predict what happens when each of the following is executed. Use the computer to check your answers. Clear the screen after each part. If the **SQUARE** and **TRIANGLE** procedures from this section are not in the computer's workspace, enter them before checking your predictions.

   (a) REPEAT 4[TRIANGLE FD 50 LT 90]

   (b) SQUARE RT 45 SQUARE

   (c) SQUARE
         PU LT 90 FD 25 PD
         SQUARE

   (d) SQUARE
         PU LT 90 FD 25 RT 90 PD
         SQUARE

   (e) REPEAT 6[TRIANGLE RT 60]

   (f) REPEAT 10[SQUARE RT 36]

   (g) REPEAT 4[TRIANGLE SQUARE FD 50 RT 90]

   (h) REPEAT 4[TRIANGLE RT 45 SQUARE RT 45]

   (i) PU BK 10 RT 90 FD 25 LT 90 PD
         REPEAT 4[TRIANGLE FD 50 LT 45 SQUARE FD 50 LT 45]
         HT

4. (a) Type the following procedure exactly as it is written and define it by using CTRL-C.

    ```
    TO TRY.ANGLE
    FD 70
    RT 60
    F 70
    RI 60
    FD70
    RT 60
    END
    ```

   (b) How many bugs can you find in the procedure? What happens if you run the procedure in this form? Does the computer list all the bugs when you try to run the procedure?

   (c) Now reenter the edit mode to correct the program in (a) to read as shown below.

    ```
    TO TRY.ANGLE
    FD 70
    RT 60
    FD 70
    RT 60
    FD 70
    RT 60
    END
    ```

   (d) Predict the result of running the new program and check to see if you were correct.

   (e) Enter the edit mode and change the name of the program from TRY.ANGLE to TRY. Define TRY using CTRL-C. Will both TRY and TRY.ANGLE produce the same figure?

5. (a) Type the following program. Then, instead of exiting the edit mode with a CTRL-C, use a CTRL-G to abort the program.

    ```
    TO CORNER
    FD 70 RT 90 FD 70
    END
    ```

    Now type CORNER, press RETURN, and observe what happens. Why did the computer respond as it did?

(b) Type the following procedure and exit the edit mode by using CTRL-C.

TO TURN
FD 70 RT 90
END

Now type **TO TURN** and exit the edit mode with CTRL-G. What happens when **TURN** is executed?

6. Write a procedure to draw Figure (a). (The **SQUARE** procedure described earlier in this section might be useful.) Now edit the procedure to draw Figure (b).

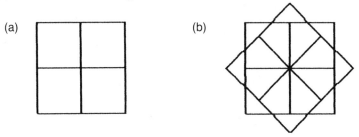

(a)   (b)

7. Use the edit mode to define procedures to draw each of the following shapes. If you can use previously defined procedures, do so. Use the names shown above the shapes as the names of the procedures.

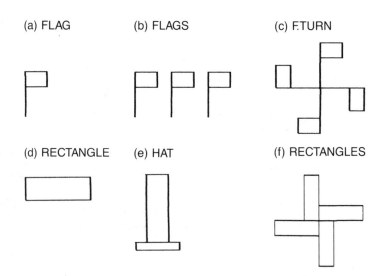

(a) FLAG   (b) FLAGS   (c) F.TURN

(d) RECTANGLE   (e) HAT   (f) RECTANGLES

(g) SQUARES   (h) HOUSE   (i) RHOMBUS

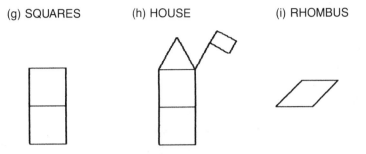

8. Write procedures to draw each of the following. Make each letter 50 units high and 30 units wide. (Make the letters in block form without curves.)

   (a) The letter L
   (b) The letter O
   (c) The letter G
   (d) The word LOGO

9. Sketch a figure of your choice on paper and then write a procedure to draw it.

☆10. Write a procedure to draw a square with a side length of 100 and with both diagonals showing.

2-2 More on the Editor and Workspace Management

Defining Several Procedures

Suppose we have just booted (started) Logo and we would like to teach the computer two new procedures called PENT and HEX. It is possible to use the edit mode to define more than one procedure at a time. To define these two procedures, we may enter the edit mode by typing TO PENT and pressing RETURN. The PENT procedure may then be typed, and the HEX procedure may be typed immediately afterward, as follows.

```
TO PENT
REPEAT 5[FD 30 RT 72]
END
TO HEX
REPEAT 6[FD 30 RT 60]
END
```

When we type CTRL-C, the edit mode is exited and both procedures are defined. The following messages are then displayed.

```
PENT DEFINED
HEX DEFINED
```

We saw in Section 2-1 that when we exited the edit mode after defining only one procedure, it was not necessary to close with the END statement. Logo assumed that we forgot it and added it for us. If the END statement had been omitted from the PENT procedure, however, the HEX procedure would have been merged with the PENT procedure and only the PENT procedure would have been defined. This points out the importance of always adding END statements to your procedures.

Editing Several Procedures

EDIT ALL
(ED ALL)

Just as it is possible to define more than one procedure at the same time, it is possible to edit several procedures at once. Suppose we decide, after several procedures have been defined, that we want the turtle to be hidden after each of the figures is drawn. Rather than edit each procedure separately, we use the EDIT (ED) command with the word ALL. When the command **EDIT ALL (ED ALL)** is used, everything in the workspace is listed in the editor. Then the required changes in all procedures can be made. After the editing is completed, CTRL-C is typed so that the procedures are redefined. For example, if we wish to hide the turtle when the PENT or HEX procedures are run, we execute ED ALL, then use CTRL-O to open a line before the END command in the PENT procedure and type HT. We then repeat this process for the HEX procedure. After the procedure have been revised, we use CTRL-C to redefine the procedures.

Remark: In Terrapin Logo version 2.0, the EDIT (ED) primitive may take a list of procedures as input—for example, ED [PENT HEX].

If there is a very long procedure or many procedures contained in the workspace when **ED ALL** is typed, more than one screen of text may need editing. In order to handle this, we need to be able to scroll large amounts of text back and forth. You can think of the screen as a window in front of a long page of text that moves up and down so that the desired text becomes available. Recall that using CTRL-P and CTRL-N moves the cursor only one line at a time. The commands shown below are useful for handling larger amounts of text in the editor.

CTRL-F Scrolls the text forward (down) one screenful.

CTRL-F

CTRL-B Scrolls the text back (up) one screenful or to the beginning of the sequence.

CTRL-B

CTRL-L Scrolls the text so that the line containing the cursor is approximately in the center of the screen.

CTRL-L

Remark: Note that CTRL-F has a different function in the edit mode than it does in the draw mode.

Examining the Workspace

Two new procedures, PENT and HEX, are now stored in the computer's workspace. In order to see the titles of all the procedures in the workspace, we use the command **PRINTOUT (PO)** with input TITLES. **PRINTOUT TITLES** can be abbreviated as **POTS**. If POTS is typed, a list of all the titles of procedures in the workspace will be printed on the screen. For example, if only PENT and HEX have been entered since the computer was turned on, typing POTS and pressing the RETURN key will cause the following two lines to be printed on the computer screen:

PRINTOUT (PO)
PRINTOUT TITLES (POTS)

```
TO PENT
TO HEX
```

It is possible to list a procedure without entering the edit mode by using the PRINTOUT (PO) command. For example, to display the procedure for PENT, we can type PO PENT and press RETURN. The following procedure is then printed on the screen. Compare this result with that obtained by typing TO PENT and pressing RETURN.

```
TO PENT
REPEAT 5[FD 30 RT 72]
END
```

Remark: In Terrapin Logo version 2.0, the PRINTOUT (PO) command can take a list of procedures as input—for example, PO [HEX PENT].

If PRINTOUT (PO) is used without an input, the most recently defined procedure will be displayed. The PRINTOUT (PO) command is normally used when the user simply wants to examine a procedure or procedures, whereas EDIT (ED) or TO is used when the user expects to make changes in one or more procedures. It is important to remember that changes in procedures can be made only in the edit mode.

Remark: If you are in the splitscreen mode and cannot see the entire text of a procedure, press CTRL-T to see the entire text screen and then CTRL-S to return to the splitscreen mode.

PRINTOUT ALL (PO ALL)

As explained previously, the workspace is a section of memory that holds all the currently defined procedures and variables. They can be viewed by typing **PRINTOUT ALL (PO ALL).** If there is more than one screenful of information, Logo will scroll rapidly through the workspace. You can think of the screen as a window moving in front of the scroll, as shown in Figure 2.7. You can stop the display from scrolling by using **CTRL-W**. Repeated use of CTRL-W will continue to advance the display one line at a time.

CTRL-W

Eliminating Procedures

ERASE (ER)

Sometimes we want to remove procedures from the workspace. To eliminate a procedure, we use the **ERASE (ER)** command. ERASE (ER) followed by the name of a procedure erases the procedure from the workspace. For example, if we type ER PENT, the PENT procedure

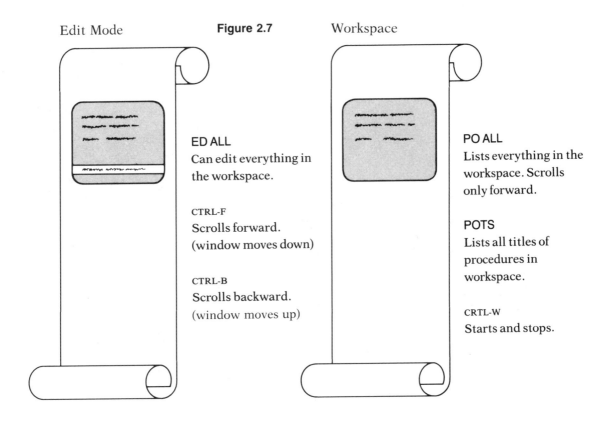

Edit Mode   **Figure 2.7**   Workspace

ED ALL
Can edit everything in
the workspace.

CTRL-F
Scrolls forward.
(window moves down)

CTRL-B
Scrolls backward.
(window moves up)

PO ALL
Lists everything in the
workspace. Scrolls
only forward.

POTS
Lists all titles of
procedures in
workspace.

CRTL-W
Starts and stops.

is removed from the computer's memory as soon as the RETURN key is pressed. Now if we type POTS, the PENT procedure is not listed on the screen.

Remark: In Terrapin Logo version 2.0, ERASE (ER) can take a list as input—for example, ER[PENT HEX].

To erase all the procedures from the workspace, you can use the commands **ERASE ALL (ER ALL)** or GOODBYE. An alternate way to clear everything out of the workspace is to shut the computer off and then reboot Logo. The advantage of using ER ALL or GOODBYE is that Logo does not have to be rebooted in order for us to continue.

**ERASE ALL
(ER ALL)**

Warning: Be careful before using ER ALL or GOODBYE, because once these commands have been executed, everything that you have been working on is erased from the workspace.

Summary of Commands

Editing Commands

CTRL-A	Moves the cursor to the beginning of the current line.
CTRL-E	Moves the cursor to the end of the current line (E stands for "end").
[1]CTRL-K	Deletes all the characters on the current line, beneath and to the right of the cursor (K stands for "kill").
CTRL-N	Moves the cursor down one line (N stands for "next").
CTRL-O	Opens a new line at the position of the cursor (O stands for "open").
CTRL-P	Moves the cursor up one line (P stands for "previous").
CTRL-F	Scrolls the text forward (down) one screenful.
CTRL-B	Scrolls the text back (up) one screenful or to the beginning of the sequence.
CTRL-L	Scrolls the text so that the line containing the cursor is approximately in the center of the screen.

Workspace Commands

[2]PRINTOUT (PO)	Takes a particular procedure name as input and prints out the text of the procedure.
PRINTOUT ALL (PO ALL)	Prints out all names and the text of procedures in the workspace. (Names are discussed in later chapters.)
PRINTOUT TITLES (POTS)	Prints out the titles of all the procedures in the workspace.
CTRL-W	Stops the screen from scrolling. Repeated typing of CTRL-W causes Logo to stop after printing the next line (or next list element). Typing another character will resume normal processing.
[2]ERASE (ER)	Takes a particular procedure name as input and erases the procedure from the workspace.
ERASE ALL (ER ALL)	Clears all procedures and names from the workspace. (Names are discussed in later chapters.)
GOODBYE	Clears the entire workspace and restarts Logo.

[1]In Terrapin Logo version 2.0, CTRL-X is used in place of CTRL-K to delete a line. CTRL-Y can be used to "yank back" (restore) the most recently deleted line.

[2]In Terrapin Logo version 2.0, PRINTOUT (PO) and ERASE (ER) can take a list of procedures as input—for example, ER [TRIANGLE SQUARE].

Problem Set 2-2

1. Type **GOODBYE** to clear all procedures from computer's work-space. Then enter both procedures listed below into the editor and define them using CTRL-C.

TO TRI	TO DIA
RT 30	TRI
REPEAT 3[FD 40 RT 120]	RT 60
END	FD 40
	RT 90
	TRI
	END

    (a) Guess the result of executing each procedure and run them to see if you were correct.
    (b) Type **EDIT** and press RETURN. What happens? Now type CTRL-G.
    (c) Type **EDIT ALL** and press RETURN. Change **FD 40** to **FD 20** in each procedure. Type CTRL-C to define each procedure.
    (d) Type **POTS**. What happens?
    (e) Type **PO ALL**. What happens?
    (f) Type **ER DIA**. What happens? Now if you type **POTS**, what appears?
    (g) Enter the following procedure, define it, guess the shape it produces, and run it to see if you were correct.

        TO DESIGN
        REPEAT 10[TRI RT 36]
        END

    (h) Will **DESIGN** be listed if you now type **POTS** and press RETURN?
    (i) Type **ER TRI** and then type **DESIGN** and press RETURN. What happens? Why?
    (j) Type **ER ALL**. Now what happens when you type **POTS**?

2. (a) Write a procedure called **SQ** to draw a square of size 20. Run the procedure.
    (b) Edit the **SQ** procedure to draw a square of size 100. Run your procedure to see that it works.
    (c) Change the name of the **SQ** procedure to **BOX**. Run **BOX** to see if it draws a square of size 100.

(d) Type **POTS**. Are both **SQ** and **BOX** listed? Why?

(e) Edit **SQ** to change it back to exactly the way it was in part (a).

3. Investigate the following while in the edit mode.

(a) How does pressing the RETURN key compare with using CTRL-N?

(b) How does pressing the space bar compare with pressing the right arrow key?

(c) Can a procedure be defined using CTRL-C if the cursor is not positioned at the end of the procedure?

4. (a) Write a procedure called **T** to draw the letter **T** so that it is 50 units high and 25 units wide.

(b) Edit the **T** procedure so that the letter that is drawn is twice as high and twice as wide as the one in part (a).

(c) Edit the **T** procedure so that the letter drawn is the same height as the one in part (a) but twice as wide.

2-3   Using Procedures as Building Blocks

Breaking Projects Down into Steps

In this section, we write procedures to draw more figures and also examine problem-solving skills and ideas of structured programming that are used in more complicated drawings. When creating a complex drawing, it is helpful to break the project down into steps. To illustrate this process, we first sketched a swing set on graph paper, as shown in Figure 2-8. The graph paper was marked off to represent the approximate size of the graphics screen, with each side of a small square representing 10 turtle steps.

Figure 2-8

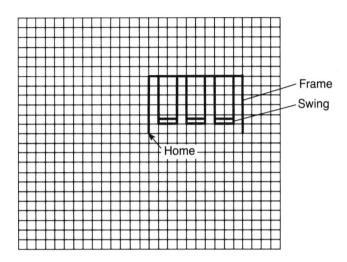

Many problems can be made easier by working on parts of them and then reassembling the parts to form the desired figure. The swing set, for example, can be broken down into parts, and a procedure can be written to draw each part. The swing set drawing is composed of the frame and the three swings. Notice that the same procedure will work for drawing each of the three swings. With the turtle at home with heading 0, a procedure to draw the swing set follows:

```
TO SWING.SET
FRAME
SWING
SWING
SWING
HT
END
```

Now try to write separate procedures for drawing the frame and a single swing. Compare your procedures with the procedures given below. Try to follow these procedures through and make sure you see how they work. If you have doubts, run them on the computer. The procedures you write may differ from the ones given here and still be absolutely correct. It is important to realize that the computer's execution of the procedure—not the book—is the final test of whether the procedure is correct.

```
TO FRAME      TO SWING
FD 60         BK 50
RT 90         RT 90
FD 100        FD 20
RT 90         LT 90
FD 60         FD 5
END           LT 90
              FD 20
              BK 20
              RT 90
              FD 45
              END
```

If we now run the **SWING.SET** procedure defined earlier, we will obtain the drawing in Figure 2-9.

Figure 2-9

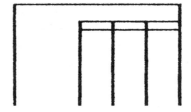

The figure here was caused by not moving the individual parts to where they belonged before we drew them. It is usually necessary to keep track not only of the turtle's position but also of its heading in order to set up the turtle for drawing the next part of a figure.

The reason that the swings are upside down is that the turtle had heading 180 when **FRAME** was completed. We can correct this by adding the line **RT 180** after **FRAME** in the **SWING.SET** procedure. If we run **SWING.SET** with the new line added, we notice that we have made progress: the swings are now right side up, as shown in Figure 2-10.

Figure 2-10

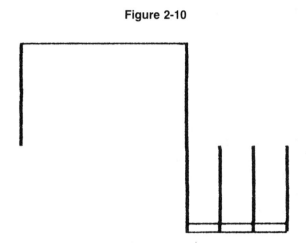

Next we need to adjust the turtle's position before drawing each swing. Because our swing was drawn by starting on the left side, we need to move the turtle to the left side of the frame first. We see from the graph in Figure 2-8 that to locate the appropriate starting point for the swings after the frame is drawn, we may move the turtle by executing the line **FD 60 LT 90 FD 90 RT 90**. Now the first swing can be drawn in its correct position. We can determine the starting point for the other two swings in a similar way. The new **SWING.SET** procedure is given below.

```
TO SWING.SET
FRAME
RT 180
FD 60 LT 90 FD 90 RT 90
SWING
RT 90 FD 10 LT 90
SWING
RT 90 FD 10 LT 90
SWING
HT
END
```

Figure 2-11

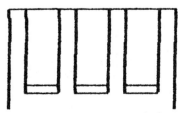

From the previous discussion we see that in each building block of a project it is important to note both the initial heading and position of the turtle and the final heading and position of the turtle. If this is not done, it is difficult to put the parts together as desired. Later we will see that it is also necessary to keep track of whether the pen is up or down and of the color of the pen if a color monitor is being used.

top-down programming

The approach to programming we have just demonstrated in the SWING.SET procedure is called **top-down programming.** It starts with a general idea and gradually begins to deal with smaller details. This is a very useful approach to many problems, although it is easier to work some problems without breaking them down into smaller parts.

In working through the swing set problem, we broke the problem down into several steps. A summary of these steps is given below. (These steps may not be appropriate for all problems.)

1. Sketch your drawing on paper, preferably graph paper, in order to get an idea of the scale to be used and of how the final picture should look.

2. Divide the drawing into parts that are repeated, that you already know how to draw, or that are smaller parts of the whole. Separate procedures to draw each individual part are easier to check than a single procedure for the whole drawing.

3. Decide how your individual procedures are going to fit together to form the complete picture. Some procedures may be necessary just to move the turtle to the right position for drawing the individual parts.

4. Write your procedures. One approach is to write individual procedures, make sure they work, and then try to put them all together to form the complete picture. Another approach is to fit the procedures together as they are completed. Either approach is an acceptable problem-solving strategy, and each has advantages in different situations.

Problem 2-2

Write a procedure for drawing the boat sketched in Figure 2-12.

Figure 2-12

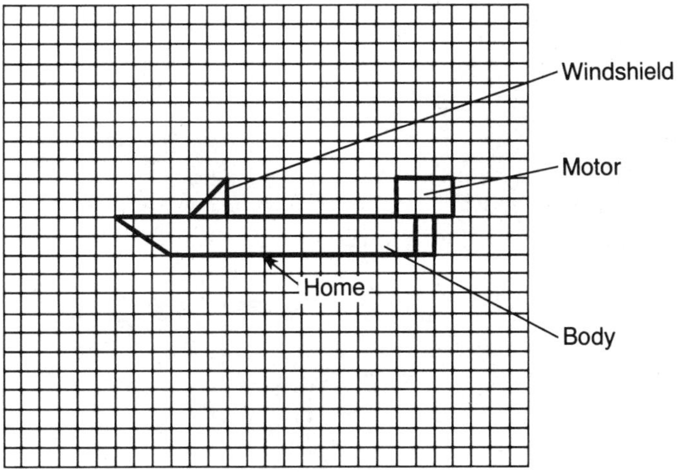

Solution

The figure can be broken down into three separate parts: the body, the windshield, and the motor. Thus, a procedure named **BOAT** to draw this figure might appear as follows:

```
TO BOAT
BODY
MOTOR
WINDSHIELD
HT
END
```

First we design a procedure called **BODY** for drawing the body. One possible procedure and its output are given in Figure 2-13.

TO BODY
LT 90 FD 50
RT 45 FD 28
RT 135 FD 150
RT 90 FD 20
RT 90 FD 80
RT 90
END

Figure 2-13

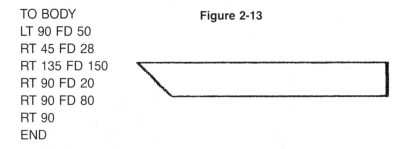

Likewise, procedures called **MOTOR** and **WINDSHIELD** can be designed to draw the other two parts, as shown in Figures 2-14 and 2-15.

TO MOTOR
FD 20 LT 90
FD 10 RT 90
FD 20 RT 90
FD 30 RT 90
FD 20 RT 90
FD 10 LT 90
FD 20 RT 90
FD 10 RT 90
END

Figure 2-14

TO WINDSHIELD
FD 20 LT 135
FD 28 LT 135
FD 20 LT 90
END

Figure 2-15

If we attempt to put these procedures together in the procedure called **BOAT** in the order previously listed, the result will be as shown in Figure 2-16.

Figure 2-16

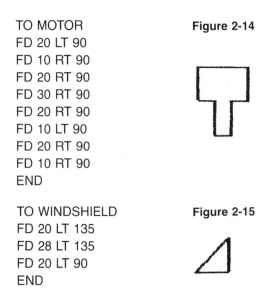

Here we have encountered the same type of problem that we met in the SWING.SET procedure. To correct the BOAT procedure so that it draws the correct figure, we must keep track of the turtle's position and heading. Sometimes it is convenient to move the turtle to the required positions and headings by using a set of procedures. The procedure below, called SETUP.M, moves the turtle to the correct position for drawing the motor. The procedure SETUP.W moves the turtle to the correct position for drawing the windshield. It is often advantageous to use such "setup" procedures in complex projects because they make debugging easier.

```
TO SETUP.M
PU RT 90 FD 80 LT 90 PD
END
```

```
TO SETUP.W
PU FD 20 LT 90 FD 100 RT 90 PD
END
```

After we edit BOAT to add these new procedures, we obtain the procedure and the picture shown in Figure 2-17.

```
TO BOAT
BODY
SETUP.M
MOTOR
SETUP.W
WINDSHIELD
HT
END
```

Figure 2-17

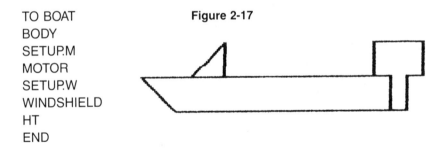

Error Messages

When a programming error occurs while a procedure is running, an error message is printed. For example, suppose we wish to draw a house using the HOUSE procedure given below. The HOUSE procedure calls on the procedure BOTTOM, which in turn calls upon another procedure called SQ. Notice the errors in SQ and in BOTTOM. We are interested in the error messages that occur when the HOUSE procedure is run. Before reading on, predict what happens if HOUSE is executed in its current form.

```
TO HOUSE
BOTTOM
REPEAT 3[FD 50 RT 120]
HT
END
```

```
TO BOTTOM      TO SQ
SQ             REPEAT 4[FD50 RT 90]
FD 50 R 30     END
END
```

When HOUSE is executed, Logo runs the program until it encounters an error. Then it types the following error message:

```
THERE IS NO PROCEDURE NAMED FD50, IN LINE
  REPEAT 4[FD50 RT 90]
AT LEVEL 3 OF SQ
```

Notice that Logo did not reach the error in the BOTTOM procedure because the SQ procedure was called first and the error in that procedure caused it to be stopped and the error message to be displayed. The error occurred because a procedure can be named by any combination of letters or letters followed by numbers, and the computer "thought" that FD50 was the name of a procedure. Because no such procedure had been defined, the computer did not find it in its memory and therefore reported the error message.

Notice that the error message contains the following pieces of information:

- a description of the error
- the line in which it occurred
- the level number at which the error occurred
- the name of the procedure that contained the error

level number   This message is self-explanatory except for the **level number.** We can think of instructions executed at the prompt as being at the top level or level 0 because no procedures (zero procedures) are involved in the execution of the command. A command in HOUSE is executed at level 1, since one procedure is involved in the execution of the command. Since BOTTOM is called by HOUSE, a command in BOTTOM is executed at level 2. Other level numbers have similar meanings. The model of the HOUSE procedure shown in Figure 2-18 may help you to understand level numbers. Similar models will be described further when procedures that call other procedures are discussed in later chapters.

Figure 2-18

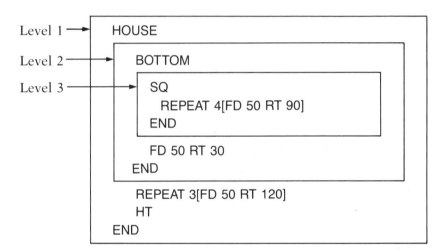

Based on this information, we should edit the SQ procedure to change the typing of FD50 to FD 50, press CTRL-C, and try the HOUSE procedure again. This time the HOUSE procedure will be executed until the error in the BOTTOM procedure is encountered. That is, a square of size 50 will be drawn, the turtle will move forward 50 units, and then the following error message will be displayed:

```
THERE IS NO PROCEDURE NAMED R, IN LINE
   FD 50 R 30
AT LEVEL 2 OF BOTTOM
```

Notice that this is a level 2 error because BOTTOM was called by HOUSE, which is a level 1 procedure. If we now edit the BOTTOM procedure to change R 30 to RT 30 and redefine the procedure using

CTRL-C, and if no other errors are present, a house should be drawn when **HOUSE** is executed.

Remark: If the entire error message is not visible in the splitscreen mode, use CTRL-T to see the entire textscreen and then CTRL-S to return to the splitscreen mode.

Problem Set 2-3

1. Write procedures to draw each of the following figures.

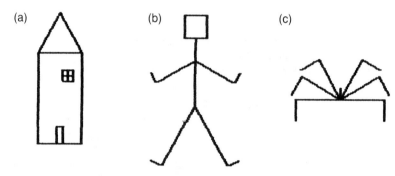

(a)   (b)   (c)

2. Copy the procedures below exactly as listed, run them to obtain an error message, and then correct the error in order to draw a rectangle.

```
TO RECT                TO CORNER
CORNER                 FD 70 RITE 90 FD 30
RT 90                  END
CORNER
RT 90
END
```

3. Predict the result of running each of the following procedures. Use the computer to check your guesses. (It is assumed that a procedure called **SQUARE**, which draws a square of size 50, is in the workspace.)

```
(a)  TO ROOF       (b)  TO HOUSE1
     RT 30              SQUARE
     FD 50              ROOF
     RT 120             END
     FD 50
     END
```

(c) TO HOUSE2
     SQUARE
     FD 50
     ROOF
     END

(d) TO HOUSE3
     SQUARE
     FD 50
     SQUARE
     FD 50
     ROOF
     END

4. Write a procedure called **BLADES** to draw the following figure.

5. Write procedures to draw the following pieces of the playground equipment. Use the names listed for the procedure names.

(a) T.TOTTER

(b) M.BARS

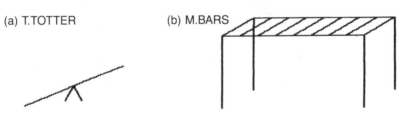

(c) SLIDE

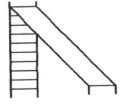

6. Write a procedure called **PLAYGROUND** that draws each playground piece designed in problem 5 to form a playground. Add more pieces to the playground if you desire.

2-4 Creating Files on a Disk

permanent memory

Once we have defined a procedure, the computer remembers it as long as it is not erased from the workspace or working memory. If the machine is turned off, all the work that is in the workspace is lost unless the material is first saved on a floppy disk. The disk acts as a **permanent memory** for storing procedures.

initialize

When a new floppy disk is purchased, it contains no information at all. Before anything can be saved on a disk, the disk must be **initialized.** When a disk is initialized, special information is placed on the disk in order for it to operate on the computer. A disk needs to be initialized only once. If it is initialized each time it is used, all previous material stored on it will be lost.

Disks for Logo are initialized using commands from Apple DOS (Disk Operating System). They can be initialized in the same way as other disks for the Apple. To initialize a disk, simply follow these instructions.

1. Place the Logo Utilities disk in the disk drive and turn on the computer's power. (Remember that the Utilities disk is different from the Logo disk.)

2. After the disk drive stops whirring, remove the Utilities disk from the drive and insert the disk to be initialized.

3. Type

    INIT HELLO

    and press RETURN. When the disk drive stops and the red light goes out, the disk has been initialized. It can be used to save files.

4. Remove the disk and label it with a felt tip pen. Do not write on it with a sharp pen. Store the disk until you need it.

Remark: A disk may also be initialized by booting the Apple System Master (or another disk that has been initialized using an Apple II+, Apple IIe, or Apple IIc), placing the new disk in the drive, typing NEW and pressing RETURN. Next type INIT HELLO and press RETURN. Incidentally, titles other than HELLO can be used to initialize disks. Some people may use their own names to initialize their disks.

Caring for Your Disk

Here are several guidelines that might help prevent an accident that could damage your disk and destroy all your work.

1. Always return a disk to its envelope after using it.

2. Store disks away from dust and heat, including direct sunlight.

3. Keep disks away from magnets or electric motors.

4. Always label your disks, but only with a felt tip pen. Never write on a disk with a sharp-pointed pen or pencil.

5. Use common sense! Never fold, throw, or drop a disk.

Cataloging a Disk

Now we experiment with saving files on a disk. The term **file** is used to refer to a body of information stored on the disk. For example, a file might be a set of procedures or a picture. To create a file, load Logo into the computer, remove the Logo disk, and insert your newly initialized disk. The command for examining the contents of your disk is **CATALOG.** If you type CATALOG and press RETURN with the new disk in the drive, Logo will respond with a list of all the files on the disk. In this case, the only file present is the HELLO file, which was created when you initialized the disk. In addition to the volume number of the disk, the HELLO file will be listed as shown.

file

CATALOG

A 002 HELLO

Remark: The A in this listing simply means that the file is written in Applesoft BASIC. The number 002 indicates that the file is two sectors in length. In all, a disk can store 496 sectors of programs and other files. You don't need to worry about these parts of the listing.

To see a listing of the files on the the Utilities disk, type CATALOG and press RETURN when the Utilities disk is in the disk drive. When you have looked at the first part of the list, press the space bar to see the names of the remainder of the files.

Saving Files on Disk

To see how to save files, type in the following procedures.

```
TO TRIANGLE
REPEAT 3[FD 60 RT 120]
END
```

TO L.ANTENNA	TO R.ANTENNA	TO BUTTERFLY
LT 15	RT 15	RT 60
FD 20	FD 20	TRIANGLE
LT 120	RT 120	RT 180
FD 10	FD 10	TRIANGLE
BK 10	BK 10	RT 120
RT 120	LT 120	R.ANTENNA
BK 20	BK 20	L.ANTENNA
RT 15	LT 15	HT
END	END	END

Before saving any procedures on a disk, we should make sure the procedures do what we want them to do. Thus, after defining the four new procedures given above, type **BUTTERFLY** and see if you get a figure that looks like a butterfly. If you do not, debug the program.

We are now ready to save the procedures on a disk. First, we choose a name for the file. Suppose we choose the name **INSECT** to remind us of what is in the file. We could have chosen the name **BUTTERFLY** instead; it does not matter that this file name is also a procedure name.

It is important to examine the contents of the workspace before saving it on a disk. There may be some procedures in the workspace that we do not want to save or we may have erased some that we intended to save. Recall that to see a list of all procedure titles in the workspace, we type **POTS**. It is more convenient to type **ND** to get into the nodraw mode before typing **POTS** so that we will have the whole screen for the title display. If there is more than one screenful of procedures, the list will scroll as it is being displayed. You can stop the scrolling by using CTRL-W. Repeated use of CTRL-W will continue to advance the display one line at a time.

If there are titles of procedures on the list that we do not want to save, we can erase the procedures with the ERASE (ER) command.

To save the desired procedures on the disk, we use the command **SAVE**, followed by the file name we chose. For example, typing

SAVE "INSECT

will save everything in the workspace in a file called INSECT. Notice that a space and a single set of quotes must appear before the file name. When the disk drive stops whirring, your file will be saved on the disk. To check this, type CATALOG. The following listing should appear on the screen.

```
A 002 HELLO
B 003 INSECT.LOGO
```

Logo files are listed with .LOGO at the end. You should not add this word when you save or retrieve files.

Remark: In Terrapin Logo version 2.0, it is possible to save selected procedures from the workspace in a file. For example, to save just the TRIANGLE procedure in the INSECT file, we type SAVE "INSECT [TRIANGLE].

Reading Files from the Disk

Before we read a file from a disk back into the workspace, we may want to clear the workspace. (Remember that this can be done in several ways; probably the easiest is simply to type GOODBYE. Be sure to save anything you want to keep before you clear the memory!) If the workspace is not cleared first, all the material from the file will be added to the present workspace contents. This may be desirable in some cases.

To read a file back into the workspace, we type the command **READ** followed by a single set of quotes and the file name, like this:

READ "INSECT

When we press RETURN, the disk drive will begin to whir, and everything stored on the disk under the name INSECT will be added to the

SAVE

READ

workspace. As the procedures are entered into the workspace, their names will appear on the screen. Once the disk drive stops, any of the procedures from the INSECT file can be used just as if it had been typed directly into the computer.

It is important to realize that only a copy of the file is transferred into the workspace. The procedures as originally saved are still stored on the disk and can be read from the disk as many times as desired. You should also note that a procedure in the workspace will be replaced if a procedure with the same name is read in from the disk.

Remark: It is often desirable to create a **backup copy** of your procedures. This can be accomplished by using a second initialized disk. You can read the material from the first disk into the workspace and then save it on the second disk. Remember to examine the workspace each time to see exactly what you are saving. A backup copy can ensure that your work will not be lost if something happens to your first disk.

Adding Procedures to a File

Procedures can be added to a file by reading the file from a disk into the workspace, entering the new procedures into the workspace, and then saving the workspace under the same file name as before. This process replaces the previous file on the disk with the new file of the same name.

Warning: If you read procedures from a file into the workspace, edit the procedures, and do not save the edited form back on a disk, the edited procedures will be lost when the computer's memory is cleared. The original file on the disk will not be changed.

Saving and Reading Pictures on a Disk

It is also possible to save pictures on a disk. This is handy if a picture is so complicated that it takes a long time to draw or if the only way to get the picture to print out on a printer is through first saving it on a disk. To save the butterfly picture on a disk, for example, run

BUTTERFLY to produce the picture and then use the **SAVEPICT** command as shown.

SAVEPICT "BUTTERFLY

Again, the name for the picture can be one of your own choosing. It doesn't have to be the same as the name of the procedure that created the picture.

To recall a picture from the disk, use the **READPICT** command with the name you gave the picture, like this.

READPICT

READPICT "BUTTERFLY

Pictures saved on a disk by using the SAVEPICT command are listed in the disk catalog with .PICT appended to their names. To see this, catalog your disk after saving the butterfly picture. When a picture is saved on a disk, it is possible to have the picture appear in a procedure by using the READPICT command.

Warning: If you name a file or picture with the same name as a file or picture already on the disk, and then save the new file, the file on the disk will be erased and replaced with the new file. It is a good idea to copy everything onto your backup disk before trying to change files, in case you make a wrong entry or some other disaster occurs.

Erasing Files and Pictures

We use the commands **ERASEFILE** and **ERASEPICT** to erase files or pictures from a disk. For example, to erase the INSECT file and the BUTTERFLY picture, we type the following:

ERASEFILE
ERASEPICT

ERASEFILE "INSECT
ERASEPICT "BUTTERFLY

Remark: Saving pictures on a disk requires a considerable amount of memory, so pictures can fill up disk space quite quickly. For this reason, you should get in the habit of erasing pictures that you really do not need.

Summary of Commands

CATALOG	Prints the names of the files on the disk in the drive.
[1]SAVE	Takes one input. Saves the contents of the workspace on disk; for example, SAVE "GOOD.STUFF.
READ	Takes one input. Reads a file from the disk; for example, READ "GOOD.STUFF.
SAVEPICT	Takes one input. Saves the picture on the screen to the disk, using the input name; for example, SAVEPICT "HOUSE.
READPICT	Takes one input. Reads the picture with the input name from the disk and displays it on the screen; for example, READPICT "HOUSE.
ERASEFILE	Takes one input. Erases the file with the input name from the disk; for example, ERASEFILE "TURTLE.TALK.
ERASEPICT	Takes one input. Erases the picture with the input name from the disk; for example, ERASEPICT "HOUSE.

[1]In Terrapin Logo version 2.0, SAVE can be used to save selected procedures from the workspace; for example, SAVE "POLYGONS [SQUARE TRIANGLE PENTAGON].

Problem Set 2-4

1. Type GOODBYE and press RETURN to clear the workspace. Then enter the four procedures given below.

```
TO SQUARE                TO PENTAGON
REPEAT 4[FD 70 RT 90]    REPEAT 5[FD 70 RT 72]
END                      END


TO HEXAGON               TO POLYGONS
REPEAT 6[FD 70 RT 60]    SQUARE
END                      PENTAGON
                         HEXAGON
                         END
```

(a) Execute POTS to see if all the titles are listed.
(b) Save these four procedures to your file disk under the name POLYGONS.

(c)   Type **GOODBYE** and then type **POTS** to see that the work-space is empty. Read in the **POLYGONS** file. Execute **POTS** to see if all the titles are listed.

(d)   Enter the following procedure.

```
TO OCTAGON
REPEAT 8[FD 70 RT 45]
END
```

Now save the workspace under the name **FIGURES**. Type **GOODBYE** and read in the **FIGURES** file. Execute **POTS** and observe the results.

(e)   Erase the **OCTAGON** procedure from the workspace and save the procedures under the name **FIGURES**. How does the **FIGURES** file compare with the **POLYGONS** file?

(f)   Erase the **FIGURES** file from the disk. Type **CATALOG** and press RETURN to make sure it is gone.

2.   Run the **POLYGONS** procedure from problem 1 to obtain a figure on the screen. Then do each of the following:

(a)   Save the picture on a disk under the name **POLYS**.

(b)   Type **CATALOG** to see if the picture was really saved to the disk.

(c)   Clear the screen and read the picture from the disk onto the screen.

(d)   Erase the picture from the disk.

Solution to the Preliminary Problem

Understanding the Problem

The problem is to design a series of procedures to create a drawing similar to the one in Figure 2-19. Once the drawing is complete, we are to save it on a disk.

Figure 2-19

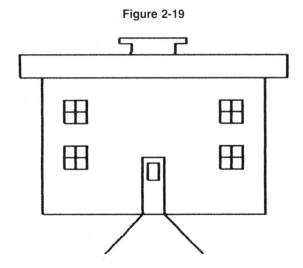

Devising a Plan

We follow the steps outlined in the chapter, beginning by drawing a sketch of the figure in order to determine a proper scale and to break the figure down into smaller parts. A sample sketch is given below in Figure 2-20.

Figure 2-20

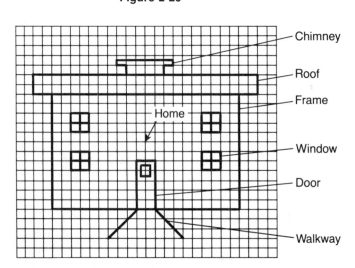

Now we can write procedures to draw each of the individual parts and put the procedures together to form the desired figure. It will take several moves in each case to get the turtle in the proper position to draw the individual parts. An overall procedure might look like the following:

```
TO HOUSE
FULLSCREEN
FRAME
ROOF
CHIMNEY
WINDOW
WINDOW
WINDOW
WINDOW
DOOR
WALKWAY
HT
END
```

Carrying Out the Plan

Using the scale from the graph paper in Figure 2-20, we can write the following procedures to draw the individual parts. The turtle starts and stops in its original position and heading in each part.

```
TO FRAME
REPEAT 2[FD 120 RT 90 FD 200 RT 90]
END
```

```
TO ROOF
REPEAT 2[FD 20 RT 90 FD 240 RT 90]
END
```

```
TO CHIMNEY
FD 10 LT 90
FD 10 RT 90
FD 5 RT 90
FD 60 RT 90
FD 5 RT 90
FD 10 LT 90
FD 10 RT 90
FD 40 RT 90
END

TO WINDOW
REPEAT 4[SQUARE RT 90]
END

TO SQUARE
REPEAT 4[FD 10 RT 90]
END

TO DOOR
FD 50 LT 90
FD 20 LT 90
FD 50 RT 180
FD 30 RT 90
PU FD 5 LT 90 PD
REPEAT 2[FD 15 RT 90 FD 10 RT 90]
PU RT 90 FD 15 LT 90 BK 30 PD
END

TO WALKWAY
LT 45 BK 50 FD 50
LT 45 FD 20 LT 45
FD 50 BK 50 RT 45
BK 20 RT 90
END
```

Next we need to move the turtle into the proper position and heading
to draw each part. If the turtle starts at home with heading 0, separate
procedures similar to the **SETUP** procedures in Problem 2-2 could be
written for each of the above procedures, but in this case we will edit

the HOUSE procedure and include the appropriate instructions in the main procedure, as follows:

```
TO HOUSE
FULLSCREEN
PU LT 90 FD 100 LT 90 FD 70 RT 180 PD
FRAME
FD 120 LT 90 FD 20 RT 90
ROOF
PU RT 90 FD 100 LT 90 FD 20 PD
CHIMNEY
PU BK 50 LT 90 FD 50 RT 90 PD
WINDOW
PU BK 40 PD
WINDOW
PU RT 90 FD 140 LT 90 PD
WINDOW
PU FD 40 PD
WINDOW
PU BK 90 LT 90 FD 60 RT 90 PD
DOOR
WALKWAY
HT
END
```

Once the house is displayed on the screen, we can save it to a disk by typing SAVEPICT "HOUSE and pressing RETURN.

Looking Back

In this step, we run the procedure to see if it produces the desired result. If not, we debug the program. Some possible related projects are given below.

1. Draw the house using a smaller scale and add a garage.

2. Add some smoke coming out of the chimney.

3. Add several trees and shrubs around the house.

Chapter 2 Problem Set

1. (a) Enter the **TRI** and **SPIN** procedures shown below and then predict the results of running each procedure. Check your predictions.

   ```
   TO TRI                    TO SPIN
   REPEAT 3[FD 50 RT 120]    REPEAT 3[TRI RT 120]
   END                       END
   ```

   (b) Edit the **SPIN** procedure to make the following changes. Predict the results of running each edited procedure, then check your predictions.

   (1) Change the input to **REPEAT** from 3 to 6 and the angle size from 120 to 60.

   (2) Change the input to **REPEAT** to 8 and the angle size to 45.

   (3) Change the input to **REPEAT** to 12 and the angle size 30.

   (4) Change the input to **REPEAT** to 24 and the angle size to 15.

2. Write procedures to draw each of the following figures, using the names above the drawings as procedure names.

   (a) TRIANGLES   (b) RECTANGLES

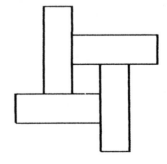

(c) MISSION   (d) KITE

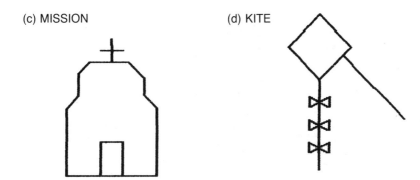

3. Write procedures to draw figures similar to each of the following.

    (a)   (b)

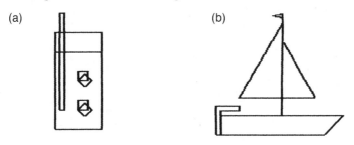

4. Write procedures to draw a figure similar to the following. Save
    the picture on your disk.

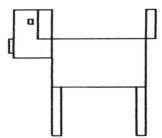

5. Create a maze on the screen and save the picture of the maze on
    a disk. Practice moving the turtle through the maze.

3

New Vocabulary in Chapter 3

Terms	Primitives	Keys
variable p. 88	TRACE p. 96	CTRL-Z p. 99
local variables p. 95	NOTRACE p. 97	
convex polygon p. 102	PAUSE p. 98	
concave polygon p. 103	CONTINUE (CO) p. 98	
congruent p. 104	PENCOLOR (PC) p. 117	
Closed Path Theorem p. 105	BACKGROUND (BG) p. 117	
Total Turtle Trip Theorem p. 105	RANDOM p. 118	
regular polygon p. 105	RANDOMIZE p. 119	
obtuse angle p. 107		
arc p. 111		
perimeter p. 113		
circumference p. 113		

Preliminary Problem

Write a procedure to draw an umbrella similar to the one shown above. Use variables so that the umbrella can be drawn in various sizes, and use color if available.

3

Procedures with Variables

Introduction

The procedures developed in Chapter 2 can be used for drawing only one size of figure. In this chapter, we introduce the concept of a variable in a procedure. Variables enable us to draw different sizes of figures using the same procedure. We also develop various procedures for drawing variable sizes of circles and arcs. In addition, we include a section on how to use color.

3-1 Procedures with Variables

Introducing a Variable

The procedure given below for drawing a square was developed in Chapter 2.

```
TO SQUARE
REPEAT 4 [FD 50 RT 90]
END
```

This procedure draws a square whose sides have size 50. To draw a different size square, we have to either edit this procedure or write a new procedure.

variable

A third alternative is to write a procedure to draw a square using a variable for the length of a side. A **variable** is a name for an unknown in algebra; it is also an unknown in a Logo procedure. Any letter, word (as long as it is not a Logo primitive), or combination of letters and numerals preceded by a colon may be used as a variable. The colon indicates to the computer that what follows is a variable. For example, when we tell the turtle to move **FORWARD :SIDE** instead of **FORWARD 50**, the command is not limited to one distance to move forward. Suppose we edit **SQUARE** and change **FD 50** to **FD :SIDE** , as shown below.

```
TO SQUARE
REPEAT 4 [FD :SIDE RT 90]
END
```

Now if we run the **SQUARE** procedure, we will obtain the following error message:

```
THERE IS NO NAME SIDE, IN LINE
  REPEAT 4 [FD :SIDE RT 90]
AT LEVEL 1 OF SQUARE.
```

When the computer executed the **SQUARE** procedure, it did not know what :SIDE was. The colon indicated that :SIDE was a variable, so the computer expected to be given a value for :SIDE. Since no value was given for :SIDE, the computer registered an error in the line **REPEAT 4 [FD :SIDE RT 90]**. Because this line appears in the **SQUARE** procedure, the error is in level 1 of **SQUARE**.

To debug the procedure and to be able to give the computer a value for the side, we need to put :SIDE in the title line. We may do this by entering the edit mode and changing the title line as follows:

```
TO SQUARE :SIDE
```

Placing :SIDE in the title line tells the computer that :SIDE will be replaced with an input when the procedure is run. The complete edited procedure follows.

TO SQUARE :SIDE
REPEAT 4 [FD :SIDE RT 90]
END

If we now type **SQUARE** and press RETURN, the procedure still will
not run. Instead, we will obtain this error mesage:

SQUARE NEEDS MORE INPUTS.

The reason for the error message is that the computer was not told
how long to make the side of the square—that is, it was not given a
value for the variable :SIDE. This can be done by typing **SQUARE**
followed by a space and a number. Figure 3-1 shows drawings created
by various executions of this procedure. (Execute **DRAW** to clear the
screen after each part.)

Figure 3-1

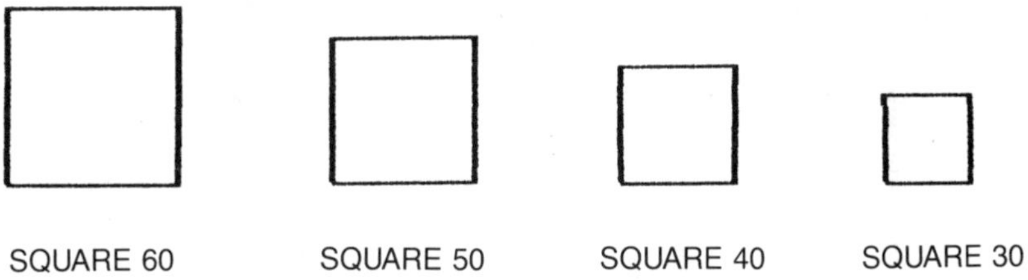

SQUARE 60   SQUARE 50   SQUARE 40   SQUARE 30

Investigate the use of variables by typing the following and clearing
the screen after each run.

(a) SQUARE :50   (b) SQUARE 0

(c) SQUARE 37+25   (d) SQUARE 37   +   25

(e) SQUARE (37+25)   (f) SQUARE 30*2

(g) SQUARE −50   (h) SQUARE 50 FD 50 SQUARE 25

If you ran parts (c), (d), (e), and (f), you discovered that a procedure
accepts arithmetic expressions as replacements for the variable :SIDE.
The computer does the arithmetic involved first and then uses the
result of the arithmetic as the replacement for :SIDE. Notice that the
spacing of the numerals and the plus sign does not matter and that
parentheses are not needed.

Using Variables with Procedures Calling Procedures

Much as we wrote the procedure to draw a square of variable size, we can write a procedure to draw a variable size triangle:

TO TRIANGLE :SIDE
REPEAT 3 [FD :SIDE RT 120]
END

The **SQUARE** and **TRIANGLE** procedures can then be used in creating other procedures. For example, we encourage you to try to write a procedure to draw a house as in Figure 3-2(a) before reading further. [Figure 3-2(b) may help.] Write your procedure so that the turtle returns to its original position and heading.

Figure 3-2

(a)

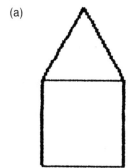

(b)

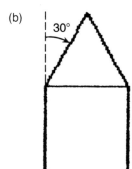

Such a procedure could first draw a square of size :SIDE, then put the turtle in the correct position to draw the triangle by moving the turtle **FD :SIDE** and turning **RT 30**, and then by drawing the triangle. To return the turtle to its original position and heading, we use the instructions **LT 30** and **BK :SIDE**. We might call the procedure **HOUSE** and write it as shown below.

TO HOUSE :SIDE
SQUARE :SIDE
FD :SIDE RT 30
TRIANGLE :SIDE
LT 30 BK :SIDE
HT
END

Using Arithmetic with Variables

Through the use of variables we gain much flexibility in writing procedures, because one procedure can be used for drawing many different sizes of figures. For example, to draw the nested squares in Figure 3-3, we could write a **NESTSQUARES** procedure using the variable :SIDE.

Figure 3-3

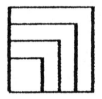

The **NESTSQUARES** procedure could draw the largest square, then draw the next largest square by making the length of the side 10 units smaller, and continue this process until all the squares are drawn, like this:

```
TO NESTSQUARES :SIDE
SQUARE :SIDE
SQUARE :SIDE - 10
SQUARE :SIDE - 20
SQUARE :SIDE - 30
END
```

Notice that the first square was drawn by using **SQUARE :SIDE**, giving :SIDE the same input as we gave for it in **NESTSQUARES :SIDE**. Then, to draw the next largest square, we decrease the input value for :SIDE by using :SIDE − 10 as the input the second time **SQUARE** is called. For example, if we start with **SQUARE 50**, the largest square will be drawn with sides of length 50. If we then call **SQUARE** with :SIDE − 10 as input, the side of the second square will have length (50 − 10), or 40. The same process can be used to draw the other two nested squares with input :SIDE − 20 and :SIDE − 30, respectively.

Now, predict the results of running **NESTSQUARES** with inputs of 60, 30, 0 and − 20. Check your predictions using the computer. Remember to clear the screen before each new run.

Problem 3-1

Write a procedure to draw a set of houses similar to the ones shown in Figure 3-4.

Figure 3-4

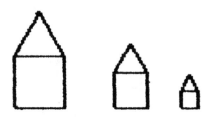

Solution

We may write a procedure similar to **NESTSQUARES** to draw the set of houses. We might call it **ROW**.

Recall that we already have a **HOUSE** procedure, as given below.

```
TO HOUSE :SIDE
SQUARE :SIDE
FD :SIDE RT 30
TRIANGLE :SIDE
LT 30 BK :SIDE
HT
END
```

ROW, the procedure to draw the set of houses, must have :SIDE as a variable input so that it can provide input to **HOUSE**. Just as the **NESTSQUARES** procedure called **SQUARE** three times, so **ROW** must call **HOUSE** three times. Each time **HOUSE** is called, we want to decrease the input by the same amount. This can be done by calling HOUSE :SIDE, HOUSE :SIDE − 10, and HOUSE :SIDE − 20.

To move the turtle into position to draw the next house after a house is drawn, we need to write a **MOVE** procedure. This can be done in many ways, and we encourage you to try it on your own. One way to write the procedure is to consider what it must do. If we draw the large house first, then we might want **MOVE** to put the pen up, turn the turtle right 90 degrees, move the turtle forward twice the length of a side of the house, turn the turtle left 90 degrees, and put the pen down. In this manner, we draw the second house, move the turtle, and draw the third house. A MOVE procedure to do these things is given below.

```
TO MOVE :SIDE
PU
RT 90
FD :SIDE*2
LT 90
PD
END
```

Here is the complete ROW procedure, combining the HOUSE procedures and the MOVE procedures.

```
TO ROW :SIDE
HOUSE :SIDE
MOVE :SIDE
HOUSE :SIDE − 10
MOVE :SIDE − 10
HOUSE :SIDE − 20
END
```

Procedures with Several Variables

In Logo, we can use more than one variable in a procedure. To do this, we must list all the variables in the title line, preceding each variable by a colon and separating each variable from the next by at least one space. For example, we could use either of the procedures below to define a rectangle with variable widths and lengths.

```
TO RECTANGLE :WIDTH :LENGTH
FD :WIDTH RT 90
FD :LENGTH RT 90
FD :WIDTH RT 90
FD :LENGTH RT 90
END
```

```
TO RECTANGLE :WIDTH :LENGTH
REPEAT 2 [FD :WIDTH RT 90 FD :LENGTH RT 90]
END
```

In Figure 3-5, we see two different runs of this procedure.

Figure 3-5

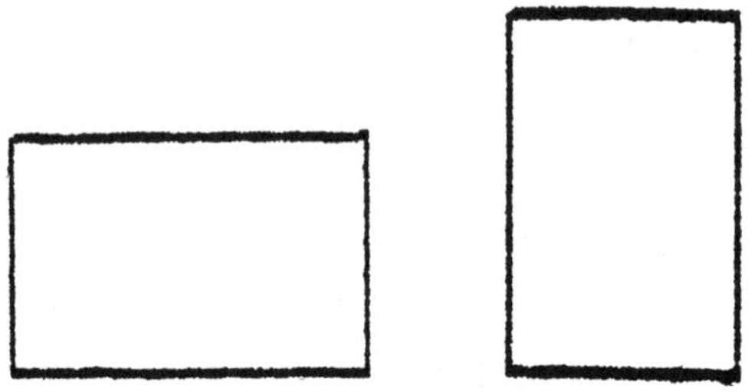

RECTANGLE 45 70   RECTANGLE 70 45

When **RECTANGLE** is run with inputs 45 70, the computer reads the first value, 45, as the value of **:WIDTH** and the second value, 70, as the value of **:LENGTH**. (These values are used only in a single run of the procedure; they must be typed in again each time.) Typing REC-TANGLE 70 45, on the other hand, produces a rectangle with a width of 70 and a length of 45. In other words, inputs are assigned to variables in the order that they are given; the first input is assigned to the first variable, and so on.

Local Variables

In this chapter, we have seen that we can write a procedure such as **HOUSE** that calls other procedures involving variables. How do the variables interact when a procedure calls another procedure that uses variables with the same names?

We explore this with an example. Suppose we want to write a procedure called **ELL** for drawing a block "L," as shown below in Figure 3-6.

Figure 3-6

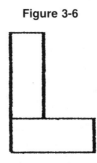

In the first line of the ELL procedure, we might use the RECTANGLE procedure to draw the lower rectangle. Then, if we move the turtle forward the width of the rectangle, we can use the RECTANGLE procedure with the width and length interchanged to draw the remainder of the "L." When writing the procedure, we must put two variables in the title line of ELL.

```
TO ELL :W :L
RECTANGLE :W :L
FD :W
RECTANGLE :L :W
END
```

If we run this procedure by typing ELL **20 50**, we will get a drawing like that in Figure 3-6. Some people, however, might expect the result to be a shape such as the one in Figure 3-7. Why did we not get such a figure?

Figure 3-7

The reason for this involves the way Logo treats variables in a procedure. The :WIDTH and :LENGTH variables in the RECTANGLE procedure are **local variables.** That is, they are private to the REC-TANGLE procedure and accessible only to RECTANGLE. ELL's variables, :W and :L, are also private to it.

local variables

Remember that any time the computer receives the instruction RECTANGLE with two numerical inputs, the first input is automatically assigned to :WIDTH and the second to :LENGTH—no matter where the numbers come from. In our example, when ELL **20 50** is executed, ELL first assigns 20 to its own :W variable and 50 to its own :L variable. Then it calls RECTANGLE and passes these values to it as inputs. RECTANGLE assigns the first input value to its local :WIDTH variable and the second to its :LENGTH variable. The turtle draws the horizontal rectangle and executes FD **20**.

ELL now calls RECTANGLE :L :W. This means that the first value passed to RECTANGLE this time is the value of ELL's :L variable, or 50, and the second value passed is ELL's :W value, or 20. Since REC-TANGLE always assigns the first value it receives to its :WIDTH variable, the value of ELL's :L variable becomes the value of RECTANGLE's :WIDTH variable. Similarly, 20, the value of ELL's :W variable, is assigned to RECTANGLE's :LENGTH variable.

Remark: In Terrapin Logo version 2.0, the primitive LOCAL allows local variables to be created inside a procedure without declaring the variables in the title line.

Try the ELL procedure with various inputs. Can you make it draw two stacked squares, as in Figure 3-8?

Figure 3-8

Debugging Commands: TRACE and NOTRACE

TRACE

Before writing more procedures, we discuss several debugging commands. The first of these is **TRACE**, a primitive that causes the computer to print each line of a procedure on the monitor screen and pause before the line is executed. The computer will pause until we type a character or press the space bar; then it will execute the line. TRACE also informs us what the inputs are for variables in a procedure and when a procedure's execution is completed. For example, if we type TRACE and then run ELL 20 50, we will see the turtle drawing the ELL and also the series of lines below.

```
TRACE
TRACING ON
?ELL 20 50
EXECUTING ELL 20 50
RECTANGLE :WIDTH :LENGTH
EXECUTING RECTANGLE 20 50
REPEAT 2 [FD :WIDTH RT 90 FD :LENGTH RT 90]
ENDING RECTANGLE
FD :WIDTH
RECTANGLE :LENGTH :WIDTH
EXECUTING RECTANGLE 50 20
REPEAT 2 [FD :WIDTH RT 90 FD :LENGTH RT 90]
ENDING RECTANGLE
ENDING ELL
```

To discontinue the use of **TRACE**, we simply type **NOTRACE**.

NOTRACE

It is possible to use both **TRACE** and **NOTRACE** within a procedure. This can be done when we wish to debug or edit a few lines of a procedure. We can type **TRACE** before the lines to be debugged and **NOTRACE** after them. When the procedure is run, the **TRACE** primitive will cause the desired section of the procedure to be stepped through one line at a time until **NOTRACE** is reached. The procedure will then continue normally.

For example, consider the execution of the procedure below using 30 and 50 as inputs to **HOUSE1** with the turtle starting with heading 0. The result is shown in Figure 3-9(a).

```
TO HOUSE1 :SIDE1 :SIDE2
RECTANGLE :SIDE1 :SIDE2
BK (:SIDE1)/3
RT 90
RECTANGLE (:SIDE1)/2 (:SIDE2)/2
FD :SIDE1
TRIANGLE :SIDE2
END
```

Figure 3-9 (a)

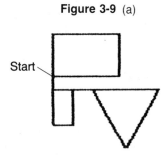

Start

To find the bugs in this procedure and edit it so that it produces a drawing similar to the drawing in Figure 3-9(b), we may edit HOUSE1 to include TRACE in the procedure after the first call to RECTANGLE and NOTRACE before the call to TRIANGLE. Then we may execute the procedure, find the bugs, and correct them. We recommend that you try this.

Figure 3-9   (b)

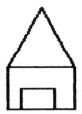

Debugging Commands: PAUSE, CONTINUE, and CTRL-Z

PAUSE

Another primitive used in debugging is **PAUSE**. The use of PAUSE in a procedure causes the procedure to stop running at the point where the computer reaches the PAUSE command. You may issue any commands you wish while the procedure is stopped. To continue the procedure, type **CONTINUE (CO)** and press RETURN. The procedure will then resume at the place where it was stopped.

CONTINUE (CO)

For example, suppose we want to see if the turtle is in the correct position to draw the second rectangle in the ELL procedure. We could add a PAUSE, as follows:

```
TO ELL :W :L
RECTANGLE :W :L
FD :W
PAUSE
RECTANGLE :L :W
END
```

Now when ELL 20 50 is run, the procedure will go on until PAUSE is reached. Then the following lines will be displayed.

```
PAUSE, IN LINE
  PAUSE
AT LEVEL 1 OF ELL
L1?
```

The meaning of level is the same as discussed in earlier chapters. At this point we might type HT to hide the turtle. Then, when we type CO, the procedure will continue with the turtle hidden.

Experiment with such commands as HT, ST, PU, and PD to see what can be done when a procedure has paused. Try typing TRIANGLE 30 during the pause. Is a triangle with side of length 30 drawn?

A procedure may also be interrupted while it is running by using CTRL-Z. CTRL-Z acts like PAUSE except that it is used while a procedure is running, whereas PAUSE is typed ahead of time as part of the procedure text. CTRL-Z may not be a line in a procedure. You may issue commands when the procedure pauses. As with PAUSE, you can continue the run after CTRL-Z by typing CONTINUE (CO). An example of the use of CTRL-Z is given in the next section.

CTRL-Z

Summary of Commands

TRACE	Accepts no inputs. Causes the computer to wait for a character to be typed before executing a procedure line. Any character except CTRL-G and CTRL-Z may be used to cause execution of the next line. TRACE can be included in a procedure before the line where you want tracing to begin.
NOTRACE	Takes no inputs. Causes the computer to turn off TRACE. Like TRACE, it can be included in a procedure.
PAUSE	Takes no inputs. Is added to a procedure at a point where you want to stop its execution. Allows you to type command lines to be executed while the procedure is stopped. Execution of procedure can be continued by typing CONTINUE (CO) if no errors have occurred during the pause.
CTRL-Z	Causes a procedure to pause. Can be used while the procedure is running. Allows commands to be inserted. Execution of procedure can be continued by typing CONTINUE (CO).
CONTINUE (CO)	Takes no inputs. Continues execution of a procedure after PAUSE or CTRL-Z is used.

Problem Set 3-1

---

1. Predict the output when the procedure below is run by typing VSQUARE 40.

   TO VSQUARE :SIDE
   REPEAT 4 [FD :SIDE RT 90 FD :SIDE]
   END

2. Use the **VSQUARE** procedure from Problem 1 to write a procedure for drawing a window of variable size, similar to the one shown below.

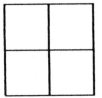

3. Use the **TRIANGLE** procedure described in this section to write a procedure that draws an equilateral triangle of variable size, turns the turtle left 20 degrees, draws another equilateral triangle, and continues this process until the turtle returns to its original position and heading.

4. Write a procedure for drawing a stack of three variable size rods, in which

   (a) the length of each rod is 10 units shorter than the length of the one below it, as shown in the figure below.

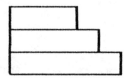

   (b) the length of each rod is half the length of the rod just below it.

5. Write procedures with variables for drawing each of the following:

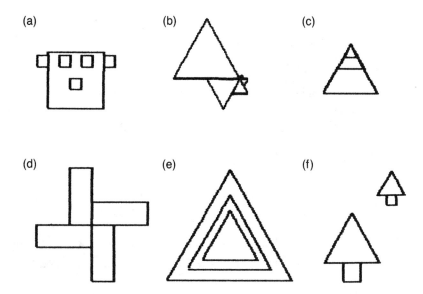

(a) (b) (c)

(d) (e) (f)

6. Edit the HOUSE1 procedure described in this section to correct the bugs.

7. (a) Predict what happens when TRAIN 20 50 is executed using the RECTANGLE procedure described in this section.

```
TO TRAIN :WIDTH :LENGTH
RECTANGLE :WIDTH :LENGTH
RT 90
FD :LENGTH
LT 90
RECTANGLE :LENGTH :WIDTH
END
```

(b) Execute TRAIN 20 50 to determine whether your prediction was correct.

8. (a) Predict what happens when DESIGN 20 50 is executed using the RECTANGLE procedure from this section.

```
TO DESIGN :WIDTH :LENGTH
REPEAT 2 [RECTANGLE :WIDTH :LENGTH FD :LENGTH]
RT 180
REPEAT 2 [RECTANGLE :LENGTH :WIDTH FD :LENGTH]
END
```

(b) Execute DESIGN 20 50 to determine whether your prediction was correct.

9. (a) Predict whether ARCH 50 20 will draw the arch shown in the picture.

    ```
    TO ARCH :WIDTH :LENGTH
    RECTANGLE :WIDTH :LENGTH
    RECTANGLE :LENGTH :WIDTH
    RT 90
    FD :WIDTH − :LENGTH
    LT 90
    RECTANGLE :WIDTH :LENGTH
    END
    ```

    (b) If ARCH 50 20 is executed, what are the values of :WIDTH and :LENGTH when FD :WIDTH − :LENGTH is executed?

    (c) If ARCH does not draw the picture shown, insert PAUSE between the first two RECTANGLE calls to see where the turtle is. Correct the bug.

10. Describe the differences between the functions of CTRL-G and CTRL-Z.

3-2 The Turtle Takes a Trip

convex polygon

A central concept in turtle geometry is total turning. If the turtle turns RT 90 and then LT 90, we say that its total turning is 0. If the turtle moves around any **convex polygon** (a polygon with no indentations or inward turns) and returns to its initial position and heading, its total turning is 360 (or − 360 if the turtle moves counterclockwise). You can understand this best by "playing turtle" and actually walking around a given convex polygon, returning to your original starting point and heading.

As an example, consider the regular octagon in Figure 3-10.

Figure 3-10

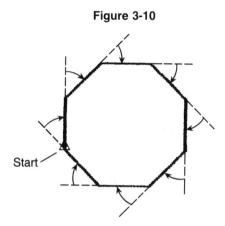

Start

The arrows show the turning angles of the turtle. If the turtle starts with heading 0 and turns as pictured, it will end with heading 0 and will have turned 360 degrees.

The 360 degree turning for a convex polygon is a special case of a general mathematical theorem called the Closed Path Theorem or, in Logo, the Total Turtle Trip Theorem. Before we state the theorem, let us consider what happens when we walk around a nonconvex (**concave**) polygon such as the one shown in Figure 3-11.

concave polygon

Figure 3-11

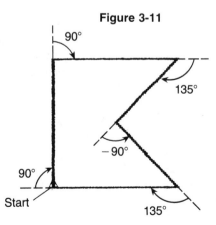

90°

135°

−90°

90°

Start

135°

If we count clockwise turns as having positive measures and counterclockwise turns as having negative measures, then the total turning for the polygon in Figure 3-11 is still 360 degrees, just as it was for the one in Figure 3-10. In this case, we have 90 + 135 + (− 90) + 135 + 90 = 360.

Problem 3-2

(a) Draw a polygon whose total turning is a negative multiple of 360. Use arrows to show the turning.

congruent   (b) What is the total turning in the walk pictured in Figure 3-12, where triangles ABC and AED are **congruent** (same size and shape)?

Figure 3-12

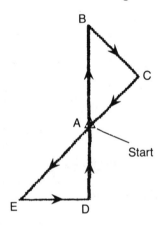

Solution

(a) One way to obtain a negative total turning is simply to walk around a convex figure in a counterclockwise direction, as shown by the arrows in Figure 3-13.

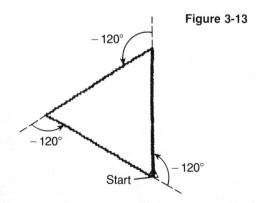

Figure 3-13

(b) In Figure 3-12, where triangles ABC and AED are congruent, the path around the figure crosses itself. If the turtle walks around triangle ABC in a clockwise direction, as pictured, and then walks around the congruent triangle in a counterclockwise direction, the total turning must be 0. Can you explain why?

Experiment with other closed drawings and use a protractor to measure the amount of turning. You should discover that the total turning in each case is a multiple of 360. This leads us to the **Closed Path Theorem** or **Total Turtle Trip Theorem**, which can be stated like this:

CLOSED PATH THEOREM (TOTAL TURTLE TRIP THEOREM)
The total turning along any closed path is a multiple of 360 degrees.

Remark: We use a multiple of 360 to mean any integer times 360— for example, 1*360, 2*360, − 1*360, or − 5*360.

Closed Path Theorem

Total Turtle Trip Theorem

Procedures for Drawing Polygons

If, as in a polygon, a closed path does not cross itself, the total turning is 360 degrees (or − 360 degrees). We use this fact to write a procedure for drawing a regular polygon. Because a **regular polygon** is both equilateral (has all sides congruent) and equiangular (has all angles congruent), it can be determined by the length of a side and the turning angle. The measure of each angle through which the turtle must turn to draw a regular polygon is determined by the number of sides of the polygon. For example, if the regular polygon has three sides, the turning angle is 360/3, or 120 degrees; if the polygon has four sides, the turning angle is 360/4, or 90 degrees; and so on. In general, for a regular polygon of n sides, the measure of the turning angle is $360/n$. If a regular polygon has eight sides, as in Figure 3-10, what is the turning angle?

regular polygon

To write a procedure to draw any regular polygon, we use two variables, :SIDE and :N, where :SIDE is the length of a side of the polygon and :N is the number of sides. The turning angle of the polygon is 360/:N. All the turtle needs to do to draw a polygon is move FD :SIDE, turn RT 360/:N, and repeat this :N times, as follows:

```
TO POLYGON :SIDE :N
REPEAT :N [FD :SIDE RT 360/:N]
END
```

Three runs of this procedure are shown in Figure 3-14, using 30 as the length of a side and 3, 6, and 8 as values for :N. Try POLYGON with other inputs, such as POLYGON 30 2, POLYGON 30 100, POLYGON 5 50, and POLYGON 3 100.

Figure 3-14

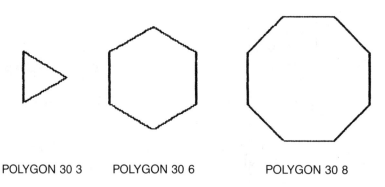

POLYGON 30 3   POLYGON 30 6   POLYGON 30 8

A many-sided regular polygon can be used to approximate a circle. If :SIDE is 1, how great must :N be before the polygon looks like a circle?

The Total Turtle Trip Theorem can also be used to draw closed figures other than polygons. Consider the regular five-pointed star in Figure 3-15(a). We will work out a procedure for drawing such a star in the following problem.

Figure 3-15

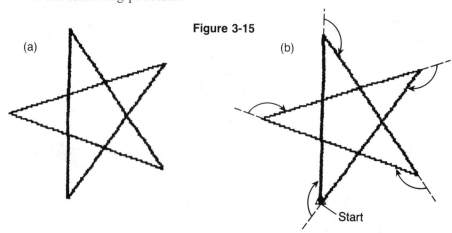

(a)

(b)

Start

Problem 3-3

Write a procedure to draw a variable size star similar to the one in Figure 3-15(a).

Solution

If we look carefully at Figure 3-15(b), we see that if the turtle moves forward some distance, turns through some angle, moves forward the same distance, and turns through the same angle as before, it can draw the star after a series of five moves.

Because the figure is to be a variable size star, we do not know the length of a side. We also do not automatically know the size of the turning angle. To actually draw the star, we may use any length for :SIDE, but we must find the size of the turning angle. The procedure called **STAR**, of the following form, will produce the desired figure. The question mark indicates that we don't know what the input to **RT** is yet.

```
TO STAR :SIDE
REPEAT 5 [FD :SIDE RT ?]
END
```

If we consider Figure 3-15(b), we can see that the turning angle of the five-pointed star appears to be an **obtuse angle**, that is, an angle of measure more than 90 degrees but less than 180 degrees. A strategy for finding the proper angle size might be a trial-and-error process in which we execute **STAR** with, say, 50 as the input for :SIDE and a specific angle size. To keep from having to type in the instructions several times (**STAR** cannot be executed as it is now), we introduce the variable :ANGLE into the **STAR** procedure, as shown below:

obtuse angle

```
TO STAR :SIDE :ANGLE
REPEAT 5 [FD :SIDE RT :ANGLE]
END
```

Before reading further, experiment with different sizes for the turning angle to find the correct size to close the figure and make the star. If you are not sure whether the angle measure you discover is the correct one, you might execute **STAR** several times with the same inputs or execute the line below with your inputs substituted for the variables. If the original star is retraced exactly, your angle size is sure to be correct.

REPEAT 20 [STAR :SIDE :ANGLE]

Now we consider a closer analysis of the problem. From the Total Turtle Trip Theorem, we know that the total turning for the star must be a multiple of 360. Thus one way to determine the turning angle is to check the quotients of multiples of 360 divided by 5. One of them should give the desired angle measure to produce the star. Some of the quotients follow:

$$(1*360)/5 = 72$$
$$(2*360)/5 = 144$$
$$(3*360)/5 = 216$$

When **STAR 50 144** is executed, a five-pointed star is obtained. Is this the angle size you found when you used the trial-and-error process discussed earlier?

Problem Set 3-2

1. How many degrees should the turtle turn at each angle in order to draw each of the following figures?

    (a) hexagon
    (b) octagon
    (c) septagon (polygon with seven sides)

2. Suppose the turtle drew a square and then walked backwards around the square. What would its total turning be?

3. (a) Write a procedure to draw a seven-pointed star.
    (b) What is the turning angle needed to draw a star that has eleven points?

4. How many sides does a regular polygon have if the turning angle is each of the following?

    (a) 12 degrees
    (b) 30 degrees

5. Can you draw a six-pointed star using the methods described in this section? Why or why not?

6. Write a procedure to draw each of the following figures.

(a) 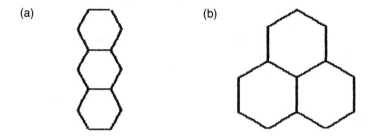 (b)

3-3 Procedures for Circles and Arcs

Logo Circles

As we mentioned previously, a circle can be approximated by a many-sided regular polygon. This approach to circles is useful in the study of geometry, particularly in finding the area and circumference of a circle. It is also a natural approach to use in Logo. The turtle cannot draw a mathematically correct circle—that is, the set of all points in a plane at a given distance from a given point. However, the turtle can make a "turtle-type" circle—that is, a polygon that looks like a circle—by drawing, for example, a polygon with 360 sides each of length 1. With this in mind, we write a CIRCLE procedure to produce the circle given in Figure 3-16. The procedure, along with its output, is shown below.

```
TO CIRCLE
REPEAT 360 [FD 1 RT 1]
END
```

Figure 3-16

Remark: You can speed up the CIRCLE procedure by hiding the turtle so that it is not drawn at each step of the repeat. Press CTRL-Z during the execution of CIRCLE and type HT during the pause. Then continue the run by typing CO. We could also edit the CIRCLE procedure to include HT as the first line in the body of the procedure.

The CIRCLE procedure draws only one size circle. To vary the size of the circle being drawn, we can vary the length of the forward movement, as seen in the VCIRCLE procedure below.

```
TO VCIRCLE :S
REPEAT 360 [FD :S RT 1]
END
```

Different circles drawn using the VCIRCLE procedure are shown in Figure 3-17.

Figure 3-17

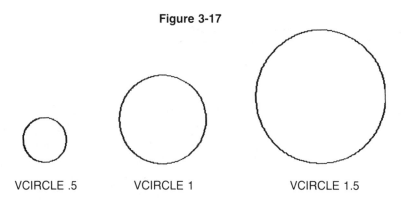

VCIRCLE .5   VCIRCLE 1   VCIRCLE 1.5

Drawing Circles Faster

As you have no doubt noticed, drawing a complete circle by running either the CIRCLE or the VCIRCLE procedure is time-consuming. We saw that it is possible to make the procedures run faster by using the command HIDETURTLE (HT) so that the turtle does not have to be drawn on the screen for each move. As you may also have discovered, you can speed up the drawing further by varying the number of repeats (which depends upon the turning angle size). To close the figure, the turtle must complete a 360-degree trip. To make sure that this happens, see that the number of times the moves are repeated multiplied by the number of degrees for each turn equals 360. For example, if we decide that the turtle should turn 15 degrees each time, the process must be repeated 360/15 or 24 times.

In addition, if we wish the size of the new circle to be approximately the same as that of the old circle, we need to make the perimeter of the polygon drawing the new circle the same as the perimeter of the polygon that drew the original approximation using the CIRCLE procedure in Figure 3-16. This can be done by adjusting the length of each side of the polygon as follows: The perimeter of the drawing in Figure 3-16 is 360*1, or 360 turtle steps. If the new figure is to have 24 sides and a perimeter of 360, then each side must have length 360/24, or 15 turtle steps. Consequently, we obtain the new procedure below.

```
TO FCIRCLE
REPEAT 24 [FD 15 RT 15 ]
END
```

As an exercise, write a procedure for drawing circles using variables for both the side and the turns. We recommend hiding the turtle before you start the drawing.

Drawing Arcs

The circle procedures just described can be adapted to draw **arcs,** or continuous parts of a circle. For example, if we wanted to draw a semicircle, we could repeat [FD 1 RT 1] 180 times instead of 360 times, as follows:

arc

```
TO SEMICIRCLE
REPEAT 180 [FD 1 RT 1]
END
```

In a similar manner, we could write procedures for an arc whose measure is 90 degrees, 45 degrees, or any other number. To create a general arc procedure, we use the number of degrees in the arc as a variable, :N, and thus repeat :N times the directions [FD 1 RT 1]. (We are assuming an integral number of degrees in the arc, although the procedure could be adapted for any positive number of degrees.) Incidentally, if we use the REPEAT command, we cannot use a negative number of degrees as an input.

```
TO RARC :N
REPEAT :N [FD 1 RT 1]
END
```

Notice that the arcs drawn by the **RARC** procedure are drawn to the right of the turtle's initial position, as shown in Figure 3-18.

Figure 3-18

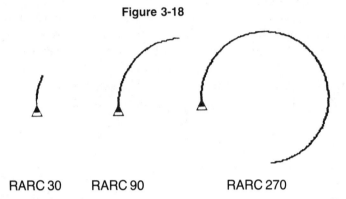

RARC 30   RARC 90   RARC 270

We could write a procedure, **LARC**, for drawing arcs to the left by changing the command **RT 1** to **LT 1**; try this as an exercise. You might also try writing procedures to draw arcs faster.

Remark: RARC and LARC may be used to draw circles to the right and left of the home position by making :N equal 360.

Problem 3-4

Write procedures for drawing variable size arcs to the right and left of the turtle's starting point.

Solution

We already know how to draw variable size circles by using the VCIRCLE procedure given below.

```
TO VCIRCLE :S
REPEAT 360[FD :S RT 1]
END
```

We can adapt the VCIRCLE procedure to draw arcs to the right of the turtle's starting position by introducing a variable :N for the number of times to repeat the command FD :S RT 1. Such a procedure, called VRARC, is given below.

```
TO VRARC :S :N
REPEAT :N [FD :S RT 1]
END
```

A similar procedure called VLARC can be written to draw variable size arcs to the left of the turtle's starting position by replacing RT 1 with LT 1 in the VRARC procedure.

```
TO VLARC :S :N
REPEAT :N [FD :S LT 1]
END
```

Drawing a Circle with a Given Radius

In order to draw a circle with a given radius, we need to remember that in Logo we are only approximating a circle with a many-sided polygon. One connection between a circle and an approximating polygon is that the **perimeter** of the polygon and the **circumference** of the circle—that is, the distance around each—must be nearly the same. The Mathematical Aside below shows the relationship between the perimeter and the circumference and how a radius of the circle is related to a side of the polygon.

perimeter
circumference

Mathematical Aside

If the polygon used to approximate a circle of radius R has a side of length S and has 360 sides, its perimeter is 360*S. If π is approximated as 3.14159, the circumference (C = 2πr) of the circle is 2*3.14159*R. Because the perimeter of the polygon and the circumference of the circle are approximately the same, we have the following:

$$360*S = 2*3.14159*R$$
$$S = 2*3.14159*R/360$$

A procedure called **RCIRCLE** with input :R for the length of the radius and which calls **VCIRCLE** with input in terms of :R is given by the following lines.

```
TO RCIRCLE :R
HT
VCIRCLE 2*3.14159*:R/360
ST
END
```

Remark: The name **RCIRCLE** was used because the circle is drawn to the right with positive input.

Try **RCIRCLE 30** to see how the procedure works. It will take some time to run. If you get tired of watching, you can use CTRL-G to abort the run.

Try to write an **LCIRCLE** procedure that draws circles to the left of the starting point, and save it for use in the problem set. You might also write some procedures for drawing arcs of differing sizes with variable radii.

If the Terrapin Logo Utilities Disk or Krell Utilities Disk is available, you should also read the **ARCS** or **CIRCLE** file (respectively) and see how the procedures work. You can save these procedures on your own disk so you can use them whenever you wish.

Problem Set 3-3

1. Write procedures for drawing each of the following variable size figures.

(a)   (b)   (c)   (d)

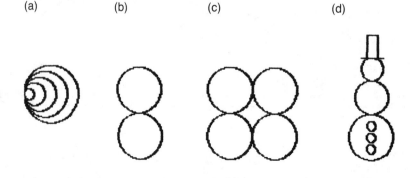

2. Generalize the **FCIRCLE** procedure to include variable sides, turns, and number of repeats.

3. Execute the **RCIRCLE** procedure using a negative input. What is the result?

4. Write a procedure called **LCIRCLE**, similar to **RCIRCLE**, that will draw circles of a given radius to the left of the starting point.

5. Write procedures called **RVRARC** and **LVLARC** that can be used to draw variable size arcs in circles with variable size radii.

6. Write procedures to draw each of the following variable size figures.

(a)   (b)   (c)

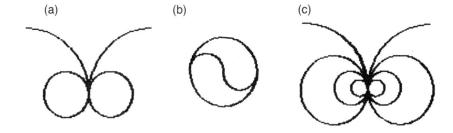

7. (a) The trademark for an automobile company is composed of four interlocking circles, as shown below. Write a procedure for drawing this symbol in variable sizes.

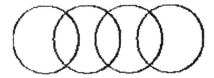

(b) The Olympic symbol is composed of five interlocking circles, as shown below. Write a procedure for drawing the Olympic symbol in variable sizes.

8. Write a procedure for drawing each of the following variable size figures.

(a)   (b)   (c)   (d)

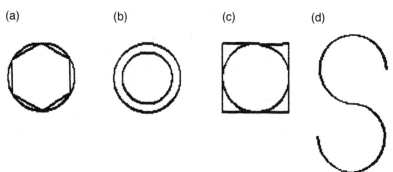

9. (a) Write a procedure to draw a variable size flower, as shown below.

(b) Write a procedure to draw a row of flowers of different sizes using the procedure you wrote for part (a).

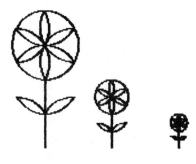

3-4 Programming with Color

When you load Logo into your computer, your monitor should initially have a black background, and when the turtle moves in the draw mode, it should leave a white trail. If you have a color monitor, however, you can use Logo primitives to change both pen color—that is, the color of the turtle trail—and background color in your drawings. The primitives that will changes these colors are called **PENCOLOR (PC)** and **BACKGROUND (BG)**, respectively. These primitives take an integer 0 through 6 as input. The colors corresponding to 0 through 5 of Logo are given below; we'll discuss 6 a little later.

PENCOLOR (PC)
BACKGROUND (BG)

Black	0
White	1
Green	2
Violet	3
Orange	4
Blue	5

As an example, suppose we type **BG 2 PC 3**. That should make the background color of the monitor screen green and the pen color violet. Check to see if your monitor has color by typing this line and then drawing a square. To reset the colors to the original ones, type **NODRAW (ND)**.

Now suppose that instead of typing **NODRAW**, we type **DRAW**. In this case the monitor screen will be cleared, but the colors of both background and pen will remain in effect. To see that this is true, type **NODRAW** followed by **BG 2 PC 3 FD 100 DRAW FD 100**. DRAW resets the turtle to the home position but uses the last background color and pen color referenced.

PENCOLOR 6 causes the background color and the pen color to be reversed on any dots that the turtle passes over with the pen down. You should experiment with the different color commands and inputs to determine which pen colors show up on which background colors.

If the background color in a drawing is changed, some of the pen color dots may be changed also. You can get interesting patterns of color by taking advantage of this feature. We suggest that you try various ways of changing colors to find those that are most pleasing to you. Note that on a black-and-white monitor or a green monitor, the "colors" will appear as gray or light green, respectively.

Erasing Drawings

Changing pen colors allows you to erase a line or a part of a drawing. You do this by changing the pen color to the background color and going back over the part of the drawing you want to erase. Be careful not to forget to change the pen color back by typing PC with the number of the original color after you have finished erasing.

If no value is given to either pen color or background color when the computer is turned on, the default colors are white and black, respectively. To see how this works, use the SQUARE procedure given earlier and type the following:

```
SQUARE 50
PC 0
SQUARE 50
PC 6
REPEAT 10 [SQUARE 50]
```

What do you think will happen if you type the following lines?

```
DRAW
BG 2
PC 3
FD 100
BG 3
```

Did you expect the line segment to disappear? Did it?

The Random Command

RANDOM

Interesting designs can be created by intentionally changing colors within a procedure. There are a variety of ways to do this. One primitive we can use to produce different colors is called **RANDOM**. The RANDOM command is used with an integer input to produce an integer at random between 0 and one less than the input, inclusive. For example, RANDOM 14 will produce one of the integers 0 through 13. If we want a random number between 1 and 13 inclusive, we can use (RANDOM 13) + 1. Do you see why parentheses are needed? Now type

RANDOM 13 + 1 and see if you can determine the difference between the two lines.

We can use the **RANDOM** primitive to change pen colors in a design, as shown in the following procedure. It uses the variable **SQUARE** procedure that we defined earlier.

```
TO CSQUARE
REPEAT 36 [SQUARE 50 RT 10 PC (RANDOM 5) + 1]
END
```

When the **CSQUARE** procedure is run, a square is drawn; the turtle turns 10 degrees to the right; the pen color is changed using the **RANDOM** primitive; and then the process is repeated. Remember that **RANDOM 5** generates an integer between 0 and 4 inclusive. We add 1 so that the pen color is not black; otherwise, if the background is black, the pen color will not show.

The same idea is used in the **RAINBOW** procedure below, which utilizes the arc procedures defined in the previous section.

```
TO RAINBOW
PC (RANDOM 5) + 1
HT
RVRARC 50 180
LT 90
FD 5
LT 90
PC (RANDOM 5) + 1
LVLARC 55 180
RT 90
FD 5
RT 90
PC (RANDOM 5) + 1
RVRARC 60 180
END
```

If we run this program, we will get a multicolored rainbow with three arcs. If we turn the computer off and run the **RAINBOW** procedure again in a later session, the rainbow we obtain then will be exactly like the one we get this time. If we wish, we can eliminate this duplication by using the primitive **RANDOMIZE**. RANDOMIZE takes no inputs and randomizes the sequence that is generated by calls to

RANDOMIZE

RANDOM. If we insert **RANDOMIZE** following the title line of the **RAINBOW** procedure, then each time the **RAINBOW** procedure is run, a new, possibly different rainbow will be drawn.

We can also use color to draw a sun. We might use the orange pen color to draw a segment and then turn the turtle 181 degrees, as shown in Figure 3-19.

Figure 3-19

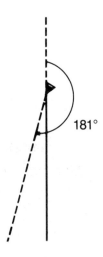

If we now draw the segment again, we have what appears as a thick band of color the length of the segment. Repeating these instructions 180 times causes the segment to act like the diameter of a circle, and if we draw enough diameters, it will appear that a circle has been filled. An example procedure follows.

```
TO SUN
HT
PC 4
REPEAT 180 [FD 25 RT 181]
PC 1
END
```

There are other procedures for "filling" circles. They include a procedure that draws a square, turns the turtle some amount, draws another square, and repeats this sequence until a filled circle is obtained. For example, if we use the previously defined **SQUARE** procedure, the program might appear as follows.

```
TO FILLCIR :S
REPEAT 360 [SQUARE :S RT 1]
END
```

By combining the HOUSE procedure, the SUN procedure, and any others you want, you can create a scene.

Summary of Commands

PENCOLOR (PC)	Takes one input, which must be an integer between 0 and 6 inclusive. Determines the color of the turtle tracks in draw mode.
BACKGROUND (BG)	Takes one input, which must be an integer between 0 and 6 inclusive. Sets the color of the monitor screen background.
RANDOM	Takes one input, a natural number, n. Outputs an integer between 0 and $n-1$ inclusive.
RANDOMIZE	Takes no inputs. Randomizes the sequence that is generated by calls to RANDOM.

Problem Set 3-4

1. Determine which pen colors show up on which background colors.
2. (a) Edit the RAINBOW procedure described in this section to make five colored arcs in the rainbow.
   (b) Write a procedure that uses the RAINBOW procedure from 2(a) and draws the rainbow on a blue sky background.
3. Edit your procedure for drawing the set of stacked rods in Problem 4 from Problem Set 3-1 to create a new set of stacked colored rods.
4. Write a procedure to draw a variable size lime lollipop on a white stick.
5. Write a procedure for drawing a four-ring target with each ring being a different color.
6. Write a procedure for drawing a double-dip ice cream cone in which the top dip is grape (colored violet) and the bottom dip is lime (colored green).

7. (a) Write a procedure for drawing a blue balloon on a string.

   (b) Write a procedure for drawing three blue balloons, as shown below.

8. (a) Write a procedure for filling a circle that involves rotating a radius.

   (b) Write a procedure for filling a circle that involves rotating a hexagon.

9. Write a procedure for drawing the figure shown below.

10. Write a procedure for drawing a hot-air balloon. Decorate the balloon however you wish and add scenery in the background.

Solution to the Preliminary Problem

Understanding the Problem

The problem is to write a procedure to draw an umbrella similar to the one in Figure 3-20. The procedure should also allow for variable sizes and colors.

Figure 3-20

The drawing shows that the umbrella top is made of a semicircle, while the bottom of the umbrella and the handle also contain semicircles.

Devising a Plan

There are three basic parts to the umbrella: the top, which is a colored semicircular region; the bottom, which appears to be composed of six semicircles; and the spike and handle, which consist of a semicircle attached to a line segment. The semicircles at the bottom of the umbrella may be formed by erasing portions of the top of the umbrella. The radii of the semicircles forming the bottom of the umbrella are related to the radius of the semicircle forming the top of the umbrella (because they divide it into six equal parts), so one variable that we could use is :R, the radius of the top of the umbrella. We could write an UMBRELLA procedure that would call UTOP to draw the top of the umbrella, UBOTTOM to draw the bottom of the umbrella, and SANDH to draw the spike and handle. The procedure might look like this:

```
TO UMBRELLA :R
UTOP :R
UBOTTOM :R
SANDH :R
END
```

Carrying Out the Plan

To carry out the plan, we need to design the UTOP, UBOTTOM, and SANDH procedures. The UTOP and UBOTTOM procedures are similar in that they draw semicircles, and we know how to draw semicircles. It appears that the size of the semicircles forming the bottom of the umbrella depends upon the size of the semicircle forming the top of the umbrella, so we need to write our procedure in such a way that the radius of the bottom semicircles depends upon the radius of the top semicircle.

We also need to devise a way for coloring the umbrella. For our example, we assume the pen color is 1 so that the umbrella will be white. How could we color a semicircle and its interior? You may recall that one way to color the interior of a circle was to essentially rotate a diameter (Section 3-4). Since we want to color only half of a circle, it might make sense to try rotating a radius through 180 degrees. Before rotating the radius, think about which direction we want the turtle to point at the start. Remember that the turtle has heading 0 when we first enter the draw mode. If we start a semicircle with the turtle headed in this direction, the umbrella may wind up on its side. (Try it.) Since we want the umbrella to be drawn as pictured in Figure 3-20, we should turn the turtle either LT 90 or RT 90 to start. We choose LT 90. After that, we could rotate the radius by first drawing the radius, :R, using FD :R, then moving the turtle back where it started using BK :R, turning the turtle RT 1, and repeating the process 180 times. We should end up with the turtle where it started so that its position will be known when we start the next procedure. Typing LT 90 will accomplish this. We combine all these steps into the UTOP procedure below.

```
TO UTOP :R
HT LT 90
REPEAT 180 [FD :R BK :R RT 1]
LT 90
END
```

To take out the color of the semicircular region drawn by UTOP when we draw the bottom of the umbrella, we need to make the pen color the same color as the background color. If the background color is black, we should place the line PC 0 in our procedure before drawing the bottom of the umbrella.

When **UTOP** completed its run, the semicircular arc at the top of the umbrella is drawn and the turtle is in the center of the bottom of the semicircle with heading 0, as shown in Figure 3-21. Now, to draw the semicircles at the bottom of the umbrella, it is reasonable to repeat this same process six times, using :R/6 as the value for the radii of the semicircles, without returning to home each time.

Figure 3-21

Recall that when we finished drawing the top of the umbrella, the turtle was at the center of the semicircular area and had heading 0. We want the turtle to be at X, the center of the first semicircular arc of the umbrella's bottom, to start. How far must we move the turtle and how much must we turn it to put it in the same relative position as it was when it started the semicircular top? Because the diameter of three semicircles on the bottom of the umbrella must fit onto a radius of the semicircle of the top of the umbrella, a radius of one of the semicircles on the bottom of the umbrella is one-sixth of the radius of the top semicircle. To move the turtle into position to draw, we should turn it **LT 90** and move it **FD 5*:R/6**. (Why?)

Now we are ready to draw the six semicircular arcs at the bottom of the umbrella. We want to repeat the process we used for drawing the top using a radius that is one-sixth of the original radius. A line to do this might look like the following:

REPEAT 6 [LT 90 REPEAT 180 [FD :R/6 BK :R/6 RT 1]]

However, recall where the turtle ends after completing each semi-circle. It stops at the center of the semicircle. Thus, before we draw the next semicircle, we must move the turtle to the center of the next semicircle. This means that we must move it the length of two radii of the smaller semicircles, or one-third of the radius of the large semicircle. We must also turn it until it has the same heading as when it started. Thus the line above must be changed to read as follows:

REPEAT 6[LT 90 REPEAT 180 [FD :R/6 BK :R/6 RT 1] FD :R/3 LT 90]

When we are finished, we move the turtle back home and change the pen color back to the umbrella color (in our example, white) by using PU HOME PD PC 1. Thus, the UBOTTOM procedure appears as follows.

```
TO UBOTTOM :R
LT 90
FD 5*:R/6
PC 0
RT 90
REPEAT 6 [LT 90 REPEAT 180 [FD :R/6 BK :R/6 RT 1] FD :R/3 LT 90]
PU HOME PD
PC 1
END
```

To draw the spike and handle, we now write the SANDH procedure. Because the turtle has heading 0, we need to move it FD :R + 10 to draw the spike. Because the handle is approximately three times as long as the radius of the top, we move the turtle BK :R*3 to draw the straight part of the handle. The curved part of the handle is another semicircle. Before drawing the semicircle, we turn the turtle RT 180 to make drawing the handle easier. If the semicircle forming the handle has radius :R/3, we can use the procedure RVRARC, written in Problem Set 3-3, Problem 5, to draw a variable size arc with a given radius. If you did not do that exercise, you can use the procedure given here.

```
TO RVARC :R :N
VRARC 2*3.14159*:R/360 :N
END
```

SANDH must call the VRARC procedure with inputs :R/3 and 180. We combine all these ideas into the SANDH procedure below.

```
TO SANDH :R
FD :R + 10
BK :R*3
RT 180
VRARC :R/3 180
END
```

Looking Back

You might try rewriting the **UMBRELLA** procedure using other procedures from the MIT Terrapin or Krell Logo Utilities Disks. Other variations include putting ribs in the umbrella and widening the handle. In addition, the umbrella was drawn starting at home. You might try drawing the umbrella while allowing the turtle to start at any point and with any heading.

Chapter 3 Problem Set

1. Predict what will happen when each of the following is run. Use the computer to check your guesses.

    (a) REPEAT 360 [FD 2 RT 1]
    (b) REPEAT 180 [FD 1 RT 2]
    (c) REPEAT 180 [FD 4 RT 2]
    (d) REPEAT 72 [FD 5 RT 5]
    (e) REPEAT 5 [FD 15 RT 72]
    (f) TO HEART
         LT 150
         FD 88 RT 120 FD 88 RT 30
         REPEAT 18 [FD 4 RT 10]
         RT 180 BK 4 LT 90 FD 3 RT 90
         REPEAT 19 [FD 4 RT 10]
         END

2. Write procedures to draw each of the following figures.

    (a)
    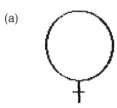

    (b)
    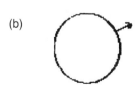

    (c)
    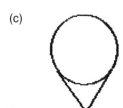

    (d)
    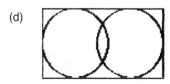

3. Use different pen colors to draw and color the set of pool balls below. You will have to repeat some colors.

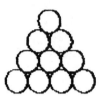

4. Design a colorful scene using pen color and background colors. Include a lake, mountains, and a city on the horizon. (You can use procedures written in Chapters 2 and 3.)

5. As another example of the use of **RANDOM**, type the following procedure and run it to see what it does.

```
TO CRAZY
REPEAT (RANDOM 30) [FD (RANDOM 50) RT (RANDOM 50)]
END
```

CHAPTER

4

New Vocabulary in Chapter 4

Terms	Primitives
recursive procedure p. 131	IF p. 135
recursion p. 131	STOP p. 135
tail-end recursion p. 132	ELSE p. 136
hypothesis p. 135	MAKE p. 145
conclusion p. 135	TEST p. 164
word p. 149	IFFALSE (IFF) p. 164
global variables p. 151	IFTRUE (IFT) p. 164
embedded recursion p. 162	NOT p. 166

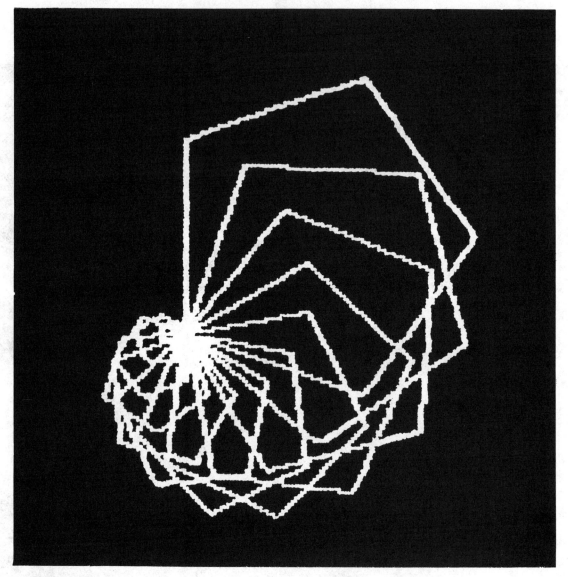

Preliminary Problem

Write a procedure that spins a pentagon, "shrinking" its size after each spin, and produces a shape similar to the one shown in the figure above.

4

Recursive Procedures

Introduction

A special case of a procedure calling another procedure occurs when a procedure calls itself rather than some other procedure. Such a procedure is called a **recursive procedure** and the process of a procedure calling itself is called **recursion.** Utilizing relatively few instructions, recursive procedures can be used to solve problems that otherwise would require long and cumbersome programs. In this chapter we look at the way turtle graphics uses recursion. Recursion is one of Logo's most interesting and powerful features.

recursive procedure

recursion

4-1 Poly and Other Recursive Procedures

Tail-end Recursion

As a first example of the use of recursion, let's write a procedure for drawing a circle that does not use a REPEAT statement. We could start the procedure with FD 1 RT 1 and make the turtle repeat this instruction by ordering it to start the procedure anew after each time the instruction is executed. Such a procedure, named CIRC, might look like this:

```
TO CIRC
FD 1 RT 1
CIRC
END
```

When CIRC is executed, the computer reads FD 1 RT 1 and causes the turtle to move forward one unit and then turn right one degree. CIRC then calls a copy of the CIRC procedure, which again executes FD 1 RT 1 and in turn calls another copy of CIRC, and so on. The process goes on and on because we have made CIRC one of the instructions in the CIRC procedure. The END statement is never reached, and the instruction FD 1 RT 1 is executed indefinitely. You may stop the execution of the procedure at any time by pressing CTRL-G, however.

tail-end recursion

The infinitely repetitive process shown in the CIRC procedure occurs in the type of recursion called **tail-end recursion**. In tail-end recursion, only one recursive call is made within the body of the procedure, and it is the final step before the END statement. Later in this chapter, in Section 4-3, we introduce another type of recursion that is sometimes called non-tail-end or embedded recursion.

The POLY Procedure

Recursion is particularly valuable when we do not know how many times to repeat a set of instructions to accomplish some goal. For example, consider the shapes that can be drawn by repeating the instruction "Go forward some fixed distance and turn right some fixed angle." A recursive procedure named POLY that does this is given below.

```
TO POLY :SIDE :ANGLE
FD :SIDE RT :ANGLE
POLY :SIDE :ANGLE
END
```

To execute the POLY procedure, we need two numeric inputs, one for :SIDE and the other for :ANGLE. Figure 4-1 shows shapes drawn by POLY with eight different inputs. The drawings were stopped using CTRL-G.

Figure 4-1

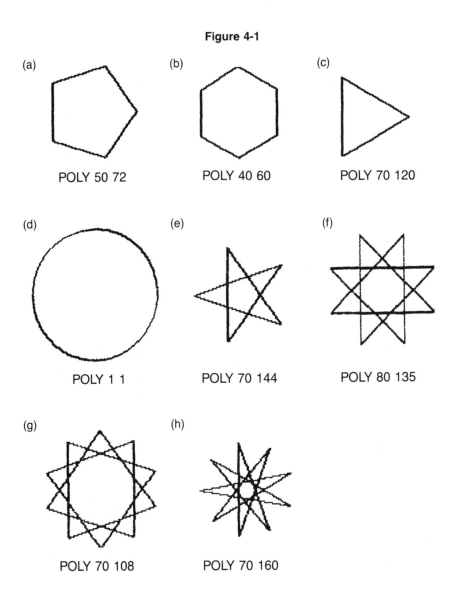

(a)

POLY 50 72

(b)

POLY 40 60

(c)

POLY 70 120

(d)

POLY 1 1

(e)

POLY 70 144

(f)

POLY 80 135

(g)

POLY 70 108

(h)

POLY 70 160

The **POLY** procedure draws regular polygons (polygons that have congruent sides and congruent angles), as in Figure 4-1 (a), (b), (c), and (d), and also star shapes, as in Figure 4-1 (e), (f), (g), and (h).

Try other executions of **POLY**, such as **POLY 50 180**, **POLY 50 181**, **POLY 60 288**, **POLY 6000 300**, and **POLY 7000 135**. As an exercise, predict which inputs produce regular polygons and which produce star shapes.

POLYSPI: A Variation of the POLY Procedure

The recursive call in the POLY procedure causes the line FD :SIDE RT :ANGLE to be executed over and over. However, recursion is a powerful idea that can be used to produce effects far beyond mere repetition. To see an example of such effects, we could modify the POLY procedure by changing the line FD :SIDE RT :ANGLE to have either a different side measure or a different angle measure each time the recursive call is made—for example, POLY :SIDE+5 :ANGLE. Such a procedure can be called POLYSPI. "SPI" suggests the spiral nature of the drawing produced by the procedure, which is shown below.

```
TO POLYSPI :SIDE :ANGLE
FD :SIDE RT :ANGLE
POLYSPI :SIDE+5 :ANGLE
END
```

Figure 4-2 shows some of the shapes that can be drawn by POLYSPI. Because each side of the POLYSPI figure is five units longer than the previous one, the sides quickly grow too large to fit the screen. The procedures describing the shapes in Figure 4-2 have therefore been stopped with CTRL-G.

Figure 4-2

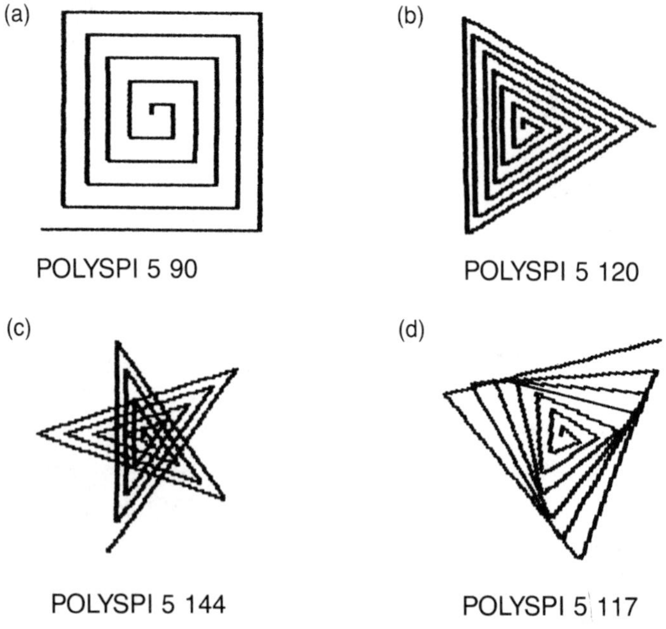

(a)

POLYSPI 5 90

(b)

POLYSPI 5 120

(c)

POLYSPI 5 144

(d)

POLYSPI 5 117

To understand how POLYSPI works, consider POLYSPI 5 90, which is shown in Figure 4-2 (a). In this procedure, the computer executes FD 5 RT 90 and then goes to the next line, which is a recursive call. POLYSPI 5 90 calls POLYSPI 5 + 5 90 or POLYSPI 10 90. POLYSPI 10 90 is executed and then calls POLYSPI 15 90, and so on indefinitely. Notice that the END statement is never reached.

The IF and STOP Commands

In Figure 4-2 we stopped the turtle by using CTRL-G. Another way to stop the turtle is to write a stop instruction in the procedure itself. This can be done with the **IF** and **STOP** primitives. For example, if we do not want the turtle to draw any segment longer than 100 units, we insert the following instruction:

IF :SIDE > 100 THEN STOP

An edited form of POLYSPI that includes a STOP instruction looks like this:

```
TO POLYSPI  :SIDE  :ANGLE
IF  :SIDE > 100 THEN STOP
FD :SIDE RT :ANGLE
POLYSPI  :SIDE + 5 :ANGLE
END
```

In this new form of the POLYSPI procedure, the IF statement tests whether a side is longer than 100 units. If a side is longer than 100 units, the turtle stops; if not, the turtle executes the next line. In general, the IF statement needs two inputs. It is used in the conditional form IF ---- THEN ----, as in the line IF :SIDE > 100 THEN STOP or as in IF :SIDE > 100 THEN PU HOME PD. The part of the IF statement following the IF primitive and preceding the word THEN is called the **hypothesis,** and the part following THEN is called the **conclusion.** The hypothesis is either true or false. The conclusion contains instructions that are carried out if the hypothesis is true. If, on the other hand, the hypothesis is false, the next line in the procedure is executed. The use of the word THEN before the conclusion is optional, and we will often omit it from our procedures. The STOP primitive causes the current procedure to stop and returns control to the calling procedure.

IF
STOP

hypothesis
conclusion

Let's examine a few examples of the IF statement. As a first example, predict the effect when the line IF :SIDE > 100 POLYSPI 5 :ANGLE is inserted in the latest version of POLYSPI instead of the line IF :SIDE > 100 STOP. This statement checks to see if the variable :SIDE is greater than 100 and calls POLYSPI 5 :ANGLE if this hypothesis is true. If this line is substituted in POLYSPI, the procedure does not stop until a CTRL-G is typed, but it never draws segments longer than 100 units in length.

Next assume that the following is a line in some procedure.

IF :SIDE > 100 THEN IF :ANGLE < 180 THEN STOP

This statement becomes less confusing if we break it into two parts. The hypothesis is :SIDE>100, and the conclusion is IF :ANGLE <180 THEN STOP. If the hypothesis is true, then the conclusion will be executed. The conclusion is another IF statement, which has a hypothesis and a conclusion of its own. The total effect of this statement is to stop the procedure if :SIDE is greater than 100 and :ANGLE is less than 180. Nested IF statements can be used in Logo when testing whether more than one condition is met.

If the hypothesis of the IF statement is true, the conclusion will be executed. If the hypothesis is false, the next line in the procedure will be executed. In fact, the line following the IF statement will be executed regardless of whether the condition in the IF statement is true or false as long as the conclusion does not contain a STOP or TOPLEVEL command. (TOPLEVEL is discussed in Chapter 5.) Beginners often mistakenly believe that the line following an IF statement will be executed only if the condition in the IF statement is false.

ELSE

Sometimes it is desirable to have a statement that is executed only if the hypothesis is false. This can be accomplished by using the **ELSE** primitive in an IF statement. For example, consider the following procedure. (An indentation implies that a line of the procedure continues.)

```
TO SIZE :ANGLE
IF :ANGLE<90 PRINT [ACUTE ANGLE] ELSE PRINT [OBTUSE
    OR RIGHT ANGLE]
END
```

This procedure will cause the computer to print either ACUTE ANGLE or OBTUSE OR RIGHT ANGLE, depending on the numerical value of

:ANGLE. The instruction after the **ELSE** primitive is executed only if the hypothesis is found to be false. Can you tell the difference between the effects of the preceding procedure and those of the following procedure?

```
TO SIZE1 :ANGLE
IF :ANGLE<90 PRINT [ACUTE ANGLE]
PRINT [OBTUSE OR RIGHT ANGLE]
END
```

In this example, OBTUSE OR RIGHT ANGLE will be printed if :ANGLE is not less than 90, but if :ANGLE is less than 90 (the hypothesis of the **IF** statement is true), then both ACUTE ANGLE and OBTUSE ANGLE OR RIGHT ANGLE will be printed!

Problem 4-1

Write a recursive procedure called **TOWER** to draw a variable size tower similar to the one shown in Figure 4-3, where the length of a side of each square is five units longer than a side of the square directly above it. Assume the turtle is at home with heading 0.

Figure 4-3

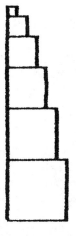

Solution

To draw the squares we can use the previously defined procedure for SQUARE that is shown below.

```
TO SQUARE :SIDE
REPEAT 4 [FD :SIDE RT 90]
END
```

We start the desired procedure with the title line **TO TOWER :SIDE**, followed by the line **SQUARE :SIDE**. This line causes the turtle to draw the bottom square and return to its original position and heading in the lower left corner. Before drawing the next square, the **TOWER** procedure must move the turtle to the top left corner of the bottom square. This can be done by executing the line **FD :SIDE**.

To draw the next square, we could use the **SQUARE** procedure with input **:SIDE − 5**. After that, if we make the next lines of the procedure **FD :SIDE − 5 and SQUARE :SIDE − 10**, **TOWER** would draw three squares. We could continue this process, but the procedure would become long. The use of recursion could shorten it considerably. Instead of using the preceding lines, we could write the **TOWER** procedure using recursion, as shown below.

```
TO TOWER :SIDE
SQUARE :SIDE
FD :SIDE
TOWER :SIDE − 5
END
```

If **TOWER 30** is run, it becomes obvious that there is a bug in our procedure, because a drawing such as the one in Figure 4-4 is obtained. The procedure must be stopped with CTRL-G or else the left tower will continue to be drawn indefinitely. Can you determine why this happens?

To debug the program, we need a line to stop the drawing before the left tower is drawn. Before we can correct the program, however, we should understand why the bug occurred. As the procedure **TOWER 30** is run, the successive procedures **TOWER 30, TOWER 25, TOWER 20, TOWER 15, TOWER 10, TOWER 5, TOWER 0, TOWER −5,** and so on are executed. When **TOWER 0** is called, no square is drawn. When **TOWER −5** is executed, the turtle draws a square by executing **REPEAT 4 [FD −5 RT 90]** and then **FD −5**. Because **FD −5** is

Figure 4-4

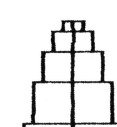

equivalent to **BK 5**, the top square on the left in Figure 4-4 is drawn and then the turtle moves down five steps, and so on. Therefore, to remove the bug, we need a line in the procedure that stops it before **TOWER** −5 is executed. The needed line could be **IF :SIDE < 0 STOP.** Where should this line be placed in the **TOWER** procedure? Consider the four possibilities shown below and predict which one draws the desired tower. Check your prediction on the computer.

(a)
```
TO TOWER :SIDE
  IF :SIDE < 0 STOP
  SQUARE :SIDE
  FD :SIDE
  TOWER :SIDE − 5
END
```

(b)
```
TO TOWER :SIDE
  SQUARE :SIDE
  IF :SIDE < 0 STOP
  FD :SIDE
  TOWER :SIDE − 5
END
```

(c)
```
TO TOWER :SIDE
  SQUARE :SIDE
  FD :SIDE
  IF :SIDE < 0 STOP
  TOWER :SIDE − 5
END
```

(d)
```
TO TOWER :SIDE
  SQUARE :SIDE
  FD :SIDE
  TOWER :SIDE − 5
  IF :SIDE < 0 STOP
END
```

In case (a), no square with side less than 0 will be drawn, and we obtain the desired tower. In case (b), **TOWER 30** executes **SQUARE 30**, **FD 30** and then calls **TOWER 25**. This executes **SQUARE 25**, **FD 25** and in turn calls **TOWER 20**, which executes **SQUARE 20**, **FD 20**, and so on until **TOWER 0** is called. **TOWER 0** calls **TOWER** −5, which executes **SQUARE** −5 and then stops. Consequently, procedure (b) does not stop the tower where we wish. Similarly, procedure (c) does not produce the desired tower because if we run **TOWER 30**, the turtle executes **SQUARE** −5 and then **FD** −5 just before stopping. The procedure in (d) does not stop at all because the line **IF :SIDE** < **0 STOP** is never reached. (Do you see why?) Thus, the only procedure that will produce the desired result is the procedure in (a).

Summary of Commands

IF	Takes two inputs. It is used in the conditional form IF----THEN----. The first input (the hypothesis) must be either true or false. The second input (the conclusion) contains instructions that are carried out if and only if the first input is true. The use of THEN is optional.
STOP	Takes no inputs. Causes the current procedure to stop and returns control to the calling procedure.
ELSE	Used in the conditional form IF----THEN----ELSE----. The instruction following ELSE is executed only if the hypothesis is false.

Problem Set 4-1

1. Use the **POLY** procedure defined in this section to predict the shapes that are drawn by executing each of the following. Check your predictions on the computer. Use CTRL-G to stop the executions.

   (a) POLY 50 180   (b) POLY 50 90

   (c) POLY 50 270   (d) POLY 50 300

   (e) POLY 50 240   (f) POLY 3 360

2. Which inputs in the **POLY** procedure produce regular polygons? Which produce star shapes?

3. Predict the shapes that are drawn by the following procedures, then check your predictions on the computer. **TRIANGLE** and **SQUARE** are defined as follows:

```
TO TRIANGLE :SIDE          TO SQUARE :SIDE
REPEAT 3 [FD :SIDE RT 120]  REPEAT 4 [FD :SIDE RT 90]
END                        END
```

(a)
```
TO L
FD 2
L
END
```

(b)
```
TO RUNSQ :SIDE
SQUARE :SIDE
RT 40
RUNSQ :SIDE
END
```

(c)
```
TO RUNTRI :SIDE
TRIANGLE :SIDE
RT 20
RUNTRI :SIDE
END
```

(d)
```
TO ROTSQ :SIDE
SQUARE :SIDE
RT 20
ROTSQ :SIDE +5
END
```

(e)
```
TO ROTRI :SIDE
TRIANGLE :SIDE
RT 20
ROTRI :SIDE − 5
END
```

(f)
```
TO TOW :SIDE
SQUARE :SIDE
FD :SIDE
TOW :SIDE * 0.6
END
```

(g)
```
TO TOW1 :SIDE
IF :SIDE < 5 STOP
SQUARE :SIDE
FD :SIDE
TOW1 :SIDE * 0.6
END
```

(h)
```
TO SPI :SIDE
IF :SIDE > 50 STOP
FD :SIDE RT 30
SPI :SIDE + 3
END
```

4. Consider the **SPIRAL** procedure defined below. Then predict the outcome of **SPIRAL 50 90**.

```
TO SPIRAL :S :A
FD :S RT :A
IF :S < 0 PU HOME PD STOP
SPIRAL :S − 5 :A
END
```

5. Write a recursive procedure that involves a **STOP** command and draws a figure similar to each of the following.

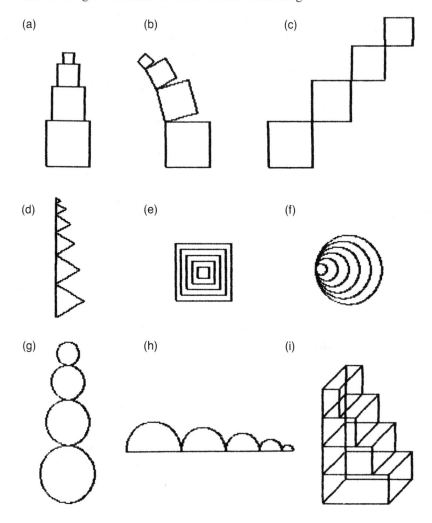

(a)

(b)

(c)

(d)

(e)

(f)

(g)

(h)

(i)

6. Write a procedure that takes three integer inputs, :A, :B, and :C, and prints the words ALL POSITIVE if all three values are greater than zero and prints NOT ALL POSITIVE if one or more of the three values is not positive.

7. Write a procedure called **TOWER1** that incorporates a **STOP** command such that **TOWER1** draws a tower along with its mirror image when **TOWER1 30** is run.

8. Write a procedure called TOWER2, including a STOP statement, which draws a tower similar to the one in Figure 4-3 but starts the drawing at the top of the tower.

9. Consider the POLYSPI1 procedure below. Answer the questions following the procedure.

```
TO POLYSPI1 :SIDE :ANGLE
FD :SIDE RT :ANGLE
IF :SIDE < 100 POLYSPI1 :SIDE + 5 :ANGLE
END
```

   (a) Predict the outcome of POLYSPI1 70 90.
   (b) Will POLYSPI1 always stop? Why?
   (c) How is POLYSPI1 related to the edited version of POLYSPI?

10. Write a recursive procedure with a STOP command that draws a figure similar to the one below.

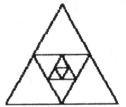

11. Write a program for drawing a shape that appeals to you. Call that program SHAPE. Then use your SHAPE procedure and recursion to create a new geometric figure.

4-2 Other Ways to Stop Recursion

We have used the STOP command to stop a recursive procedure in which the length of a side was incremented. A procedure can also be stopped when the angle is incremented, as will be discussed in the next section. But how can we stop a procedure like POLY, in which neither the length of the side nor the measure of the angle changes?

Notice that with each recursive call of the **POLY** procedure below, it is the turtle's heading that changes.

```
TO POLY :SIDE :ANGLE
FD :SIDE RT :ANGLE
POLY :SIDE :ANGLE
END
```

If **DRAW** is executed, the turtle starts at home and its heading is 0. At the time when **POLY** starts to repeat itself, that is, when no new parts of the figure are drawn, the turtle has returned to its original heading. If the turtle's initial heading is 0, we may stop **POLY** before it repeats itself by telling the computer to determine if the heading is again 0. To check the turtle's heading, we use the Logo primitive **HEADING**. We try to write **POLYSTOP**, a modified version of the **POLY** procedure, by inserting the line **IF HEADING = 0 STOP** in an appropriate place in the procedure. The following are two possible versions of the **POLYSTOP** procedure.

(a)
```
TO POLYSTOP :SIDE :ANGLE
IF HEADING = 0 STOP
FD :SIDE RT :ANGLE
POLYSTOP :SIDE :ANGLE
END
```

(b)
```
TO POLYSTOP :SIDE :ANGLE
FD :SIDE RT :ANGLE
IF HEADING = 0 STOP
POLYSTOP :SIDE :ANGLE
END
```

The version of **POLYSTOP** in (a) does not draw any figures if the turtle starts at home with heading 0. Why?

If the turtle starts at home with heading 0, the second version of **POLYSTOP** accomplishes its goal of making the turtle stop and closes the figure when we execute procedures such as **POLYSTOP 50 144** or **POLYSTOP 70 135**. However, if we execute **POLYSTOP 50 360/7**, the turtle draws a heptagon (7 sides) but does not stop. This is because Logo rounds the value of 360/7, and when the turtle makes seven turns its heading is not exactly 0. **POLYSTOP** can be edited so that it stops for angle values like 360/7, 360/11, and 360/29 as well as for integral values by replacing the line **IF HEADING = 0 STOP** with a line that instructs the turtle to stop if the heading is very close to 0 but not necessarily exactly 0. If we decide that the turtle should stop when its heading is between 0.001 and 359.999, the following two lines will accomplish this:

IF HEADING < 0.001 STOP
IF HEADING > 359.999 STOP

Edit POLYSTOP in this way and check to see whether it stops for an angle input like 360/7.

Stopping POLY When the Turtle's Initial Heading Is Not Known

For our next discussion, assume that the angle input in POLYSTOP is an integer and hence that POLYSTOP stops when the corresponding figure closes. In the previous discussion, we assumed that the turtle started at home with heading 0. Now let's change the initial heading. For example, execute DRAW RT 30 and POLYSTOP 50 144. POLYSTOP does not stop. Why?

When the turtle's initial heading is not 0, the figure closes only when the initial heading is again reached. Thus, in case of an initial heading of 30 degrees, we could replace the line IF HEADING = 0 STOP by IF HEADING = 30 STOP. In general, it is desirable to have a procedure that records the turtle's initial heading and stops when the POLY figure closes.

We next investigate writing a new POLYSTOP procedure. To record the initial heading, we could name it H (or anything else) using the Logo command MAKE. The statement MAKE "H HEADING gives H a value equal to whatever heading the turtle has at a given moment. In general, the **MAKE** statement accepts two inputs: the first is the name of the variable we are defining, and the second is the value of this new variable. For example, in the statement MAKE "H HEADING, H is the name of the new variable and HEADING (which is a number greater than or equal to 0 and less than 360) is the value that H acquires. The double quotation mark before the variable name indicates that H is the actual name of the new variable. Because H is now a variable, it must be preceded by a colon. We discuss the MAKE statement further at the end of this section.

MAKE

We now return to the task of writing the new POLYSTOP procedure. To record the turtle's initial heading, we insert the statement MAKE "H HEADING immediately following the title line and include the line IF HEADING = :H STOP, as shown below.

```
TO POLYSTOP :SIDE :ANGLE
MAKE "H HEADING
FD :SIDE RT :ANGLE
IF HEADING = :H STOP
POLYSTOP :SIDE :ANGLE
END
```

If we now execute POLYSTOP 50 160, the turtle does not stop. Do you see why?

If the turtle's initial heading is 0, the MAKE statement assigns H the value 0. When the next line is executed, the turtle turns 160 degrees; therefore, its new heading is 160. Thus HEADING = :H is false because 160 ≠ 0. Consequently the procedure does not stop, and the next line is executed; that is, POLYSTOP calls a copy of itself. The statement MAKE "H HEADING assigns the present heading of 160 to H. When the next line is executed, the heading becomes 160 + 160, or 320. Because 320 ≠ 160, the procedure does not stop. Indeed, the process never stops because HEADING is never equal to :H; they always differ by 160 degrees.

The reason :H changed was because POLYSTOP called a copy of itself and forced the computer to change the value of H. In order to allow the POLYSTOP procedure to stop, we need a way to keep :H, the initial heading, constant throughout the execution of the procedure. In order to achieve this we eliminate the line MAKE "H HEADING from POLYSTOP and create a new procedure called POLYHALT that takes the same inputs as POLYSTOP and records the turtle's initial heading before calling POLYSTOP. Rather than executing POLYSTOP we would execute POLYHALT. The edited POLYSTOP and the new POLYHALT procedures are given below.

```
TO POLYSTOP :SIDE :ANGLE          TO POLYHALT :SIDE :ANGLE
FD :SIDE RT :ANGLE                MAKE "H HEADING
IF HEADING = :H STOP              POLYSTOP :SIDE :ANGLE
POLYSTOP :SIDE :ANGLE             END
END
```

Figure 4-5 shows some drawings made with POLYHALT.

Figure 4-5

(a)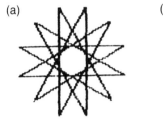

(b)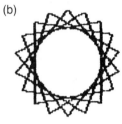

(c)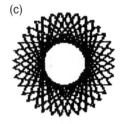

POLYHALT 80 150   POLYHALT 60 100   POLYHALT 70 130

The POLYROLL Procedure

Other drawings made with the POLYHALT procedure are given in Figure 4-6.

Figure 4-6

(a)

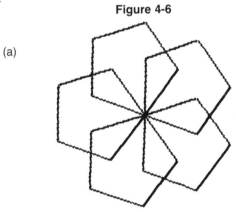

REPEAT 5 [POLYHALT 50 72 RT 72]

(b)

REPEAT 10 [POLYHALT 50 80 RT 36]

(c)

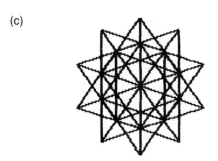

REPEAT 10 [POLYHALT 60 144 RT 36]

The shapes in Figure 4-6 as well as other shapes can be obtained from a single PROLL procedure, defined as follows:

TO PROLL :N :SIDE :ANGLE1 :ANGLE2
REPEAT :N [POLYHALT :SIDE :ANGLE1 RT :ANGLE2]
END

Can you write a recursive procedure called POLYROLL for drawing shapes similar to those in Figure 4-6, assuming that the turtle starts with a heading of 0? POLYROLL needs three inputs, :SIDE and :ANGLE1 for POLYHALT and :ANGLE2, a new variable that tells the POLYHALT figures how much to turn. The POLYROLL procedure is given below.

TO POLYROLL :SIDE :ANGLE1 :ANGLE2
POLYHALT :SIDE :ANGLE1
RT :ANGLE2
IF HEADING = 0 STOP
POLYROLL :SIDE :ANGLE1 :ANGLE2
END

Various figures drawn by POLYROLL are shown in Figure 4-7.

Figure 4-7

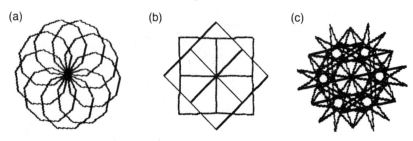

(a)   (b)   (c)

POLYROLL 20 40 40   POLYROLL 40 90 45   POLYROLL 50 160 60

Why does POLYROLL work without editing the definition of POLY-HALT so that it has :ANGLE1 rather than :ANGLE as a variable? Consider what happens when POLYROLL is executed. Executing POLY-ROLL 20 90 45 assigns 20 to the variable :SIDE, 90 to the variable :ANGLE1, and 45 to the variable :ANGLE2. The three variables, :SIDE, :ANGLE1, and :ANGLE2 are called local variables because their values are local to the procedure in whose title they appear. As you may remember from Chapter 3, local variables are accessible only to the procedure in which they appear. As soon as the END statement of that procedure is reached, their values are discarded. For example, the variables :SIDE and :ANGLE1 are accessible to POLYHALT because POLYHALT is called in the POLYROLL procedure with these two variables. Notice that POLYHALT does not have access to the variable :ANGLE2, however. POLYHALT assigns the values of :SIDE and :ANGLE1 to its own variables :SIDE and :ANGLE, respectively.

Logo Words, the MAKE Statement, and Global Variables

The primitive MAKE introduced earlier uses Logo words. To indicate a **word** in Logo, a string of characters (one character or more) made from almost any keyboard symbols is prefixed by a single set of double quotation marks. For example, "HOUSE, "AX33, and "M3.4 are all words in Logo. Numbers may or may not be prefixed by the double quotation marks. For example, PRINT "1 and PRINT 1 have the same effect. If we type PRINT "AXBB, the computer displays AXBB. If, on the other hand, we type PRINT AXBB, the computer displays the error message THERE IS NO PROCEDURE NAMED AXBB because AXBB without a quotation mark is interpreted as a name of a procedure and not a Logo Word.

word

Consider the statement MAKE "N "NUMBER. In this way we have assigned the word NUMBER to the variable :N.If we type PRINT :N, the computer displays NUMBER. On the other hand, if we type PRINT "N, the computer displays N. If we type PRINT N, the computer gives this error message:

THERE IS NO PROCEDURE NAMED N.

We can summarize this discussion as follows:

"N means the word N.

:N means the value associated with N.

N means a procedure named N.

Here are two more examples, including the computer's responses.

```
?MAKE "X "BOAT
?PRINT :X
 BOAT

?PRINT "X
 X
?PRINT X
 THERE IS NO PROCEDURE NAMED X.
```

To see how **MAKE** statements can affect a procedure, consider the SQUARE procedure below.

```
TO SQUARE :SIDE
REPEAT 4 [FD :SIDE RT 90]
END
```

If we type **SQUARE 15**, the computer displays a square of side 15. Suppose we type **MAKE "SIDE 40** and then **PRINT :SIDE**. The computer displays 40 . Now if we type **SQUARE :SIDE**, the computer displays a square of side 40.

To understand what happened, it is helpful to think about the variable :SIDE in the SQUARE procedure as this procedure's private storage container. When **MAKE "SIDE 40** is typed, the value 40 is associated with the name :SIDE, which is a global variable and thus a different storage container than the local one called :SIDE belonging to SQUARE. Therefore, the value 40 stays in the container named "SIDE until it is replaced by another value through a MAKE statement such as **MAKE "SIDE 60**. If **SQUARE 20** is typed now, the local variable :SIDE is assigned the value of 20. However, outside of the SQUARE procedure this local variable is not available and the value of :SIDE is the global one assigned by the last MAKE statement. Once the execution of SQUARE 20 is completed, the local value 20 of :SIDE is discarded. Suppose we now type **MAKE "SIDE 60** and then **SQUARE**

:SIDE. We obtain a square of side 60 because the global variable :SIDE has now the value 60. However, if SQUARE by itself is typed, Logo displays an error message:

SQUARE NEEDS MORE INPUTS.

The variables defined by a MAKE statement are accessible to all procedures. Such variables are called **global variables.** It is important to keep in mind that the name of a global variable may not appear in the title lines of procedures that use its value. Also keep in mind that a value assigned to a local variable does not affect the value of a global variable with the same name. Global variables are sometimes easier to use than local variables because once a global variable is defined, it can be used by any procedure without a declaration in the procedure's title line. On the other hand, experienced programmers prefer to use local variables rather than global variables whenever possible because changing the value of a global variable in one procedure affects all other procedures that use that global variable, whereas changing the value of a local variable in one procedure does not affect other procedures that use a variable with the same name.

global variables

The MAKE statement combined with the REPEAT command may be used to create procedures having an effect similar to that of recursive procedures with a STOP command. For example, using the MAKE statement and the REPEAT command we can write the following NEWTOWER procedure, which draws a tower made of :N squares similar to the one shown in Figure 4-3.

```
TO NEWTOWER :S :N
REPEAT :N [SQUARE :S FD :S MAKE "S :S – 5]
END
```

To try NEWTOWER, move the turtle to a position on the screen 80 units below home and execute NEWTOWER 40 6.

Summary of Commands

MAKE   Takes two inputs. The first, preceded by a quotation mark, is the name of the new variable. The second is the value of the new variable.

Problem Set 4-2

1. Use the following **TRI** procedure to write a recursive program with a **STOP** command that produces a shape similar to the one below. The shape is obtained by drawing **TRI**, turning the turtle right by 30 degrees, and repeating this sequence until no new parts of the shape can be drawn.

```
TO TRI
REPEAT 3 [FD 50 RT 120]
END
```

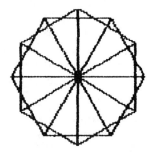

2. Use the **POLYHALT** procedure to obtain a design similar to the following.

3. Use recursion and a **STOP** command to write a procedure that spins **POLYSPI** figures in a way similar to **POLYROLL**.

4. The following **POLYROLL1** procedure along with **POLYSTOP1** makes the same design as **POLYROLL**. Run **POLYROLL1 75 90 30** and compare it with **POLYROLL 75 90 30**.

```
TO POLYROLL1 :S :A1 :A2          TO POLYSTOP1 :S :A :H
POLYSTOP1 :S :A1 HEADING         FD :S RT :A
RT :A2                           IF HEADING = :H STOP
IF HEADING = 0 STOP              POLYSTOP1 :S :A :H
POLYROLL1 :S :A1 :A2             END
END
```

5. Consider the following programs:

```
TO INCREASE :X                   TO TEX :X
MAKE "X :X + 2                    PRINT :X
PRINT :X                         INCREASE :X
END                              PRINT :X
                                 END
```

Now predict what appears on the screen for each of the following, and check your predictions on the computer.

(a) INCREASE 8
(b) TEX 8

6. Predict the outcome when WALK 5 and JOG 5 are run in the procedures defined below.

```
TO JOG :S                        TO WALK :S
FD :S RT 90                      FD :S RT 90
MAKE "S :S + 10                  MAKE "S :S + 10
JOG :S                           WALK :S − 10
END                              END
```

7. Define TRIANGLE as follows:

```
TO TRIANGLE :SIDE
REPEAT 3 [FD :SIDE RT 120]
END
```

Type MAKE "SIDE 50. Then predict the outcome when the following are run consecutively without clearing the screen.

(a) PRINT :SIDE
(b) TRIANGLE :SIDE
(c) TRIANGLE 20
(d) PRINT "SIDE

8. The following **SPIN** procedure spins a "growing" polygon 15 times.

    TO SPIN :S :N
    REPEAT 15 [POLYGON :S :N RT 15 MAKE "S :S+3]
    END

    TO POLYGON :S :N
    REPEAT :N [FD :S RT 360/:N]
    END

    Use **SPIN** to spin the following.

    (a) a "growing" square
    (b) a "growing" pentagon
    (c) a "growing" hexagon

4-3 Further Variations on the POLY Procedure

In Section 4-1 we found that increasing **:SIDE** by a certain number of steps in the **POLY** procedure yielded a procedure that drew spirals. We called that procedure **POLYSPI**. In the **POLYSPI** procedure we increased the side by five units. It is possible to make this increment a variable. Such a procedure, called **POLYSPIRAL**, is given below along with the "old" **POLYSPI** procedure for comparison. The procedures **POLYSPI 5 144** and **POLYSPIRAL 5 144 5** draw identical figures.

(a) TO POLYSPIRAL :SIDE :ANGLE :INCREMENT
     FD :SIDE RT :ANGLE
     POLYSPIRAL :SIDE + :INCREMENT :ANGLE :INCREMENT
     END

(b) TO POLYSPI :SIDE :ANGLE
     FD :SIDE RT :ANGLE
     POLYSPI :SIDE + 5 :ANGLE
     END

We can create another modification of the POLY procedure by calling the original procedure with the angle increased by five units or, indeed, by any number of units. We call the new procedure INSPI and give it below.

```
TO INSPI :SIDE :ANGLE
FD :SIDE RT :ANGLE
INSPI :SIDE :ANGLE + 5
END
```

The INSPI procedure produces drawings with various symmetries, depending upon the inputs for :ANGLE. Some of these drawings are shown in Figure 4-8.

Figure 4-8

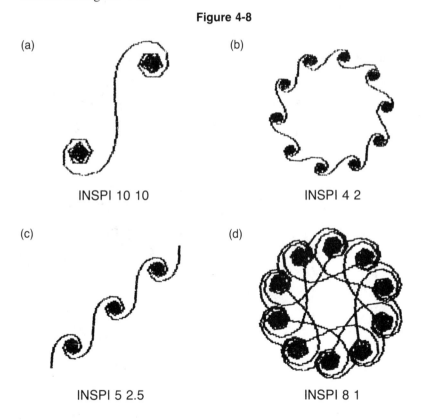

(a)

INSPI 10 10

(b)

INSPI 4 2

(c)

INSPI 5 2.5

(d)

INSPI 8 1

Try some of your own inputs and see what drawings they produce.

Still other modifications of the POLY procedure can be made. For example, suppose we want the turtle to move forward always the same number of steps, but to alternate the turning between 20 degrees and 40 degrees, and in general between A and 2A degrees. Before reading on, try to write such a procedure, called **NEWPOLY**, with the length of the side being :S and the amount of turning angle being :A.

To write such a procedure, we need to repeat indefinitely the set of instructions **FD :S RT :A FD :S RT :A * 2**. A procedure to do this can be defined as follows:

```
TO NEWPOLY :S :A
FD :S RT :A FD :S RT :A * 2
NEWPOLY :S :A
END
```

Figure 4-9 shows shapes drawn by **NEWPOLY** for various inputs.

Figure 4-9

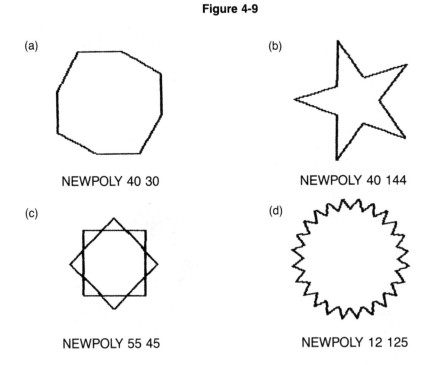

(a)

NEWPOLY 40 30

(b)

NEWPOLY 40 144

(c)

NEWPOLY 55 45

(d)

NEWPOLY 12 125

Now execute **NEWPOLY** with 20 for the value of :S and the following angle inputs: 60, 120, 179, 90, 720/7, 720/9, 720/11, 3 * 360/7. Then try the **NEWPOLY1** procedure below with various inputs and compare the results with the results obtained by **NEWPOLY**.

```
TO NEWPOLY1 :S :A
FD :S RT :A
NEWPOLY1 :S :A * 2
END
```

If you run NEWPOLY1, you should see that it stops after a short time. Why does it stop?

Another variation of the POLY procedure is a generalization of the NEWPOLY program. This procedure, which we call GPOLY (G for generalized), has four variables and is given below.

```
TO GPOLY :S1 :A1 :S2 :A2
FD :S1 RT :A1 FD :S2 RT :A2
GPOLY :S1 :A1 :S2 :A2
END
```

Figure 4-10 shows shapes drawn by GPOLY for different inputs.

Figure 4-10

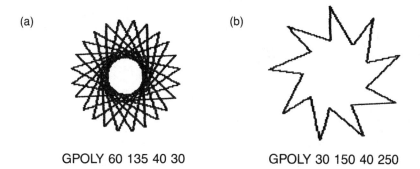

(a) GPOLY 60 135 40 30

(b) GPOLY 30 150 40 250

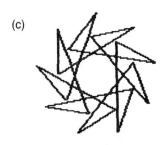

(c) GPOLY 80 120 40 160

Problem Set 4-3

1. (a) Edit the INSPI procedure so that instead of adding five to the angle each time, it adds a variable (call it :INC) to the angle each time, so the new title line is INSPI :SIDE :ANGLE :INC.

   (b) Use the INSPI procedure from part (a) to run the following:
   - (i)   INSPI 50 0 90
   - (ii)   INSPI 10 0 120
   - (iii) INSPI 40 45 180
   - (iv)   INSPI 30 0 45
   - (v)   INSPI -10 (-45) 90
   - (vi)   INSPI 30 60 180

   (c) Execute INSPI 30 5 90. Notice that the resulting figure is quite different from the figures produced by the first version of INSPI. Find other inputs for INSPI to produce still different figures.

2. (a) Write a procedure called SNEWPOLY with a STOP command and variables :SIDE, :ANGLE1, and :ANGLE2, which produces a figure obtained by rotating NEWPOLY through a variable angle :ANGLE2.

   (b) Run SNEWPOLY for the following:
   - (i)   SNEWPOLY 20 144 30
   - (ii)   SNEWPOLY 8 125 20
   - (iii) SNEWPOLY 20 100 15

4-4 Embedded Recursion

Consider the following procedures:

```
TO DOWN :N              TO SUB :N
IF :N = 0 STOP          IF :N = 0 STOP
PRINT :N                SUB :N - 1
DOWN :N - 1             PRINT :N
END                     END
```

As expected, DOWN 3 prints 3, 2, 1 and stops. Before reading further, predict what happens when SUB 3 is run.

Quite surprisingly, SUB 3 prints 1, 2, 3 and stops. To understand why this occurs, we must understand how recursion works. Remember that a recursive procedure calls a copy of itself. We will introduce a model that explains how this is done. However, we first discuss the model in a more familiar setting, in which a procedure calls another procedure and so on.

Consider the three procedures shown below:

```
TO PROCEDURE1
PR 5
PROCEDURE2
PR 0
END


TO PROCEDURE2
PR 1985
PROCEDURE3
REPEAT 2[PR 13]
END


TO PROCEDURE3
REPEAT 3[PR 10]
END
```

Predict the result of running PROCEDURE1 and check to see if the result is the same as the one given below.

```
5
1985
10
10
10
13
13
0
```

Here is a telescoping model that describes **PROCEDURE1**.

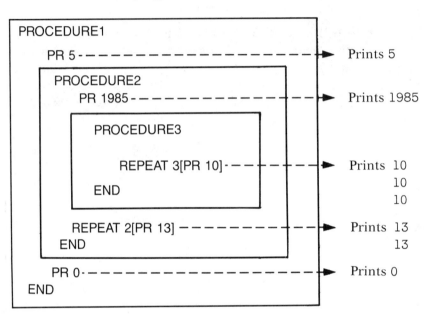

When **PROCEDURE1** is run, it proceeds until it encounters the call for **PROCEDURE2**. At this point, all the lines of **PROCEDURE2** are inserted. They are executed in order until **PROCEDURE2** calls **PROCEDURE3**, whose lines are then executed. **PROCEDURE3** does not call any other procedure, so its **END** statement is reached. After **PROCEDURE3** has been completed, control is returned to the procedure that called it, namely **PROCEDURE2**. It is as if **PROCEDURE3** completed its job and reported back to the superior that had called on it. Now **PROCEDURE2** continues where it left off; it executes **REPEAT** 2[PR 13], ends, and returns control to **PROCEDURE1**. Finally, **PROCEDURE1** prints 0 and then encounters its own **END** statement.

We can use the same telescoping model to see how the **SUB** procedure introduced at the beginning of this section works (it is given again below for easy reference). The model also shows how recursion in general works.

```
TO SUB :N
IF :N = 0 STOP
SUB :N − 1
PRINT :N
END
```

Fitting **SUB 3** into our model, we have the following:

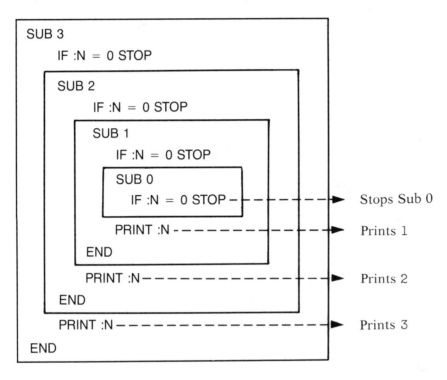

Notice that when :N = 0, in **SUB 0** the **STOP** command is finally reached. However, **STOP** stops only the procedure it is in and not the calling procedure. As in our previous example, control is then returned to the previous procedure, and so on.

From our model, we see that recursion works according to the following rules:

(1) Executions in Logo programs proceed line by line. When a procedure calls itself, it puts on hold any of its instructions that are written after the call and inserts a copy of itself at the point where the call occurs. If the called procedure stops, control is returned to the calling procedure at the point where the call occurred. The remainder of the lines in the calling procedure are then executed.

(2) The process in (1) applies to any successive calls.

embedded recursion

DOWN, the other procedure given at the beginning of this section, incorporates tail-end recursion, while SUB incorporates non–tail-end or **embedded recursion.** In a procedure that uses embedded recursion, there are instructions following the recursive call or calls—that is, the recursive call is not the last or "tail-end" call before the END statement. Apply the telescoping model to the DOWN procedure. Does the model give the result you expect?

Many people think that a recursive procedure such as DOWN simply loops back to its beginning, as shown below.

```
TO DOWN :N
IF :N = 0 STOP
PRINT :N
DOWN :N - 1
END
```

In the case of tail-end recursion, the looping model does give the same results as the telescoping model. However, it is important to remember that the looping model is not the correct model for all recursive procedures. For example, consider the DOWN1 procedure given below.

```
TO DOWN1 :N
IF :N = 0 STOP
PRINT :N
DOWN1 :N - 1
PRINT [NOT TAIL-END]
END
```

Applying the looping model, some people might expect either of the following outputs for DOWN1 3:

(a)   3
        2
        1

(b)   3
        2
        1
        NOT TAIL-END

In reality, the following is the result obtained when **DOWN1 3** is executed.

```
3
2
1
NOT TAIL-END
NOT TAIL-END
NOT TAIL-END
```

To see why this happens, apply the telescoping model to **DOWN1 3**.

As one last experiment to see the difference between tail-end and embedded recursion, execute **DOWN 200** and **DOWN1 200**. **DOWN 200** produces the expected results, as seen in (a) below.

(a)   200
      199
      198
       .
       .
       .
       1

(b)   200
      199
      198
       .
       .
       .
      87
      NO STORAGE LEFT! IN LINE DOWN1 :N − 1
      AT LEVEL 114 OF DOWN1.

DOWN1 200 produces the result in (b). **DOWN 200**, with tail-end recursion, is treated as simple looping and does not use up memory, but the embedded recursion in **DOWN1** requires memory space to store the copies of **DOWN1** "waiting" to be evaluated. Thus memory quickly fills up, and we get the error message shown above. This error message tells us that there was no storage left after 114 copies of **DOWN1** were executed.

Other Examples of Embedded Recursion

To test your understanding of recursion, predict the output of the SHAPE procedure given below and then run it to see if you are correct.

```
TO SHAPE
FD 30 RT 60
IF HEADING = 0 STOP
SHAPE
FD 30 LT 60
END
```

When SHAPE is run, it calls itself repeatedly until the heading is 0. The sixth time that SHAPE is run, the turtle has turned 60 degrees six times. Thus its heading is 0, and the last SHAPE procedure that was called stops. After stopping, it returns control to the procedure that called it, which executes the next lines in the procedure: FD 30 LT 60 and END. This process is executed only five times (Why?), and therefore the sixth segment is not drawn. The figure drawn by SHAPE is shown in Figure 4-11.

Figure 4-11

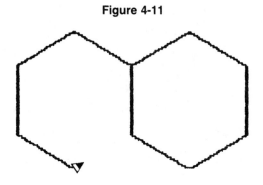

TEST

IFTRUE (IFT)

IFFALSE (IFF)

It is possible to modify the SHAPE procedure to obtain two closed hexagons. One way to do this is to introduce the Logo primitives TEST, IFTRUE (IFT), and IFFALSE (IFF). The **TEST** primitive checks for the truth or falsity of a condition. In the lines following the TEST condition, the primitives IFTRUE or IFFALSE should be used. The instructions following **IFTRUE (IFT)** on the same line will be executed if the condition tested by TEST is true, and the instructions following **IFFALSE (IFF)** on the same line will be executed if the tested condition is false. For example, consider the following three procedures:

```
TO RACK :N              TO PILE :N              TO ROLL :N
PRINT :N                TEST :N = 0             IF :N = 0 STOP
TEST :N = 0             IFFALSE PILE :N − 1     ROLL :N − 1
IFFALSE RACK :N − 1     PRINT :N                PRINT :N
END                     END                     END
```

Before reading on, try to predict the results if each of the procedures is run with input 3.

The runs are as follows:

RACK 3	PILE 3	ROLL 3
3	0	1
2	1	2
1	2	3
0	3	

Both PILE and ROLL incorporate embedded recursion. PILE 3 prints 0, while ROLL 3 does not. Why? PILE 3 calls PILE 2, which calls PILE 1, which calls PILE 0. Because :N = 0 is true, the next line IFFALSE PILE :N − 1 is not executed. The next executed line is PRINT :N, which for :N = 0 prints 0, and PILE 0 finishes its job; that is, it executes the line PRINT :N for :N = 1 and prints 1. PILE 1 was called by PILE 2; hence, 2 is printed. Similarly, 3 is printed. In contrast, when :N = 0 in the ROLL procedure, the procedure stops and therefore PRINT 0 is not executed.

The PILE procedure suggests a way to write a recursive procedure that produces two closed hexagons, as in Figure 4-12. Try to write such a procedure and check it on the computer. The procedure is given next to the figure.

```
TO SHAPE1
FD 30 RT 60
TEST HEADING = 0
IFFALSE SHAPE1
FD 30 LT 60
END
```

Figure 4-12

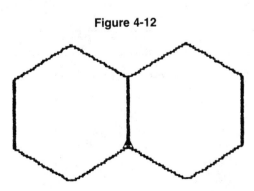

Notice that the **SHAPE1** procedure draws two closed hexagons because **SHAPE1** calls a copy of itself as long as **HEADING** is not 0.

NOT

In the **SHAPE1** procedure, the primitive **NOT** can be used to accomplish the same thing as the primitives **TEST** and **IFFALSE**. **NOT** is a primitive that outputs FALSE if its input is true and outputs TRUE if its input is false. For example, **NOT** $(3 = 5)$ outputs TRUE, and **NOT** $(2 = 4/2)$ outputs FALSE. Thus we can edit the **SHAPE1** procedure as follows:

```
TO SHAPE1
FD 30 RT 20
IF NOT (HEADING = 0) SHAPE1
FD 30 LT 60
END
```

> ### Summary of Commands and Logo Primitives
>
> TEST   Takes one input, a condition, and checks the condition for truth or falsity. Executions of subsequent lines depends upon the result of the test.
>
> IFTRUE (IFT)   The instructions following **IFTRUE** are executed if the condition tested by **TEST** is true.
>
> IFFALSE (IFF)   The instructions following **IFFALSE** are executed if the condition tested by **TEST** is false.
>
> NOT   Takes one input. Outputs FALSE if the input is true; outputs TRUE if the input is false.

Problem Set 4-4

1. Predict the outcome for each of the following when the value of :N is 3.

(a)
```
TO DEC :N
IF :N < 0 STOP
PRINT :N
DEC :N - 2
END
```

(b)
```
TO INC :N
IF :N < 0 STOP
INC :N - 2
PRINT :N
END
```

(c)
```
TO MAX :N
TEST :N < 0
IFFALSE MAX :N - 2
PRINT :N
END
```

2. Predict what figures will be drawn by each of the following:

(a) TO P
    FD 4 RT 20
    IF HEADING = 0 STOP
    P
    FD 4 LT 20
    HT
    END

(b) TO Q
    FD 4 RT 20
    TEST HEADING = 0
    IFFALSE Q
    FD 4 LT 20
    HT
    END

(c) REPEAT 5[P]

(d) REPEAT 5 [Q]

3. Generalize the SHAPE1 procedure for variable inputs :SIDE and :ANGLE. Call the new procedure GSHAPE1 and run it for the following inputs:

(a) GSHAPE1 50 120
(c) GSHAPE1 50 135
(e) GSHAPE1 5 (− 10)

(b) GSHAPE1 50 100
(d) GSHAPE1 5 10
(f) GSHAPE1 1 1

4. Predict the outcomes for each of the following when :S is 60.

(a) TO FIG :S
    IF :S < 10 STOP
    REPEAT 4 [FD :S RT 90]
    RT 90 FD :S LT 90
    FIG :S / 2
    END

(b) TO FIG1 :S
    IF :S < 10 STOP
    FIG1 :S / 2
    REPEAT 4 [FD :S RT 90]
    RT 90 FD :S LT 90
    END

(c) TO FIG2 :S
    TEST :S < 10
    IFFALSE FIG2 :S / 2
    REPEAT 4 [FD :S RT 90]
    RT 90 FD :S LT 90
    END

(d) TO FIG3 :S
    TEST :S > 10
    IFTRUE FIG3 :S / 2
    REPEAT 4 [FD :S LT 90]
    RT 90 FD :S LT 90
    END

5. Do the procedures in 4 (c) and 4 (d) always produce the same figures for the same inputs of :S? Why or why not?

6. Write a procedure utilizing embedded recursion to draw a figure similar to the following:

7. Predict the outcome of each of the following for :X = 50.

(a) TO WOW :X
    IF :X < 1 STOP
    FD :X RT 87
    WOW :X − 2
    LT 87 BK :X
    END

(b) TO WOW1 :X
    REPEAT 4[WOW :X RT 90]
    END

(c) TO WOW2 :X
    IF :X < 1 STOP
    FD :X RT 87
    WOW2 :X − 2
    PC 0 LT 87 BK :X
    END

(d) TO WOW3 :X
    IF :X < 1 STOP
    FD :X RT 118
    WOW3 :X − 2
    LT 118 BK :X
    END

8. Predict the result when the following procedure is executed when the initial heading is 0.

    TO SHAPE2
    FD 30 RT 20
    TEST HEADING = 0
    IFFALSE SHAPE2
    PC 0 FD 30 RT 20
    END

9. Predict what happens when **HOUSES 30** is executed. Check your prediction on the computer. (**SQUARE** is a procedure that draws a variable size square, and **TRIANGLE** is a procedure that draws a variable size equilateral triangle.)

```
TO HOUSES :S
IF :S < 1 STOP
SQUARE :S
PU RT 90 FD :S * 2 LT 90 PD
HOUSES :S - 10
PU LT 90 FD :S * 2 RT 90 PD
FD :S RT 30
TRIANGLE :S
LT 30 BK :S
END
```

10. Predict what happens when **REFLECT.POLYGON 8** is executed. Check your prediction by executing the procedure.

```
TO REFLECT.POLYGON :N
IF :N < 3 STOP
REPEAT :N [FD 30 RT 360/:N]
REFLECT.POLYGON :N - 1
REPEAT :N [FD 30 LT 360/:N]
END
```

☆11. Predict the outcome of **GEE 8** and **GEE 32**, where **GEE** is defined as follows:

```
TO GEE :S
IF :S < 2 STOP
LT 45 FD :S
GEE :S/2
BK :S RT 90 FD :S
GEE :S/2
BK :S LT 45
END
```

☆12. Predict the output of the following procedure.

```
TO SHE
FD 30 RT 60
IF HEADING = 0 ELSE SHE
FD 30 LT 60
END
```

Solution to the Preliminary Problem

Understanding the Problem

The problem is to write a procedure that will spin a pentagon while "shrinking" its size, producing a shape similar to the one shown in Figure 4-13. The figure is made of pentagons with one common vertex. If we start with the largest pentagon, we see that each following pentagon is smaller than the preceding one. It seems that the first few pentagons are spun in such a way that the angle between a side of any pentagon and a corresponding side in the previous pentagon is always the same.

Figure 4-13

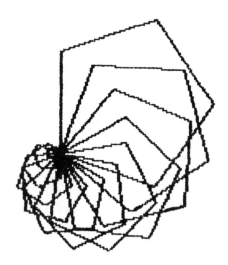

Devising a Plan

Because the figure is made of pentagons of different sizes, it is desirable to have a **PENTAGON** procedure to draw a variable size pentagon. To obtain a shape similar to the one in Figure 4-13, we could draw the first pentagon, then turn the turtle to the right a certain number of degrees (for example, 20) and draw the next pentagon with a side a certain number of units shorter than the side in the first pentagon. We choose the side of the second pentagon to be 5 units shorter than the side of the first pentagon. Next we turn the turtle 20 degrees to the right and draw a pentagon with a side 5 units shorter than the side of the previous pentagon, and so on. Because of the repetitive nature of the process, a recursive procedure could be utilized. The process should be stopped when the side of the pentagon becomes negative. (Compare this with the solution of Problem 4-1.)

Carrying Out the Plan

The procedure to draw a variable size pentagon is given below (note that the turtle needs to turn each time by 360/5, or 72 degrees).

```
TO PENTAGON :S
REPEAT 5 [FD :S RT 72]
END
```

We call the procedure that spins a pentagon and "shrinks" its size SPINPENT. We start our procedure with the title line **TO SPINPENT :S** and then type in the next line **PENTAGON :S**. This causes the turtle to draw a pentagon and return to its original position and heading. Before calling the **SPINPENT** procedure again, the procedure must turn the turtle right 20 degrees. To utilize the power of recursion, we need now to call **SPINPENT** with an input 5 units smaller, that is, **SPINPENT :S** − 5. To stop the process, we need to insert the line **IF :S** < 0 **STOP** right after the title line. (Will the procedure draw the same figures if this line is inserted elsewhere? Why?) The **SPINPENT** procedure is shown below.

```
TO SPINPENT :S
IF :S < 0 STOP
PENTAGON :S
RT 20
SPINPENT :S − 5
END
```

Looking Back

The shape in Figure 4-13 could be generated by starting with a small pentagon and spinning it while letting its size "grow," rather than the reverse as in the previous procedure. Also, we could write a general procedure for spinning and "shrinking" any polygon or any other figure.

Another Looking Back activity concerns the use of the STOP command. We used the statement IF :S < 0 STOP. Assuming that the turtle's initial heading is 0, could the statement IF HEADING = 0 STOP be used instead? What are the advantages and disadvantages of each statement? If each statement has some advantages, could the two statements be used together so that the turtle stops when :S < 0 or when HEADING = 0, whichever happens first? In Chapter 5 we will introduce the command ANYOF, which can accomplish this. Meanwhile, could you write such a procedure using the commands introduced so far?

Chapter 4 Problem Set

1. Write recursive procedures with STOP statements that draw variable size figures similar to each of the following:

(a)   (b)   (c)

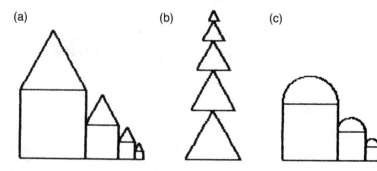

2. Write a recursive procedure with a **STOP** statement that will spin a square while "shrinking" its size, as shown below.

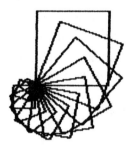

3. Write a recursive procedure with a **STOP** statement that draws the following variable size figure made of squares.

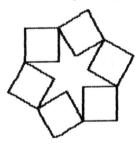

4. Predict the outcome when **TOP 50 5** is run. The procedure **TOP** is defined as follows:

```
TO TOP :S :N                TO SQUARE :S
IF :N < 0 STOP              REPEAT 4 [FD :S RT 90]
SQUARE :S                   END
FD :S RT 90 FD :S / 4 LT 90
TOP :S - 10 :N - 1
END
```

5. (a) Predict the outcome when **TT 30 5** is run. The procedure **TT** is defined as follows:

```
TO TT :X :N                 TO TRI :X
IF :N = 0 STOP              REPEAT 3 [FD :X RT 120]
TRI :X                      END
FD :X
TT :X - 5 :N - 1
END
```

(b) Execute the following and count the number of triangles drawn in each case. (i) **TT 50 2** (ii) **TT 35 4** (iii) **TT 30 5**

(c) Based on your answers to part (b), how many triangles do you think **TT 25 6** will draw? Now execute **TT 25 6** and explain the result.

6. Predict the outcomes when the following are executed. Check your predictions on the computer.

```
MAKE "H "HOUSE
PR :H
PR "H
PR H
```

7. Define **DOUBLE** as shown. Then predict the outcome when **DOUBLE 1** is executed.

```
TO DOUBLE :N
IF :N > 10000000 STOP
PR :N
MAKE "N :N * 2
DOUBLE :N
END
```

8. Consider the **VE** and **VE1** procedures defined below and answer the questions that follow.

```
TO VE :S :A            TO VE1 :S :A
FD :S RT :A            FD :S RT :A
MAKE "H HEADING        VE1 :S HEADING
VE :S :H               END
END
```

(a) What shapes do you expect **VE 3 3** to draw? Now execute **VE 3 3** to check your guess.

(b) Find the first eight angles by which the turtle turns when **VE 3 3** is executed.

(c) Predict the outcomes of each of the following: (i) **VE 20 30** (ii) **VE 20 45** (iii) **VE 20 60**

(d) Compare **VE1** to **VE**. Does **VE1** produce different shapes for the same inputs? Why?

9. Use embedded recursion to write a procedure that draws the following figure.

10. Assuming that the turtle starts at home with heading 0, edit the **SPINPENT** procedure in the solution to the Preliminary Problem so that the turtle will stop **IF :S < 0** or **IF HEADING = 0**, whichever happens first. (Hint: Use the **TEST** and **IFTRUE** commands.)

☆11. Predict the drawing obtained by executing **BOXES 30** if the procedure **BOXES** is defined as follows:

```
TO BOXES :SIDE
IF :SIDE < 10 STOP
REPEAT 4 [FD :SIDE BOXES :SIDE / 2 RT 90]
END
```

5

New Vocabulary in Chapter 5

Terms	Primitives
tessellate p. 179	SETX p. 180
Cartesian coordinate system p. 179	SETY p. 180
origin p. 180	SETXY p. 182
line segment p. 184	SQRT p. 186
distance formula p. 184	XCOR p. 186
Pythagorean Theorem p. 185	YCOR p. 186
absolute value p. 201	TOWARDS p. 187
regular tessellation p. 217	SETHEADING (SETH) p. 188
	OUTPUT (OP) p. 189
	ANYOF p. 198
	ALLOF p. 203
	TOPLEVEL p. 216
	CHAR 7 p. 230

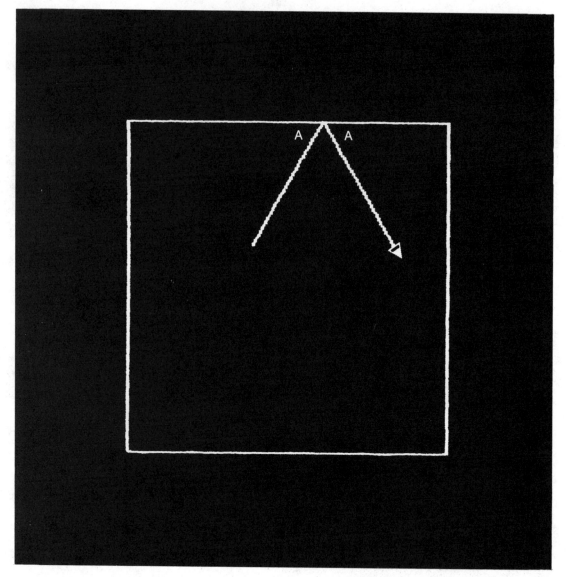

Preliminary Problem

Write a procedure that will draw a large square on the screen, as shown above. Next, write a procedure so that when the turtle is placed inside the boundary of the square at some random heading, it starts moving along a segment and "bounces off" the boundary at the same angle as it hits the boundary, then continues on its path.

5

The Coordinated Turtle

Introduction

In this chapter, we introduce primitives for using the turtle with coordinates. We then develop procedures to do geometry constructions and to **tessellate** the monitor screen, that is, to fill the screen with no holes and no overlapping. The chapter also explains how to use coordinates to develop traditional geometry concepts.

tessellate

5-1 Coordinating the Turtle

In Logo, it is possible to specify a location on the monitor screen and send the turtle directly to that position. This is done through the use of the primitives SETX, SETY, and SETXY. Logo treats the screen as a **Cartesian coordinate system** where each point of the screen is associated with an ordered pair of numbers (a,b). The number a is the x-coordinate; it is positive to the right of a vertical line drawn through home and negative to the left of the line. The number b is the y-coordinate and is positive above a horizontal line drawn through home and negative below the line. Figure 5-1, for example, pictures

**Cartesian
coordinate system**

origin

the point (−30,20). The **origin,** the point at the turtle's home position, has coordinates (0, 0).

Figure 5-1

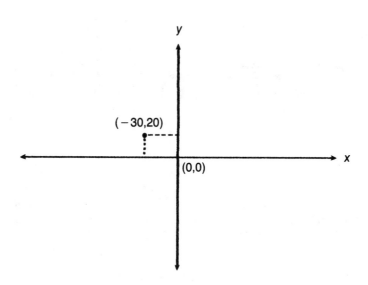

SETX

SETX is used with a number input to move the turtle in a horizontal direction to the position whose x-coordinate is the given input. This command changes neither the turtle's heading nor its y-coordinate. For example, if the turtle is at home and we type SETX 50, the turtle moves horizontally until the x-coordinate is 50. Similarly, if we now type SETX −75, the turtle moves horizontally to the point on the screen where its x-coordinate is −75. In each case, the turtle's heading is unchanged.

Suppose the turtle starts at home and we type the commands below. What is the final position of the turtle?

SETX 50 SETX (−50)

Did you expect the turtle to end up at home? Did it?

SETY

SETY works in the same way with the y-coordinates. For example, if the turtle is again at home and we type SETY 50, the turtle moves vertically up to the point where it has 50 as its y-coordinate. If we now type **SETY** −75, the turtle moves down to the point where the y-coordinate is −75. In each of these cases, as with **SETX**, the turtle's heading is unchanged. You should explore what inputs to **SETX** and **SETY** cause the turtle to wrap around the screen.

As an example of the use of **SETX** and **SETY**, suppose we start with the turtle at home and type **SETX 50 SETY 70 SETX** −30 **SETY** −50. The turtle's final position has coordinates (−30, −50), and it follows the trail pictured in Figure 5-2.

Figure 5-2

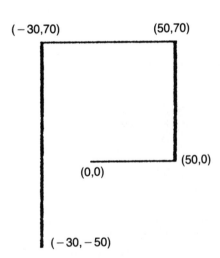

With the **SETX** and **SETY** primitives, the final position of the turtle is partly dependent upon its input value and partly on its initial position. For example, if the turtle is at home and we type **SETX 50**, the turtle moves along a horizontal line through home until its x-coordinate is 50. (The y-coordinate remains 0.) If the turtle's initial position had been 50 turtle steps to the left of home when the command **SETX 50** was issued, it would still have moved along a horizontal line until its x-coordinate was 50, with the y-coordinate remaining 0. However, if the turtle was at the point with coordinates (10, 10) when **SETX 50** was typed, the y-coordinate would be 10 while the turtle moved along a horizontal line until its x-coordinate was 50. **SETY** works the same way as **SETX**.

Problem 5-1

Write a procedure called **FILLRECT** that uses the **SETY** command to fill (color in) a rectangle that has length 50 and width 30. Assume that the turtle starts at home with heading 0.

Solution

One way to write the **FILLRECT** procedure is to have the procedure fill the rectangle as the rectangle is drawn by using a **REPEAT** statement. We could first draw one end of the rectangle by having the turtle start at home and using **SETY 30** to make it move vertically. **SETY 0** would return the turtle to its original position. To make the turtle move to the right one step to be ready to draw the next vertical line, we could issue the instructions **RIGHT 90 FORWARD 1 LEFT 90**. We could then repeat the entire process 50 times. The whole **FILLRECT** procedure might look like this.

```
TO FILLRECT
REPEAT 50 [SETY 30 SETY 0 RIGHT 90 FORWARD 1 LEFT 90]
END
```

SETXY

To place the turtle at the point with coordinates $(-30, -50)$, we could type **SETX** -30 and then **SETY** -50. However, with the **SETXY** primitive, we can do this operation in one step. **SETXY** requires two inputs; the first is the x-coordinate, and the second is the y-coordinate. Typing **SETXY** with two inputs, :A and :B, moves the turtle to the point with coordinates (:A, :B) without changing its heading. For example, typing **SETXY 30 50** moves the turtle from its present position to the point with coordinates (30, 50) without changing its heading. Do you think that typing **SETXY** -30 -50 will move the turtle to the point with coordinates $(-30, -50)$? Try it.

If you tried the above experiment and it did not do what you thought it would, you probably forgot that in Logo, the computer treats -30 -50 as -80. To keep Logo from treating this as a subtraction, we can use parentheses to rewrite the command as **SETXY** -30 (-50).

To demonstrate that the heading does not change as the turtle moves when we use **SETXY**, type the following series of commands and observe the original and final turtle positions and headings.

DRAW
PENUP
SETXY 30 40
PENDOWN
SETXY −50 60
SETXY −80 (−90)

Wherever the turtle starts, **SETX 50 SETY 50** or **SETXY 50 50** takes the turtle to the same final position. Note, however, that if the pen is down when the commands are given, the turtle leaves a different trail in each case, as shown in Figure 5-3(a) and (b), respectively.

Figure 5-3

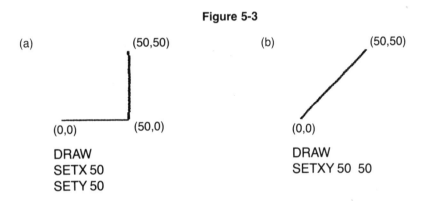

(a)

(0,0)   DRAW
        SETX 50
        SETY 50

(b)

(0,0)   DRAW
        SETXY 50 50

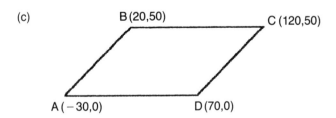

(c)

The **SETX** and **SETY** commands are not sufficient to draw segments AB and CD in Figure 5-3(c). Figure 5-3(c) could be drawn with the following set of commands:

```
PENUP
SETXY  -30 0
PENDOWN
SETXY 20 50
SETXY 120 50
SETXY 70 0
SETXY  -30 0
```

Remark: We could have used SETX 120 and SETX −30 in the place of SETXY 120 50 and SETXY −30 0 above.

Using SETXY to Draw Line Segments

line segment

As the previous example showed, the SETXY primitive is useful for drawing many geometrical figures. We now use it in a procedure to draw a line segment. **A line segment** is determined by two points, its endpoints, and all points between them. We use the notation $\overline{AB}$ to denote the line segment with endpoints A and B. If a line segment has endpoints with coordinates (− 10, 25) and (30, 50), we might write the following instructions for drawing the segment:

```
PENUP
SETXY  -10 25
PENDOWN
SETXY 30 50
```

In general, we can draw a line segment through the points with coordinates (:X1, :Y1) and (:X2, :Y2) with the following procedure:

```
TO SEGMENT :X1 :Y1 :X2 :Y2
PENUP
SETXY :X1 :Y1
PENDOWN
SETXY :X2 :Y2
END
```

Finding the Length of a Line Segment

distance formula

It is possible to find the length of line segments by using coordinates. We can find the length of a segment with the **distance formula,**

$d = \sqrt{(x_1 - x_2)^2 + (y_1 - y_2)^2}$. For example, consider points $A(-10, 20)$ and $B(20, 40)$. To find the distance between A and B, we use the distance formula and find the distance to be $\sqrt{(-10-20)^2 + (20-40)^2}$, or $\sqrt{1300}$, or approximately 36.0555. The distance formula is developed using the Pythagorean Theorem, as described in the Mathematical Aside below.

Mathematical Aside

Consider the line segment $\overline{AB}$ in Figure 5-4 whose endpoints have coordinates $A(x_1, y_1)$ and $B(x_2, y_2)$. If we draw perpendiculars to the x- and y-axes from A and B respectively, we find that the coordinates of point C are (x_1, y_2). (Why?) Now triangle ABC is a right triangle with legs $\overline{AC}$ and $\overline{BC}$ and hypotenuse $\overline{AB}$. We denote the length of segments $\overline{AB}$, $\overline{AC}$, and $\overline{BC}$ by AB, AC, and BC, respectively.

Figure 5-4

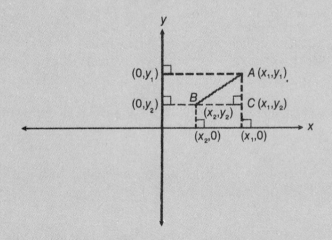

In right triangle ABC as pictured, $BC = x_1 - x_2$ and $AC = y_1 - y_2$. The **Pythagorean Theorem** states that the square of the length of the hypotenuse $\overline{AB}$ of triangle ABC equals the sum of the squares of lengths of the legs, $\overline{AC}$ and $\overline{BC}$; that is, $(AB)^2 = (AC)^2 + (BC)^2$. Equivalently, we have $AB = \sqrt{(AC)^2 + (BC)^2}$. From Figure 5-4, we see that $AB = \sqrt{(x_1 - x_2)^2 + (y_1 - y_2)^2}$. The distance between any two points in the coordinate plane can be found using this formula.

Pythagorean
Theorem

SQRT

We can translate the distance formula just developed into a Logo procedure by using the primitive **SQRT,** which takes one numeric input and outputs the square root of that input. For example, SQRT 2 gives RESULT: 1.41421. A possible procedure called DISTANCE1, with inputs :X1, :Y1, :X2, and :Y2 for the coordinates of two points, is given below.

```
TO DISTANCE1 :X1 :Y1 :X2 :Y2
SQRT (:X1 − :X2)*(:X1 − :X2) + (:Y1 − :Y2)*(:Y1 − :Y2)
END
```

However, if we execute, say, DISTANCE1 − 10 20 20 40, we obtain this error message:

```
YOU DON'T SAY WHAT TO DO WITH 36.0555, IN LINE
   SQRT (:X1−:X2)*(:X1−:X2)+(:Y1−:Y2)*(:Y1−:Y2)
AT LEVEL 1 OF DISTANCE1
```

One possible way to avoid this problem is to use a **PRINT** statement, as shown in DISTANCE2 below.

```
TO DISTANCE2 :X1 :Y1 :X2 :Y2
PRINT SQRT (:X1 − :X2) * (:X1 − :X2) + (:Y1 − :Y2) * (:Y1 − :Y2)
END
```

If we execute DISTANCE2 − 10 20 20 40, we see the following:

```
36.0555
```

DISTANCE2 now provides the length of a line segment if we input the coordinates of the endpoints of that segment.

XCOR

YCOR

DISTANCE2 can also tell us the distance of the turtle from a point with given coordinates even if we do not know the exact coordinates of the turtle. Logo has two primitives, XCOR and YCOR, that can be used to tell us the coordinates of the turtle. If we type **XCOR** and RETURN the computer prints the x-coordinate of the turtle. Similarly, typing **YCOR** and RETURN yields the y-coordinate of the turtle. With this in mind, we can use the following instruction to find the distance of the turtle from a point with coordinates (10, − 20) when the turtle's present location is (XCOR, YCOR).

DISTANCE2 – 10 20 XCOR YCOR

DISTANCE2, however, has its limits, as we will see.

Consider drawing a square if given the coordinates of two consecutive vertices of the square. For example, to draw a square ABCD where we know the vertices A(– 10, 20) and B(0, 40), we need to know the length of $\overline{AB}$ and to make each of the other sides the same length. Because the figure is a square, we also know that all angles are right angles, each having a measure of 90 degrees. Such a square is pictured in Figure 5-5.

Figure 5-5

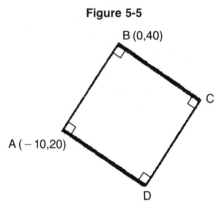

B (0,40)

C

A (– 10,20)

D

A procedure called **CORSQUARE** might first put the pen up and move the turtle to A(– 10, 20). Now we want the procedure to draw the square with sides the same length as $\overline{AB}$. We can find the length of $\overline{AB}$ using **DISTANCE2**. However, if we do not know the turtle's initial heading, we do not know how to make the turtle turn to make the 90-degree angles off the square and go through point B. That is, we must know the heading of the turtle when it draws segment $\overline{AB}$ in order to make the required 90-degree angle between segments $\overline{AB}$ and $\overline{BC}$.

We can determine the initial heading of the turtle by using the **HEADING** primitive. Two other Logo primitives can be used to determine the heading that will assure that the square has point B as a vertex. The first of these is **TOWARDS**. **TOWARDS** takes two numeric inputs that are interpreted as the x- and y-coordinates of a point. TOWARDS outputs the heading the turtle would have in going from

TOWARDS

its present position to the point with the coordinates given in the inputs. For example, assume that the turtle is at home and each of the following is typed. The results are given in the right-hand column.

TOWARDS 10 0	RESULT : 90
TOWARDS 0 10	RESULT : 0
TOWARDS 0 (− 10)	RESULT : 180
TOWARDS − 10 0	RESULT : 270

**SETHEADING
(SETH)**

TOWARDS gives the heading towards some point from the turtle's current location, but it does not actually set the heading. To have the turtle turn so that it has the desired heading requires use of another primitive, **SETHEADING (SETH)**. This primitive requires one input and turns the turtle to the heading indicated by the input. SET-HEADING does not change the position of the turtle, only its heading. For example, Figure 5-6 shows the result of using **SETHEADING** when the turtle starts at home with heading 0. Similar results are found with another starting position.

Figure 5-6

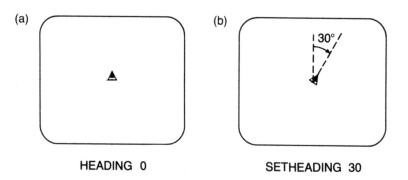

| (a) HEADING 0 | (b) SETHEADING 30 |

To return to our problem of drawing a square, recall that we needed to know the heading of the turtle in order to draw the square. If the turtle is at A(− 10, 20), we can determine the desired heading by typing TOWARDS 0 40 where (0, 40) are the coordinates for B. To actually turn the turtle toward (0, 40) so that we can draw the line segment, we use TOWARDS 0 40 as input to SETHEADING, like this:

SETHEADING TOWARDS 0 40

Now that the turtle has the desired heading and because all sides of the square are the same length and all angles are 90 degrees, we can draw the square by repeating the instruction FORWARD DISTANCE2 − 10 20 0 40 RIGHT 90 four times. We combine all these instructions in the following procedure:

```
TO CORSQUARE
PENUP
SETXY −10 20
PENDOWN
SETHEADING TOWARDS 0 40
REPEAT 4 [FORWARD DISTANCE2 −10 20 0 40 RIGHT 90]
END
```

If we execute CORSQUARE, however, we obtain the following error message:

```
DISTANCE2 DIDN'T OUTPUT, IN LINE
    REPEAT 4 [FORWARD DISTANCE2 −10 20 0 40 RIGHT 90]
AT LEVEL 1 OF CORSQUARE.
```

The computer was not able to use the value, 36.0555, that was obtained from DISTANCE2. This is because the primitive PRINT can only provide a result to be printed; it prints the result on the screen but the computer does not keep it in memory. Thus, PRINT cannot provide input to a calling procedure. The Logo primitive **OUTPUT (OP)** will prove more useful here. OUTPUT takes one input and causes the current procedure to stop and output the result to a calling procedure. For example, consider the following:

OUTPUT (OP)

```
TO ADD          TO ADD1          TO ADD2
PRINT 3+5       OUTPUT 3+5       PRINT ADD1+ADD1
END             END              END
```

If we execute each of these procedures, we obtain the following results:

```
ADD             ADD1             ADD2
8               RESULT: 8        16
```

The ADD2 procedure used the results of ADD1 to produce the sum 16. (As an experiment, you might replace ADD1 with ADD in the ADD2 procedure. You will find that the result is not 16 but an error message, because PRINT cannot pass an input to a calling procedure.)

Thus, we see that we need to change the DISTANCE2 procedure to include an OUTPUT statement instead of a PRINT statement to make it more useful. The new procedure, called DISTANCE, is given below.

```
TO DISTANCE :X1 :Y1 :X2 :Y2
OUTPUT SQRT (:X1 – :X2)*(:X1 – :X2) + (:Y1 – :Y2)*(:Y1 – :Y2)
END
```

If we edit the CORSQUARE procedure to replace DISTANCE2 with DISTANCE, and then execute CORSQUARE – 10 20 0 40, we obtain the result in Figure 5-7.

Figure 5-7

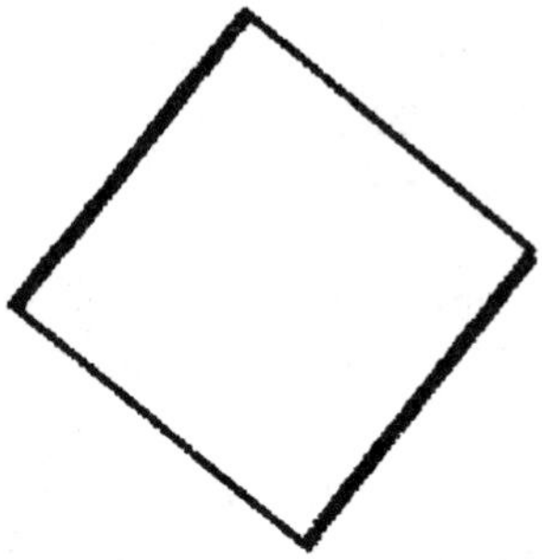

The CORSQUARE procedure can be generalized to start with the coordinates of any two points. The generalized procedure, which we call SQUARE2POINTS, is given below.

```
TO SQUARE2POINTS :X1 :Y1 :X2 :Y2
PENUP
SETXY :X1 :Y1
PENDOWN
SETHEADING TOWARDS :X2 :Y2
REPEAT 4 [FORWARD DISTANCE :X1 :Y1 :X2 :Y2 RIGHT 90]
END
```

Using Coordinates with Circle Procedures

Recall that in Chapter 3, we drew circles by repeating the instructions FORWARD some "small" distance and RIGHT a "small" angle. We also developed some procedures for drawing circles by specifying the radii of the circles. We now apply the **SETXY** primitive to the problem of drawing a circle when given various information about the circle.

Problem 5-2

Write a procedure to draw a circle that has radius 50 and that passes through a point with coordinates $(-20, -40)$, as shown in Figure 5-8.

Figure 5-8

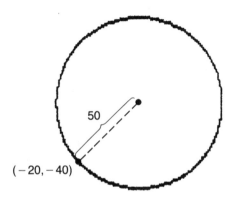

$(-20, -40)$

Solution

In Chapter 3, we saw how to draw a circle with a given radius by using the **VCIRCLE** and **RCIRCLE** procedures given below.

```
TO VCIRCLE :SIDE
REPEAT 360 [FD :SIDE RT 1]
END
```

```
TO RCIRCLE :RAD
VCIRCLE 2*3.14159*:RAD/360
END
```

When the **RCIRCLE** procedure is called, it draws a circle with a given radius, starting wherever the turtle is. Thus, it seems that all we need to do to solve our problem is to move the turtle to the point with coordinates $(-20, -40)$ and call **RCIRCLE 50**. To move the turtle to $(-20, -40)$, we use **SETXY** -20 (-40). If we do not wish the turtle to leave a trail on the way to $(-20, -40)$, we can use the **PENUP** command. Once the turtle is at that point, however, we should use the PENDOWN command. A procedure to do all these things, called PCIRCLE, follows.

```
TO PCIRCLE
PENUP
SETXY −20 (−40)
PENDOWN
RCIRCLE 50
HT
END
```

Can you draw a different circle that satisfies the conditions of the problem? How many such circles can be drawn?

The PCIRCLE procedure can be generalized so that it will draw a variable size circle passing through any given point on the screen. To accomplish this, we could edit the PCIRCLE procedure to draw a circle that has radius :RAD and passes through a point with coordinates (:X, :Y), as follows:

```
TO PCIRCLE :X :Y :RAD
PENUP
SETXY :X :Y
PENDOWN
RCIRCLE :RAD
HT
END
```

The precise location and size of a circle is determined by its radius and its center. We will explore a way of drawing a circle given its center and radius in the next problem.

Problem 5-3

Write a procedure called CIRCLE1 for drawing a circle, in which the coordinates of the center of the circle and the radius are inputs. For example, CIRCLE1 40 70 20 should draw a circle whose center has coordinates (40, 70) and whose radius is 20. A circle with this center and radius is pictured in Figure 5-9.

Figure 5-9

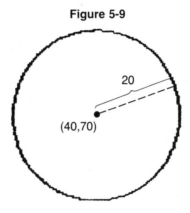

(40,70)

20

Solution

Consider the circle in Figure 5-10(a). If we were to draw the circle with a compass, we would put the tip of the compass at the center, open the compass the width of the radius, and then begin to draw the circle.

Figure 5-10

(a)   (b)   (c)

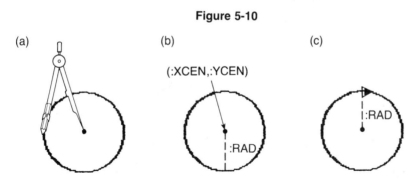

(:XCEN,:YCEN)

:RAD

:RAD

We already know how to draw a circle when given its radius, using the RCIRCLE procedure. If we want to draw a circle whose center has coordinates (:XCEN, :YCEN) and whose radius is :RAD, as in Figure 5-10(b), where should we position the turtle? One possible position from which the turtle could start drawing the circle is shown in Figure 5-10(c). Observe that the turtle is :RAD units away from the center and perpendicular to the radius. To put the turtle in such a position and heading, we could first move the turtle to the center of the circle using PENUP SETXY :XCEN :YCEN, then move the turtle forward :RAD, and finally make the turtle turn right 90 degrees. At this point we put the pen down, and the turtle is ready to draw the circle using RCIRCLE :RAD. The CIRCLE1 procedure below summarizes this process.

```
TO CIRCLE1 :XCEN :YCEN :RAD
PENUP
SETXY :XCEN :YCEN
FORWARD :RAD
RIGHT 90
PENDOWN
RCIRCLE :RAD
END
```

A circle can be uniquely determined by its center and one point on the circle. Consider a circle with center at (:XCEN, :YCEN) and passing through the point with coordinates (:PXCOR, :PYCOR), as shown in Figure 5-11.

Figure 5-11

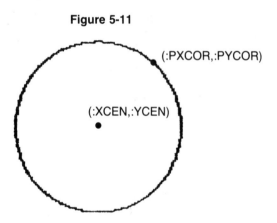

If we knew the radius of the circle, we could draw the circle using the CIRCLE1 procedure we just created. We can find the length of the radius by using the DISTANCE procedure introduced earlier in the chapter.

Let's call our new circle procedure CIRCLE2. It will use the variables :XCEN and :YCEN for the coordinates of the center and :PXCOR and :PYCOR for the coordinates of the point on the circle. CIRCLE2 calls CIRCLE1 with inputs :XCEN and :YCEN as coordinates of the center, and DISTANCE :XCEN :YCEN :PXCOR :PYCOR as the length of the radius.

```
TO CIRCLE2 :XCEN :YCEN :PXCOR :PYCOR
CIRCLE1 :XCEN :YCEN DISTANCE :XCEN :YCEN :PXCOR :PYCOR
END
```

Executing CIRCLE2 − 10 20 20 40 yields a circle with center coordinates (− 10, 20) and passing through the point with coordinates (20, 40).

Summary of Commands

SETX	Takes one number input and moves the turtle horizontally to the point with that x-coordinate. Draws a trail if the pen is down.
SETY	Takes one number input and moves the turtle vertically to the point with that y-coordinate. Draws a trail if the pen is down.
SETXY	Takes two number inputs, A and B, and moves the turtle to the point with the given coordinates (A, B). Draws a trail if the pen is down.
SQRT	Takes one positive number input and yields the square root of that input.
XCOR	Takes no inputs; outputs the turtle's current x-coordinate.
YCOR	Takes no inputs; outputs the turtle's current y-coordinate.
TOWARDS	Takes two number inputs, which are interpreted as x- and y-coordinates of a point, and outputs the heading from the turtle to that point.
SETHEADING (SETH)	Takes one number input and rotates the turtle to point in the direction specified.
OUTPUT (OP)	Takes one input and causes the current procedure to stop and output the result to the calling procedure.

Problem Set 5-1

1. Write a procedure called **AXES** that uses the **SETXY** primitive to draw x- and y-axes with the origin placed at home.

2. Write a procedure for drawing a line segment that has one endpoint with coordinates (:X, :Y), a length of :LEN, and a heading of :H.

3. If given two vertices of a square, how many squares could you draw?

4. Given the coordinates A(:X1, :Y1) and B(:X2, :Y2) of the endpoints of a diagonal of a square, write a procedure to draw the square.

5. Edit the **CIRCLE1** procedure to have the turtle mark the center of the circle.

6. Use the **CIRCLE1** procedure to write a procedure to draw five circles with a common center at $(-38, -49)$, showing all on the screen at once when the procedure is executed.

7. Write a procedure that will draw a square using the **SQUARE2POINTS** procedure and will print the x- and y-coordinates of the square's four vertices.

8. Write a procedure called **SUN** that draws a sun similar to the one shown below.

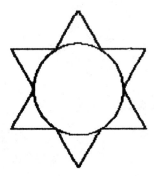

5-2 Constructing Triangles with the Turtle

Trying to determine the smallest number of parts of a figure that is sufficient to construct the figure can be a challenging problem in mathematics as well as in Logo. The ancient Greeks became very adept at constructing triangles from various parts of a triangle. In this section we consider some triangle constructions that use parts of a triangle. Traditional geometry makes use of a compass and straightedge to construct a triangle given two sides and an included angle of the triangle (SAS), two angles and an included side of the triangle (ASA), two angles and a nonincluded side of the triangle (AAS), or all three sides of the triangle (SSS). In this section we write procedures for constructing triangles that are useful not only for their mathematical value but also for constructing intricate pictures containing triangles that are not necessarily equilateral.

Constructing a Triangle Using SAS

In Logo, the easiest triangle construction among the ones just mentioned involves the use of two sides and an included angle (SAS). In triangle HPQ of Figure 5-12, angle P is the included angle between sides $\overline{HP}$ and $\overline{PQ}$. Consider how the turtle might walk around the triangle in Figure 5-12, and think about how the three parts could be used to construct the triangle.

Suppose the turtle starts at home, H, the first vertex. It might first walk backwards the length of the first side to point P, the second vertex. To continue the walk, the turtle needs to turn so that the interior angle at this vertex is of the desired measure. Once it has turned, it may walk the length of the second side. This takes the turtle to the third vertex, Q. Now if it just returns to home, H, the triangle is completed.

Figure 5-12

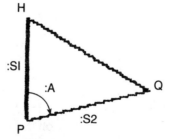

The walk just described gives us the necessary steps for writing a procedure to draw a triangle if we are given two sides, :S1 and :S2, and the included angle, :A. Because there is no triangle with an angle whose measure is greater than or equal to 180, we need a line in our procedure to tell us that no triangle is possible in these cases. This could be accomplished by using two **IF** commands in the procedure. Another way to do this utilizes the **ANYOF** primitive.

ANYOF

The primitive **ANYOF** normally takes two inputs but can take more if parentheses are used as shown in (d) and (e) below. ANYOF outputs TRUE if at least one of its inputs is true; otherwise it outputs FALSE. For example, try the following to determine the results.

(a) ANYOF (2 + 2 = 4)(3 + 5 = 8)

(b) ANYOF (2 + 2 = 4)(3 + 5 = 9)

(c) ANYOF (1 + 7 = 9)(3 = 19)

(d) (ANYOF (2 + 2>4)(3 + 5 = 8)(3 = 1))

(e) (ANYOF (2 + 2 = 4)(3 + 5<8)(10/2 = 5))

To continue the work on the **SAS** procedure, we use **ANYOF** to test the angle size, as follows:

```
IF ANYOF (:A > 180) (:A = 180) THEN
     PRINT [NO TRIANGLE IS POSSIBLE.] STOP
```

Here is the complete **SAS** procedure.

```
TO SAS :S1 :A :S2
IF ANYOF (:A>180) (:A = 180) THEN
     PRINT [NO TRIANGLE IS POSSIBLE.] STOP
BK :S1
RT :A
FD :S2
HOME
HT
END
```

This procedure depends upon the turtle starting at home. As an exercise, use the **RANDOM** and **MAKE** commands to edit the **SAS** procedure so that the turtle can start anywhere on the screen and draw a triangle given two sides and the included angle.

Remark: Note that the line after the title line in **SAS** could have been written as IF NOT :A < 180 PR [NO TRIANGLE IS POSSIBLE.] STOP.

Constructing a Triangle Using ASA

The next procedure we attempt is to construct a triangle given two angles and an included side. For example, in Figure 5-13(a), $\overline{AB}$ is the included side between angle ABC and angle BAC. In Figure 5-13(b) we want to use only angles :A1 and :A2 and the side marked :S to construct the triangle.

Figure 5-13

(a)   (b)

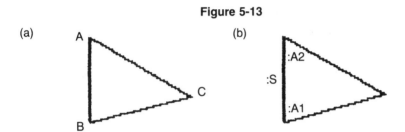

There are many ways to write a procedure called ASA that would construct the triangle, but to use the turtle effectively, we proceed as follows. Our procedure could have the turtle first draw side :S by starting at home with heading 0 and moving backward. (To write this procedure having the turtle move forward is left as an exercise.) Then it could turn the turtle so that it has a heading :A1, since one of the given angles has measure :A1. Now the turtle could start drawing the next side, as in Figure 5-14.

Figure 5-14

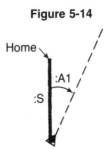

We do not know how far the turtle should move to make this side. However, we do have one more piece of information that we have not made use of :A2, the measure of the other angle.

It would be useful to have a procedure called **CHECKHEAD** that would move the turtle forward a bit and then check the angle that would be formed if the turtle returned home from that point. This process of moving and checking should be repeated recursively until the turtle reaches a point where the angle that would be formed if a triangle were drawn from that point to home is the required angle. Including CHECKHEAD, a procedure called ASA with inputs :A1, :S, and :A2 could be designed as follows.

```
TO ASA :A1 :S :A2
BK :S
RT :A1
CHECKHEAD
HOME
HT
END
```

Now we need to design the CHECKHEAD procedure. Initially CHECKHEAD should turn the turtle towards home. Then it needs to determine whether the angle that would be formed if a triangle were drawn from that point to home will give the required angle. Consider Figure 5-15 where H is home.

Figure 5-15

If we have the desired angle and the turtle is located as in Figure 5-15(a), then its heading is $360 - $:A2. (Figure 5-15(b) may help you understand why.) Thus, our CHECKHEAD procedure must determine whether or not the turtle's heading when turned toward home is $360 - $:A2. This could be done by determining if HEADING $= 360 - $:A2, or equivalently if HEADING $- (360 - $:A2$) = 0$.

Writing a Continuous Checking Procedure

The CHECKHEAD procedure is important because it is similar to a whole class of continuous checking procedures that use a trial-and-error process of moving and checking recursively. As mentioned previously, the procedure needs first to turn the turtle towards home. Next it needs to determine whether the angle that would be formed if a triangle were drawn from that point to home gives the required angle. (Look again at Figure 5-15, where H is located at home.) If the condition is true, we want to stop the CHECKHEAD procedure and send the turtle home. If the condition is not true, we want to move the turtle along the side with heading :A1 to another point to check the heading there.

It is impossible to have a check at every single point; in fact, there is no point "next to" another point. Because the turtle may not happen to stop at the exact point that was required to find the desired heading, the process may fail. What can we do about it?

The approach just described may not allow us to obtain exactly the triangle we want. However, it seems that we could obtain a triangle very much like the desired one. If we cannot get the triangle that we want, how closely can we approximate it?

We must decide what approximation is acceptable to us. For example, we might say that an acceptable point is one at which the difference in HEADING and 360 − :A2 is less than 2. That is, if the difference is less than 2, we want the CHECKHEAD procedure to stop and the triangle to be drawn. An appropriate line in the CHECKHEAD procedure might look as follows:

IF (HEADING − (360 − :A2))<2 STOP

This line still contains a flaw. It will work part of the time. However, if (360 − :A2) is greater than HEADING, then a negative number is obtained and the condition is met whether or not a suitable triangle could be drawn from that point. What we really want is to draw the triangle if the absolute value of the difference is not greater than 2. The **absolute value** of a number may be informally defined as the distance that the number is from 0 on a number line. Because distance is always positive or 0, the absolute value of a number also is always positive or 0.

absolute value

Suppose, then, that we have a procedure called ABS to find absolute value and use it to complete the CHECKHEAD procedure. The desired line will now be IF ABS (HEADING − (360 − :A2))<2 STOP. If the condition is not met, we want to turn the turtle back along the side it is drawing by using SETHEADING :A1, then proceed to move

FORWARD 1 and run the CHECKHEAD procedure again. The complete CHECKHEAD procedure may be written as follows:

```
TO CHECKHEAD
SETHEADING TOWARDS 0 0
IF ABS (HEADING − (360−:A2))<2 STOP
SETHEADING :A1
FORWARD 1
CHECKHEAD
END
```

The only remaining task is to write the procedure ABS, which determines the absolute value of a number. If the number is less than 0, the absolute value of the number is its opposite. If the number is not less than 0, the absolute value of the number is the number itself. To allow the ABS procedure to give input to CHECKHEAD, we use the primitive OUTPUT. The ABS procedure can be written as follows:

```
TO ABS :VALUE
IF :VALUE <0 OUTPUT − :VALUE
OUTPUT :VALUE
END
```

Now our ASA procedure should draw the desired triangle except for one possible error. Suppose we attempt to execute ASA 130 50 80. In this case, the measures of the known angles of the triangle are 130 and 80. It is impossible to draw a triangle having angles with those measures because the sum of the angles is greater than 180, but if we run ASA 130 50 80, we do obtain a triangle. The triangle is not the one we are seeking, because there is no triangle for which two of its angles can have 210 as the sum of their measures.

If we look at our ASA procedure, we see that we never told the computer that we could not have angles with those measures. We need a line to check the sum of the angle measures and determine whether the sum of :A1 and :A2 is less than 180. If it is not, the computer should print a message telling us that no triangle is possible.

The primitive NOT can be used to help us with this check. Recall that NOT outputs TRUE if its input is false and outputs FALSE if its input is true. Thus, in our error check, we might use the following line:

IF NOT (:A1 + :A2<180) PRINT [NO TRIANGLE IS POSSIBLE.] STOP

Edit the **ASA** procedure to include this line. Now, for further practice, try to write a general procedure for **ASA** that does not depend upon the turtle starting at home.

A procedure for drawing a triangle involving two angles and a nonincluded side, as marked in Figure 5-16, can be readily written by calling the **ASA** procedure. Try writing this new procedure as an exercise.

Figure 5-16

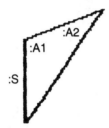

Constructing a Triangle Using SSS

Our last construction involves drawing a triangle given the lengths of the three sides, :S1, :S2, and :S3, as shown in Figure 5-17. We call the procedure to draw this triangle **SSS**.

Figure 5-17

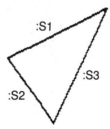

Our **SSS** procedure may contain checks to guarantee that a triangle with the given sides can exist. For example, can a triangle with sides of length 30, 50, and 20 be constructed?

In general, no triangle can be constructed unless the sum of the measures of every two sides of the triangle is greater than the measure of the third side. To determine if this condition is met, we use the primitives **NOT** and ALLOF. **ALLOF** normally takes two inputs but can

ALLOF

take more if parentheses are used, as in (c) and (d) below. It outputs TRUE if all of the inputs are true; otherwise, it outputs FALSE. For example, try the following lines on your computer to determine the result.

(a) ALLOF (2+2=4) (3+5=8)

(b) ALLOF (1+7=9) (3=1)

(c) (ALLOF (2+2=4)(3+5=8)(3=1))

(d) (ALLOF (1+7=8) (3=6) (3+5=8))

If the condition involving the three sides is met, then a triangle can be drawn. If not, we need a message to tell the user that no triangle can be drawn. A line to determine whether the condition is met is quite lengthy because there are several cases to check. Such a line might look like this:

IF NOT (ALLOF (:S1 + :S2 > :S3) (:S1 + :S3 > :S2)
    (:S2 + :S3 > :S1)) PRINT [A TRIANGLE WITH THESE
    SIDES IS NOT POSSIBLE.] STOP

Suppose our checking procedure shows that a triangle can be constructed. Now what should we do? To draw a triangle given the lengths of three sides, starting with the turtle at home with heading 0, we might first have the turtle move forward the length of :S1. This will determine the first two vertices, H and B. Now, although we do not know the angle through which to turn the turtle to draw the next side, we do know the length of the next side, :S2. Because vertex A of the triangle must be :S2 units from B, we know that A must be somewhere on a circle whose radius is :S2 and whose center is B, as shown in Figure 5-18.

Figure 5-18

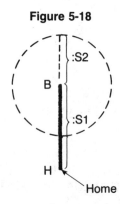

To find A, we begin to draw the circle with the pen up. We need to write a checking procedure called **CHECKSIDE**, similar to the **CHECKHEAD** procedure we used for **ASA**, to determine which point on the circle is the desired third vertex. The required point will be reached when the distance from the point being checked and the starting point H is the length of :S3. If A is the required point, then triangle HBA, shown in Figure 5-19, is the desired triangle.

Figure 5-19

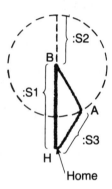

To write the whole **SSS** procedure, we see from Figure 5-19 that we need to draw :S1, put the pen up, and move the turtle **FORWARD** :S2. The turtle is now at the end of a diameter of the circle that was discussed earlier. To start the circle, we turn the turtle **RIGHT 90**, as shown in Figure 5-20.

Figure 5-20

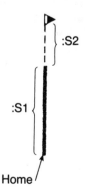

We now want to use the **CHECKSIDE** procedure to move the turtle along the circle, but at the end of each turtle step we must check the distance from the turtle's position to home. If the turtle's position is the one we want, we tell the computer to remember this point (:X, :Y). If not, we tell the turtle to continue along the circle to another point. When the desired point is reached, we return the turtle to home. To draw the triangle we put the pen down, move the turtle **FORWARD** :S1, and then move it using **SETXY** :X :Y to the point with coordinates (:X,:Y), and return the turtle home. The **SSS** procedure, which combines all of these features, looks like this.

```
TO SSS :S1 :S2 :S3
IF NOT (ALLOF (:S1 + :S2 > :S3) (:S1 + :S3 > :S2)
    (:S2 + :S3 > :S1)) PRINT [A TRIANGLE WITH THESE
    SIDES IS NOT POSSIBLE.] STOP
HT
FD :S1
PENUP
FD :S2
RT 90
CHECKSIDE
HOME
PENDOWN
FD :S1
SETXY :X :Y
HOME
END
```

We still need to write the **CHECKSIDE** procedure. This procedure should check the distance from the turtle's current position to home. If the turtle is at the desired point, we want the computer to remember the turtle's current coordinates as (:X,:Y) and stop the **CHECKSIDE** procedure; if not, we want it to move the turtle along the circle to another point and check again. As shown in Figure 5-21, at each point we want to check to determine if the length of the side determined by the turtle's current position and home is the same as :S3.

Figure 5-21

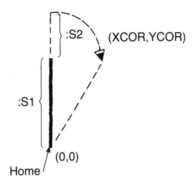

To determine the distance between the points with coordinates (0, 0) and (XCOR, YCOR), where XCOR and YCOR are the coordinates of the turtle's current position, we use the DISTANCE procedure by calling DISTANCE XCOR YCOR 0 0. If :S3 is equal to DISTANCE XCOR YCOR 0 0, then the third vertex is found. The CHECKSIDE procedure should stop at that point, and the triangle should be drawn. If this condition is not true, we want the turtle to move another step along the circle and have CHECKSIDE determine if that point satisfies the desired condition.

As in the ASA procedure, the quantities :S3 and DISTANCE XCOR YCOR 0 0 may never be equal, so again we use the ABS procedure and consider a point to be the desired point when the absolute value of the difference between the values of the real and desired points is a small positive number. Once more we choose the small positive number 2. The only thing that remains is to tell the turtle how to move along the circle if ABS (:S3 − (DISTANCE XCOR YCOR 0 0)) is not less than 2.

The RCIRCLE procedure developed in Chapter 3 can be used to draw a circle with radius :S2. However, we want the turtle to take only one step at a time along the circle and then check the distance to home, rather than drawing the entire circle. Recall that this turtle-type circle is actually a regular polygon with 360 sides. Thus, to draw a circle with a given radius, we actually determine the length of a side of an approximating polygon in terms of the radius. As we saw in Chapter 3, the side :S of an approximating polygon is given by the following equation:

:S = 2*3.14159*:S2/360

Therefore, to have the turtle move along the circle, we want it to move FORWARD 2*3.14159*:S2/360 and turn RIGHT 1 before the next check. The complete CHECKSIDE procedure follows.

```
TO CHECKSIDE
IF (ABS (:S3 − DISTANCE XCOR YCOR 0 0)) < 2
    MAKE "X XCOR MAKE "Y YCOR STOP
FORWARD 2*3.14159*:S2/360
RIGHT 1
CHECKSIDE
END
```

You should note that when the CHECKSIDE procedure is run, the values for :X and :Y change each time the procedure is run. Can you figure out why?

Summary of Commands

ANYOF   Takes two inputs that are either true or false and outputs TRUE if any of the inputs are true and FALSE otherwise. It may take more inputs if parentheses are used.

ALLOF   Takes two inputs that are either true or false and outputs TRUE if all are true and FALSE otherwise. It may take more inputs if parentheses are used.

Problem Set 5-2

---

1. Edit the ASA procedure to allow the turtle to start drawing a triangle at any point instead of just at home.

2. Edit the ASA procedure to have the turtle first move forward instead of backwards.

3. Write a procedure for drawing a triangle using two given angles and a nonincluded side. Call this new procedure AAS.

4. Edit the **SSS** procedure to allow the turtle to start drawing a triangle at any point instead of just at home.

5. Write a procedure that draws a large square on the screen with sides parallel to the axes, places a point at random on the screen, and then tells whether or not the point is inside the square. (Hint: The use of **ANYOF** may help.)

6. When a ruler and a compass are used to construct a triangle given two angles and an included side, the final construction may have segments longer than the required sides, as shown below.

   If this is allowed, a simple procedure that draws the triangle can be written. Write such a procedure.

7. Run the following edited version of **ASA** and then answer the questions below.

```
TO ASA :A1 :S :A2
FD :S
RT 180 – :A1
CHECK
END


TO CHECK
FD 1
SETH TOWARDS 0 0
MAKE "H HEADING
IF ABS (:H – (180 + :A2))<2 HOME STOP
LT :A1 + :H – 180
CHECK
END
```

   (a) Is :H fixed throughout the execution of the edited **ASA** procedure? Why or why not?

   (b) Explain how the angle :A1 + :H – 180 was found and for what purpose it is used in line **LT :A1 + :H – 180**.

8. Will your procedures in problems 2–4 work if the initial heading is not 0? If not, edit them so they will work for any initial heading.

5-3   Strips and Tessellations

Logo, because of its graphic capabilities, provides a natural tool to draw patterns in a plane. In this section, we investigate how to design strips of geometric figures as on wallpaper and how to tessellate the screen.

One type of pattern that we can draw is very much like a border that would be used on wallpaper near the floor or ceiling of a room. In this type of pattern, a single figure is repeated at intervals.

We use a five-pointed star similar to the one on the United States flag to make our first strip. As you may remember from Chapter 4, a star can be drawn with the POLY procedure. We can also write a procedure to draw a variable size star, as follows:

```
TO STAR :S
REPEAT 5 [FD :S RT 144]
HT
END
```

An example of a star drawn by this procedure is given below.

Figure 5-22

To combine several stars into a strip, we can write a procedure called STARSTRIP. We would like STARSTRIP to draw stars on the screen in a vertical pattern but not to wrap around the screen, and we would like the stars to touch at one vertex. For drawing purposes, we restrict the x-coordinates to values from -120 to 120 and the y-coordinates to values from -100 to 100 inclusive.

If we use the **STAR** procedure to start drawing the strip with the turtle at home with heading 0, we must be sure that when a star is drawn, no y-coordinate is ever greater than 100, so that when the next star is drawn, the current y-coordinate plus the length of a side of the star :S will not be greater than 100. Otherwise the star will go off the screen when we draw it. A line to check for this condition might look like the following:

IF YCOR + :S >100 STOP

If the star stays within the boundary, then our procedure should draw the star.

After a star is drawn, the turtle returns to its initial position and heading, as shown in Figure 5-23.

Figure 5-23

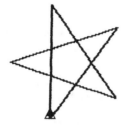

Before another star is drawn, the turtle must be moved forward :S units. After the turtle has moved :S units, the computer should again check to see if another star can be drawn without going out of the boundaries. This can be accomplished using recursion, as shown below.

```
TO STARSTRIP :S
IF YCOR + :S>100 STOP
STAR :S
FD :S
STARSTRIP :S
END
```

If **STARSTRIP 30** is executed with the turtle starting at home with heading 0, a drawing similar to the one in Figure 5-24 is produced.

Figure 5-24

We can now write a procedure called **WALL** to produce a monitor screen full of stars, as shown in Figure 5-25.

Figure 5-25

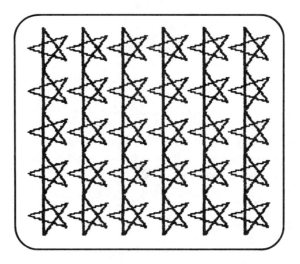

Our **WALL** procedure might first use a **SETUP** procedure to move the turtle to the lower left area of the screen, to a point with coordinates (:XPT, :YPT). Once the turtle is in the desired position, a recursive procedure called **WALLPAPER** may be used to draw successive vertical strips of stars. Within **WALLPAPER** we may use **STAR-STRIP :S** to draw the strips of stars. Because **STARSTRIP** has variable input **:S**, **WALL** needs three variable inputs, **:XPT**, **:YPT**, and **:S**. The **WALL** procedure might look like this:

```
TO WALL :XPT :YPT :S
SETUP :XPT :YPT
WALLPAPER :S
END
```

Now we must write the **SETUP** procedure. To move the turtle to a point with coordinates (:XPT, :YPT), we use two inputs, :XPT and :YPT, with the **SETXY** primitive. Because we do not want the turtle to leave a trail, we put the pen up, use the **SETXY** command, and then put the pen down, like this:

```
TO SETUP :XPT :YPT
PENUP
SETXY :XPT :YPT
PENDOWN
END
```

Finally, to write the **WALLPAPER** procedure, we use the **STARSTRIP** procedure, move the turtle to draw the next strip using the **SETUP** procedure, and repeat the process. But to keep the turtle from wrapping, we need to determine if it will go off the screen not only at the top, but also at the bottom and at each of the sides.

We need to edit the **STARSTRIP** procedure to include these checks. There are many ways to do this. One is to include several **IF** commands in the procedure. Another is to use the **ANYOF** primitive to make sure that certain conditions are met before a star is drawn. The **STARSTRIP** procedure needs to check whether each of the following is true or false before drawing any strip:

```
XCOR − :S< − 120
XCOR + :S>120
YCOR − :S< − 100
YCOR + :S>100
```

If any of these conditions is true, we want the computer to stop. (STOP stops the current procedure being executed but allows the computer to complete a procedure calling the one stopped.) If none of the conditions is true, we want the computer to continue. To include all of the conditions referred to, the ANYOF statement should appear like this:

```
IF (ANYOF (XCOR − :S < −120) (XCOR + :S > 120)
    (YCOR − :S < −100) (YCOR + :S > 100)) STOP
```

Now let's edit STARSTRIP to include this statement:

```
TO STARSTRIP :S
IF (ANYOF (XCOR − :S < −120) (XCOR + :S > 120)
    (YCOR − :S < −100) (YCOR + :S > 100)) STOP
STAR :S
FD :S
STARSTRIP :S
END
```

Next we need to write the WALLPAPER procedure. After drawing a strip using STARSTRIP, WALLPAPER needs to move the turtle to start the next strip. This can be done with the SETUP procedure. Once the move is made, we want to repeat the whole process with a call to WALLPAPER.

We must now determine the inputs in the SETUP procedure. Consider Figure 5-26, which shows the final position of the turtle after a strip is drawn if the turtle starts with heading 0.

Figure 5-26

Notice where the turtle completes the strip. If we want to draw another strip vertically, we need to put the pen up and then move the turtle down the screen and horizontally over to where we want to start the next strip. If we knew the x-coordinate the turtle had each time a strip was complete, we could move the turtle until it had that x-coordinate and its original y-coordinate, :YPT. This would put the turtle where it was when it started drawing the current strip. By moving the turtle over the length of a side, :S, without changing its heading, and putting the pen down, we would be ready to draw the next strip, as shown in Figure 5-27.

Figure 5-27

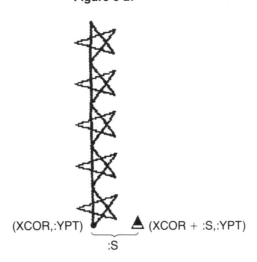

(XCOR,:YPT)   (XCOR + :S,:YPT)

:S

Part of this is easy because the original y-coordinate was :YPT. However, the x-coordinate changes with each strip. Using XCOR + :S would give us the x-coordinate at the start of each strip. Thus the inputs to **SETUP** are XCOR + :S and :YPT. The **WALLPAPER** procedure follows.

```
TO WALLPAPER :S
STARSTRIP :S
PU
SETUP (XCOR+ :S) :YPT
PD
WALLPAPER :S
END
```

Remark: WALLPAPER, as written, cannot be executed but is dependent on WALL for :YPT to have a value in the line SETUP (XCOR + :S) :YPT.

An execution of WALL − 100 (−80) 15 draws a screen of stars, but it does not stop when the turtle reaches the right side of the screen. This is because the STOP command in the STARSTRIP procedure stops only the current procedure being run. It then allows the calling procedure to be completed. The procedure calling STARSTRIP is WALLPAPER. When XCOR + :S>120, STARSTRIP stops, but WALLPAPER does not. It calls STARSTRIP again, and another strip is drawn. We can make WALLPAPER stop by inserting the line below just after the title line of WALLPAPER.

IF XCOR + :S > 120 STOP

TOPLEVEL

There are also other ways to stop WALLPAPER. The primitive TOPLEVEL may be used. TOPLEVEL is different from the STOP command because STOP stops only the current procedure (not the calling procedure), whereas TOPLEVEL stops all procedures. We utilize TOPLEVEL to stop the procedure when XCOR + :S>120 by inserting the line below in the STARSTRIP procedure.

IF XCOR + :S>120 TOPLEVEL

The edited STARSTRIP procedure follows.

```
TO STARSTRIP :S
IF XCOR + :S>120 TOPLEVEL
IF (ANYOF (XCOR − :S < −120) (XCOR + :S > 120)
    (YCOR − :S < −100) (YCOR + :S > 100)) STOP
STAR :S
FD :S
STARSTRIP :S
END
```

Remark: If we execute WALL − 100 (−80) 20, an unexpected result occurs due to the way decimals are rounded in Logo. Interested readers should try this.

Other types of wallpaper designs can be drawn using the same approaches. However, a more interesting type of design geometrically is a tessellation, a drawing that completely covers the screen with no holes and no overlapping. Examples of tessellations are given in Figure 5-28.

Figure 5-28

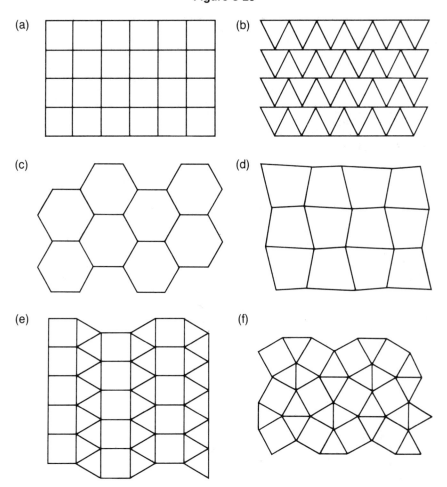

(a)

(b)

(c)

(d)

(e)

(f)

Consider how the drawings in Figure 5-28 (c) fit together to tessellate the screen. Observe that the sum of the angles in the tessellation around any vertex is 360 degrees.

Here we consider only **regular tessellations,** that is, tessellations of regular polygons. (Recall that regular polygons are polygons that have all sides congruent and all angles congruent.) Is it possible to

**regular
tessellation**

tessellate the screen with any regular polygon—for example, a pentagon or a dodecagon (12 sides)? It can be shown that the only regular polygons that can tessellate a plane by themselves, and hence the screen, are squares, equilateral triangles, and hexagons.

Mathematical Aside

To show that the only regular polygons that tessellate are squares, equilateral triangles, and hexagons, we need to know something about the size of interior angles in a regular polygon. We know that all of the angles of a regular polygon are congruent, and that if the regular polygon is to tessellate the plane, the sum of the measures of the angles around a point must be 360 degrees. Thus, 360 divided by the measure of an interior angle of the regular polygon being used must give the number of polygons that are fitted together. As a result, the measure of an interior angle of the polygon must be a divisor of 360. The divisors of 360 are 1, 2, 3, 4, 5, 6, 8, 9, 10, 12, 15, 18, 20, 24, 30, 36, 40, 45, 72, 90, 120, 180, and 360.

On the other hand, given the number of sides of a polygon, we can find the measure of its interior angles. The Total Turtle Trip Theorem tells us that the sum of the measures of the exterior angles of any n-sided polygon is 360. Thus, the measure of any exterior angle of an n-sided polygon is $360/n$. Because the sum of the measure of an exterior angle and the measure of an interior angle of a polygon is 180, we know that the measure of an interior angle of a regular polygon must be $180 - 360/n$. The chart below gives some values of n, the type of polygon related to each, and the angle measure of an interior angle found using the expression $180 - 360/n$.

Number of Sides	Polygon	Angle Measure of Interior Angle
3	Triangle	60
4	Square	90
5	Pentagon	108
6	Hexagon	120
7	Heptagon	900/7
8	Octagon	135
9	Nonagon	140
10	Decagon	144
.	.	.
.	.	.
.	.	.

Only the triangle, square, and hexagon are possible candidates to tessellate the plane because those are the only polygons whose interior angles have measures that are divisors of 360. (Note that the only divisors of 360 greater than 120 are 180 and 360. No polygon can have an interior angle with measure either 180 or 360.)

Tessellating with Squares

In order to tessellate the screen with squares, we need to recall the SQUARE procedure introduced in Chapter 3.

```
TO SQUARE :S
REPEAT 4 [FD :S RT 90]
END
```

To create a procedure for drawing a strip of squares, we imitate the STARSTRIP procedure used earlier in this chapter. Once one square is drawn with SQUARE, starting with heading 0, the turtle is left in the lower left-hand corner of the square. We need to move the turtle to the upper left-hand corner with heading 0 to start the next square, as shown in Figure 5-29.

Figure 5-29

To keep the drawings from going too high, too low, too far to the right, and too far to the left, we use the same condition checks we used in the STARSTRIP procedure. Thus, our SQUARESTRIP procedure might look like this:

```
TO SQUARESTRIP :S
IF XCOR + :S>120 TOPLEVEL
IF (ANYOF (XCOR − :S < −120) (XCOR + :S > 120)
    (YCOR − :S < −100) (YCOR + :S > 100)) STOP
SQUARE :S
FD :S
SQUARESTRIP :S
END
```

As an exercise, write a procedure to tessellate the screen with squares using the SQUARESTRIP procedure.

Tessellating with Triangles

Our next goal is to write procedures for drawing strips of triangles that fit next to each other, as shown in Figure 5-30, so they can be used to tessellate the screen.

Figure 5-30

To start, recall the procedure for drawing an equilateral triangle:

```
TO TRIANGLE :S
REPEAT 3 [FD :S RT 120]
END
```

A procedure for drawing a strip of equilateral triangles like the one shown in Figure 5-30 can be accomplished in many ways. We invite you to try it before you read further.

The drawing in Figure 5-31 may help you determine where to place the turtle to start the second triangle. Do you see that moving the turtle **FORWARD :S** and turning it **RIGHT 60** puts it in the desired position? After the second triangle is drawn, **LEFT 60** puts the turtle in a position to draw the third triangle. (Why?)

Figure 5-31

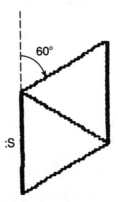

We combine all these steps into our first attempt at a **TRISTRIP** procedure, as follows:

```
TO TRISTRIP :S
TRIANGLE :S
FD :S
RT 60
TRIANGLE :S
LT 60
END
```

Remark: Do you see why the **TRISTRIP** procedure calls **TRIANGLE** twice, while the **STARSTRIP** procedure called **STAR** only once and the **SQUARESTRIP** procedure called **SQUARE** only once?

This **TRISTRIP** procedure has no set of checks to make sure that the turtle does not wrap. To incorporate those checks and to draw patterns with **TRISTRIP** that will tessellate the screen, we need to determine the height of an equilateral triangle. It can be shown that if the triangle has side of length :S, its height is :S*(SQRT 3)/2.

Mathematical Aside

By the Pythagorean Theorem, the square of x (the height) plus the square of s/2 must equal the square of the hypotenuse s, as shown in Figure 5-32. Thus we have the following:

$$x^2 + (s/2)^2 = s^2$$
$$x^2 + s^2/4 = s^2$$
$$x^2 = s^2 - s^2/4$$
$$x^2 = 3*s^2/4$$
$$x = (s \sqrt{3})/2$$

Figure 5-32

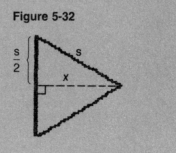

In the **TRISTRIP** procedure, we need to use both the length of a side and the height to incorporate the necessary checks. Because the triangle is being drawn starting with turtle heading 0 and is being drawn to the right, we need to know that the x-coordinate of the starting point is not less than −120 and also that the sum of the x-coordinate and :S*(SQRT 3)/2 is less than 120. (Why?) Similarly, because the drawing does not go lower than the original starting position, we need to be sure that the y-coordinate is greater than −100 and that the sum of the y-coordinate and :S is less than 100. An edited **TRISTRIP** procedure incorporating these checks follows.

```
TO TRISTRIP :S
IF XCOR + :S>120 TOPLEVEL
IF (ANYOF (XCOR< − 120)(XCOR + :S*(SQRT 3) / 2 > 120)
    (YCOR < − 100) (YCOR + :S > 100)) STOP
TRIANGLE :S
FD :S
RT 60
TRIANGLE :S
LT 60
TRISTRIP :S
END
```

To write a corresponding **WALLPAPER**, we need to devise appropriate **WALL**, and **SETUP** procedures. The **WALL** procedure is analogous to the **WALL** procedure we wrote earlier in the section, and the **SETUP** procedure is the same as the one written earlier. However, the inputs to **SETUP** when called by the **WALLPAPER** procedure must be changed. We need change only the x-coordinate input. The new x-coordinate is obtained by adding the height of the triangle, :S*(SQRT 3)/2, to the old x-coordinate. (See Figure 5-33.) We leave the completion of the corresponding **WALLPAPER** procedure to you as an exercise.

Figure 5-33

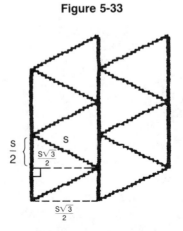

Tessellating with Hexagons

The final tessellation we will consider is one involving hexagons, as shown in Figure 5-34.

Figure 5-34

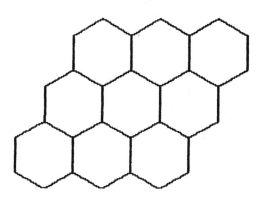

A procedure for drawing a hexagon can be defined as follows.

```
TO HEXAGON :S
REPEAT 6 [FD :S RT 60]
END
```

We start the procedure for drawing a strip of hexagons much as we did the **TRISTRIP** procedure. Because a regular hexagon can be divided into six equilateral triangles, a regular hexagon with sides of length :S has width :S*SQRT 3 at its widest part, as can be seen in Figure 5-35.

Figure 5-35

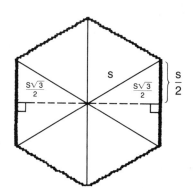

To draw a a strip of hexagons, we want to draw a hexagon, then put the turtle in the appropriate position to draw the next hexagon and continue the process. Suppose the first hexagon is drawn and the turtle is left in the position shown in Figure 5-36.

Figure 5-36

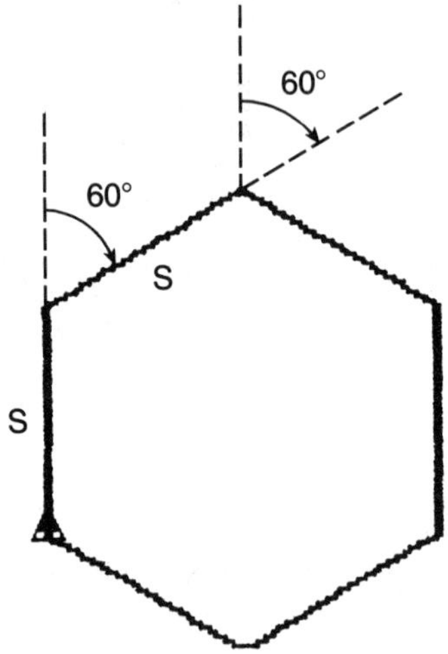

There are several ways to move the turtle to an appropriate position to draw the next hexagon. One possibility, based on Figure 5-36, is the following:

FD :S RT 60 FD :S LT 60

We now add the restrictions to keep the turtle from going off the screen and combine the steps into the HEXSTRIP procedure below.

```
TO HEXSTRIP :S
IF XCOR+:S>120 TOPLEVEL
IF (ANYOF (XCOR < -120) (XCOR + :S * (SQRT 3) > 120)
    (YCOR < -100) (YCOR + :S * 3 > 100)) STOP
HEXAGON :S
FD :S RT 60
FD :S LT 60
HEXSTRIP :S
END
```

Remark: Figure 5-35 may be used to investigate why the condition YCOR+ :S*3 > 100 is used.

Figure 5-37 shows a run of the **HEXSTRIP** procedure where the turtle starts at home with heading 0.

Figure 5-37

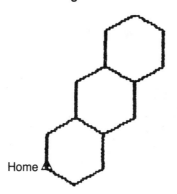

Home

We leave it to you to write a wallpaper-type procedure that tessellates the screen with hexagons. Readers may approach this problem differently depending on their mathematical and Logo backgrounds.

Summary of Commands

TOPLEVEL   Stops all procedures.

Problem Set 5-3

1. (a) Draw any figure that you wish.
   (b) Write a procedure to draw a vertical strip of these figures.

2. Which of the following figures, if any, will tessellate a plane?

   (a) Rhombus
   (b) Parallelogram
   (c) Trapezoid
   (d) Circle

3. Write a procedure that calls the **SQUARESTRIP** procedure of this section and tessellates the screen with squares.

4. (a) Write a procedure to draw a rectangle.
   (b) Write a procedure to draw a vertical strip of rectangles.

(c) Write a wallpaper-type procedure, using your rectangle procedure, that will tessellate the screen.

5. Write a procedure that calls the **HEXSTRIP** procedure of this section and tessellates the screen with hexagons.

6. Will the following drawing made of a regular octagon and a square tessellate the plane? Justify your answer.

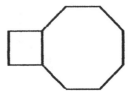

7. One method for determining whether a figure will tessellate the plane is to determine whether or not a group of the figures will fit around a point without overlapping. For example, these trapezoids fit around a point, as shown below.

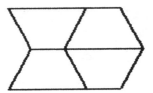

Will repeated drawings of any triangle with no two sides the same length fit around a point? Justify your answer.

8. A pavement is made of tiles of the type shown below. Each tile is made of three regular hexagons from which three sides have been removed. Write a procedure to draw a strip with such tiles.

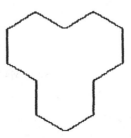

☆9. Write a procedure to tessellate the screen with the figure below.

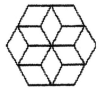

Solution to the Preliminary Problem

Understanding the Problem

The problem is to write a procedure to draw a large square on the screen as a boundary, place the turtle inside the boundary, and let the turtle move at some random heading until the turtle hits a boundary, in which case we want it to "bounce off" at the same angle as it hit the boundary. This is shown in Figure 5-38, where angles 1 and 2 are the same size.

Figure 5-38

(a)

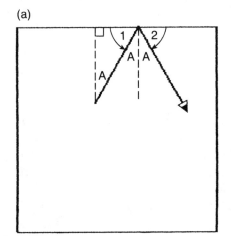

(b)

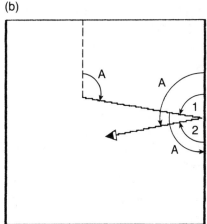

In Figure 5-38(a), the turtle has heading A before bouncing off the boundary. It can be shown that the turtle's new heading after it continues its path is 180 − A. In the situation pictured in Figure 5-38(b), it can be shown that the heading after the turtle bounces is 360 − A, or −A, that is, the opposite of the heading that it had before it bounced.

Devising a Plan

The plan is first to write a procedure to put a large square on the screen, incorporating the use of SETXY and the previously defined SQUARE procedure. Next, we need to write a procedure to place the turtle at a random point inside the square with a random heading. Finally, we need to write procedures to make the turtle move and bounce off the boundary of the square at the desired angle. To make the turtle move as desired, a process of moving and checking recursively is necessary. This process should be similar to the CHECKHEAD and CHECKSIDE procedures in this chapter.

Carrying Out the Plan

A procedure named BOUNDARY, which will draw a square whose sides have length 200, can be written using the SQUARE procedure given earlier.

```
TO BOUNDARY
FULLSCREEN
PENUP
SETXY − 100 ( − 100)
PENDOWN
SETHEADING 0
SQUARE 200
END
```

Placing the turtle at a random point inside the square and with random heading can be accomplished using the RANDOM primitive. From Chapter 3, we know that RANDOM :N, where :N is a positive integer, produces a positive integer from 0 to :N − 1 inclusive. Here we want to produce a positive integer from − 100 to 100 inclusive. The use of RANDOM 201 would produce a positive integer from 0 to 200 inclusive. Thus what we need to do is to subtract 100 from RANDOM 201 to obtain the numbers in the desired interval. Therefore, to choose x- and y-coordinates with range -100 to 100 inclusive, we might use the following:

SETXY ((RANDOM 201) -100) ((RANDOM 201) -100).

Similarly, we can set the heading at random using SETH RANDOM 360. We combine these lines into the SETTURTLE procedure shown below.

```
TO SETTURTLE
PENUP
SETXY ((RANDOM 201) - 100) ((RANDOM 201) - 100)
SETH RANDOM 360
PENDOWN
END
```

The MOVE procedure that starts the turtle's motion should first move the turtle forward a bit, 1 unit, and then test to determine whether or not the turtle is close enough to the boundary to bounce. If so, the turtle's heading should be changed; if not, MOVE should be called recursively. If the testing is done by a procedure called BOUNCE?, then the MOVE procedure follows:

```
TO MOVE
FORWARD 1
BOUNCE?
MOVE
END
```

The BOUNCE? procedure must first determine when the turtle hits the boundary or when it is very close to the boundary in order to tell when it must "bounce." We may decide that the turtle bounces if any of the following is true.

XCOR >100

XCOR <-100

YCOR >100

YCOR <-100

In Figure 5-38 we saw that if A is the original heading, the heading of the turtle after the bounce is 180 − A if the turtle bounces off the top (or bottom) and 360 − A, or − A, if it bounces off the sides. We need lines in the procedure to handle each of these cases. These two lines are as follows:

```
IF ANYOF (XCOR>100) (XCOR< − 100) SETH  − HEADING
IF ANYOF (YCOR>100) (YCOR< − 100) SETH 180 − HEADING
```

Remark: Although it is not explicitly stated, the above lines also handle the case when the turtle bounces off the corner. (Why?)

The complete **BOUNCE?** procedure follows.

```
TO BOUNCE?
IF ANYOF (XCOR>100)(XCOR< − 100) SETH  − HEADING
IF ANYOF(YCOR>100) (YCOR< − 100) SETH 180 − HEADING
END
```

To finish carrying out the plan, we need a procedure called **SQUAREBOUNCE** that calls the other procedures. SQUAREBOUNCE follows.

```
TO SQUAREBOUNCE
BOUNDARY
SETTURTLE
MOVE
END
```

Looking Back

CHAR 7

As a Looking Back activity, you may want to experiment with the commands PRINT1 **CHAR 7**. PRINT1 CHAR 7 causes the computer to make a sound. Edit the BOUNCE procedure so that each time the turtle hits the boundary, the line PRINT1 **CHAR 7** is executed and a sound is made. Another Looking Back activity is to write a procedure that will make the turtle bounce off a rectangle or a circle.

Chapter 5 Problem Set

1. Use the SETX, SETY, and SETXY primitives to draw the largest rectangle possible on your monitor screen.

2. Write a procedure to place a point at random on the screen and then print its x- and y-coordinates.

3. Write a procedure to draw x- and y-axes on the screen with home as the origin. Then mark the axes at each 10-step interval, as shown below.

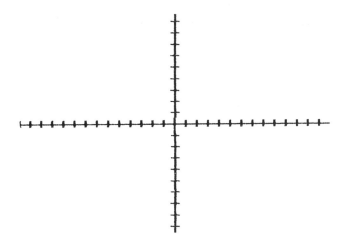

4. Write a procedure to pick two points at random on the screen and make one of these points the center of a circle and the other a point on the circle. Your procedure should then draw the circle or give an error message saying the circle will not fit on the screen.

5. Write a procedure to pick three positive numbers at random, make these three numbers the lengths of segments, draw a triangle with the three segments if possible, and if not, print a message saying that the construction is impossible.

6. If you had a procedure for using two angles and a nonincluded side of a triangle to draw the triangle, how could you edit the procedure to draw a triangle if you were given two angles and the side included between those angles?

7. Edit the **SQUARESTRIP** procedure developed earlier to tessellate the screen using the figure below.

8. Explain why the headings are what they are to make the turtle bounce off the boundary in the solution to the preliminary problem.

9. Write a procedure to make the turtle "bounce off" a rectangle at the same angle as it hits the boundary and to make it continue on its path. Have the procedure place the turtle at a random position and with random heading inside the rectangle.

6

New Vocabulary in Chapter 6

Terms	Primitives
real number p. 236	QUOTIENT p. 236
simplest form p. 245	REMAINDER p. 236
prime p. 245	ROUND p. 237
repeating decimal p. 246	INTEGER p. 237
repetend p. 246	PRINT1 p. 248
terminating decimal p. 246	SIN p. 283
N-factorial p. 251	COS p. 283
arithmetic sequence p. 254	ATAN p. 283
difference p. 254	
ratio p. 254	
geometric sequence p. 254	
Fibonacci sequence p. 255	
composite p. 257	
Least Common Multiple (LCM) p. 260	
similar p. 271	
relatively prime p. 276	
rational p. 276	
Euclidean Algorithm p. 277	

Preliminary Problem

Write a recursive procedure to draw squares within squares as shown above. Each square, other than the largest one, is obtained by joining the midpoints of the sides of the next larger square.

6

Using Arithmetic Operations in Procedures

Introduction

In previous chapters we used numbers and arithmetic operations in turtle graphics. In this chapter we introduce additional arithmetic primitives and use them to solve both arithmetic and geometric problems. In the last section of this chapter we see how Logo explorations may lead to various mathematical concepts. We also use mathematics to investigate properties of figures generated by the POLY procedure of Chapter 4.

6-1 Arithmetic Operations Revisited

In Chapter 1, we used results of arithmetic operations as inputs to Logo commands such as PRINT, RIGHT, or FORWARD. We used such results as inputs to procedures in later chapters. Outside of a procedure, if a command does not precede an arithmetic operation, Logo displays the result of the operation (or operations) preceded by the word RESULT. For example, if we type 8 + 2 * 5 and press RETURN, the following appears:

RESULT: 18

Notice that RESULT: 18 is also printed when we execute the following procedure:

TO COMPUTE
OUTPUT 8 + 2 * 5
END

This indicates that the Logo prompt outside the edit mode functions much like an OUTPUT statement. If we type PRINT COMPUTE, the number 18 is printed without the word RESULT. If we type PRINT 8 + 2 * 5, the number 18 is also printed.

Operations on Real Numbers

real number

Positive and negative integers as well as decimals can be used in Logo. Any number that can be written as a decimal is referred to as a **real number.** The numbers 5, or 5.0, and 3.14159 are decimals. Adding, subtracting, or multiplying integers always produces an integer as a result, but division of two integers may result in a noninteger. If we type 3/4, for example, we obtain the result .75.

QUOTIENT
REMAINDER

Two useful primitives that accept numeric values and output integral (integer) values are **QUOTIENT** and **REMAINDER.** QUOTIENT requires two number inputs; it outputs the integer part of the result of dividing the first number by the second. REMAINDER also requires two number inputs; if the inputs are either both positive or both negative, it outputs the remainder obtained when the first number is divided by the second. For example, if 17 is divided by 3, we have

$$
\begin{array}{r}
5 \\
3\overline{)17} \\
\underline{15} \\
2
\end{array}
$$

or 17 = 5 * 3 + 2. We say that the quotient is 5 and the remainder is 2. Sometimes it is convenient to know just the quotient or just the remainder. In Logo, these can be obtained by using the QUOTIENT or REMAINDER primitives respectively, as shown below.

QUOTIENT 17 3
RESULT: 5

REMAINDER 17 3
RESULT: 2

Can QUOTIENT and REMAINDER accept 0 as a second input? Why? We investigate the result of using noninteger inputs to QUOTIENT and REMAINDER later in the chapter.

Remark: Notice that the order of the inputs for the QUOTIENT and REMAINDER primitives is important. For example, REMAINDER 17 3 is not the same as REMAINDER 3 17.

The primitives ROUND and INTEGER accept real number inputs and output an integer. To see how these commands work, try each of the following and guess how it works.

(a) ROUND 7.4   (b) ROUND 7.6

(c) ROUND 7.5   (d) ROUND 8.5

(e) ROUND − 3.499   (f) ROUND − 3.2

(g) ROUND − 3.5   (h) INTEGER 7.4

(i) INTEGER 7.6   (j) INTEGER 7.5

(k) INTEGER 8.5   (l) INTEGER − 3.499

(m) INTEGER − 3.2   (n) INTEGER − 3.5

You may have guessed that the **ROUND** primitive outputs the integer nearest to its input, whereas the **INTEGER** primitive outputs an integer by simply discarding the decimal part of the input (if there is any). When ROUND is applied to a number with only a 5 after the decimal point, as in 7.5, the result is the nearest integer greater than the number if the number is positive and the nearest integer less than the number if the number is negative. Thus, ROUND 7.5 would give 8, whereas ROUND − 7.5 would give − 8.

ROUND
INTEGER

Both **QUOTIENT** and **REMAINDER** are designed as integer operations. However, as shown below, these primitives can accept noninteger inputs.

QUOTIENT 6.2   3.1   REMAINDER 7.2   3.1
RESULT: 2   RESULT: 1

Logo converts the noninteger inputs into integers. For example, QUOTIENT 6.2   3.1 is treated as QUOTIENT ROUND 6.2 ROUND 3.1 or QUOTIENT 6   3.

Problem 6-1

Write a procedure that converts a person's height from inches to centimeters, rounded to the nearest centimeter. (One inch = 2.54 centimeters.)

Solution

We would like this procedure to take any number of inches as input and convert that number to the nearest whole number of centimeters. Since 1 inch is 2.54 centimeters, then **2.54 * :INCHES** will give the number of centimeters for an input for :INCHES. A procedure called **METRIC.HEIGHT** could make use of the **ROUND** primitive like this:

```
TO METRIC.HEIGHT :INCHES
PRINT [THE NUMBER OF CENTIMETERS ROUNDED]
PRINT [TO THE NEAREST CENTIMETER IS]
PRINT ROUND 2.54 * :INCHES
END
```

We have seen that Logo performs decimal computations. To see to how many places Logo will carry out a computation, try 1/3. Logo outputs RESULT: .333333. Results of arithmetic operations on real numbers are accurate to at most six decimal places in Logo.

Logo allows only integers between -2^{31} and 2^{31}, that is, greater than $-2,147,483,648$ and less than $2,147,483,648$. If integer computations exceeding this range are attempted, Logo displays an approximate answer even if the answer is actually an integer. For example, consider the following:

2147483646 + 1   2147483647 + 1
RESULT: 2147483647   RESULT: 2.14748E9

In the second example, Logo displays the result in exponential notation—that is, **2.14748E9**, which means $2.14748 * 10^9$ or 2,147,480,000. The letter E in the exponential notation stands for "exponential" or "exponent."

Remark: Numbers in exponential notation can be used as inputs for INTEGER.

Now execute 2147483646/2. Again Logo displays the result in exponential notation, that is, **1.07374E9**, which is not the exact answer. Whenever division of two numbers results in a number equal to or greater than 1,000,000, Logo displays the result in exponential notation accurate to the first six digits. If we execute

PRINT 2/1000000

Logo displays 2.N6, which means $2 * 10^{-6}$, or 0.000002. The letter N in 2.N6 indicates that the exponent is negative.

Summary of Commands

QUOTIENT	Requires two number inputs. Rounds the inputs to integers if they are not integers already. Outputs the integer part of the result of dividing the first integer by the second.
REMAINDER	Requires two number inputs and rounds them to integers if necessary. Outputs the remainder obtained when the first integer is divided by the second.
ROUND	Requires one numeric input. Outputs the integer nearest to its input. When ROUND is applied to a number with only 5 after the decimal point, as in 7.5, the result is the nearest integer greater than the number if the number is positive and the nearest integer less than the number if the number is negative.
INTEGER	Requires one numeric input. Outputs the integer obtained by discarding the decimal part of the input, if any.

Problem Set 6-1

1. Predict the exact outcome if each of the following is executed. Check your predictions on the computer.

   (a) PRINT 13 * 13   (b) 13 * 13   (c) PR 2.7 + 9.3

   (d) 2000 * 2000   (e) 3000000/2   (f) 3/1000000

   (g) 7 + 3 * 11   (h) (7 + 3) * 11 (i) 5/9

2. Perform each of the following operations using the computer.

   (a) 134 * (19 * 19 + 1)   (b) 3.14 * 50.83 * 50.83 * 0.5

   (c) 173.4 + 3.14   (d) 50.83 − 173.81

3. Translate each of the following into regular arithmetic notation.

   (a) 2E3   (b) 2.783E6   (c) 5.N3

   (d) 4.08N3   (e) −1.055N2

4. Predict the output for each of the following. Check your predictions on the computer.

   (a) ROUND 7.35   (b) PRINT ROUND 7.35

   (c) ROUND −5.8   (d) ROUND 7.5

   (e) INTEGER 7.5   (f) INTEGER 5N3

   (g) INTEGER −6.5   (h) 3 * INTEGER 0.6

   (i) QUOTIENT 20 6   (j) QUOTIENT 6 20

   (k) REMAINDER 20 6   (l) REMAINDER 6 20

5. Write a procedure called METRIC.WEIGHT with variable :POUNDS that converts weight from pounds to kilograms. (1 kg = 2.2 lbs)

6. (a) Write a procedure for converting degrees Fahrenheit into degrees Celsius using the formula $C = \frac{5}{9} (F - 32)$.

   (b) Use the procedure from part (a) to convert the following Fahrenheit temperatures to Celsius.

      (i) 212°F   (ii) 101.6°F   (iii) 32°F   (iv) −42°F

7. Write a procedure that will print a table of squares of integers from 1 through any given positive integer X.

6-2 Arithmetic Procedures

In this section, we write procedures using the arithmetic operations and primitives previously discussed. For example, consider how we might write a procedure called **POWER2**, which computes the product of a given number times itself. One version is given below.

```
TO POWER2 :X
PRINT :X * :X
END
```

We can also write arithmetic procedures with two or more variables. For example, the following procedure finds the average of two given numbers.

```
TO AVERAGE :X :Y
PRINT (:X + :Y)/2
END
```

Thus, **AVERAGE 6 4** prints the value 5.

As we saw earlier, Logo procedures may be combined to create new procedures. For example, suppose we want to use the procedures just described to create a new procedure called **AVSQ**, which finds the average of the squares of two given numbers. We might write the **AVSQ** procedure like this:

```
TO AVSQ :X :Y
PRINT AVERAGE POWER2 :X   POWER2 :Y
END
```

When we execute **AVSQ 3 4**, we might expect the answer 12.5, which is the result of $(3^2 + 4^2)/2$. However, we obtain the following:

```
9
POWER2 DIDN'T OUTPUT, IN LINE
  PRINT AVERAGE POWER2 :X POWER2 :Y
AT LEVEL 1 OF AVSQ
```

The reason for the error message is that **POWER2** 3 and **POWER2** 4 are not accessible to **AVERAGE**. Before **AVSQ** can call **AVERAGE**, the

values of POWER2 3 and POWER2 4 must be found and passed to
AVERAGE. When AVSQ calls POWER2 3 the PRINT statement in
POWER2 merely displays the number 9 on the screen. This value,
however is not accessible to AVSQ. In order to send this value back
to AVSQ we must use the OUTPUT primitive instead of PRINT. We
can edit the POWER2 and AVERAGE procedures to change the PRINT
command to OUTPUT, as shown below.

```
TO POWER2 :X
OUTPUT :X * :X
END
```

```
TO AVERAGE :X :Y
OUTPUT (:X + :Y)/2
END
```

If we plan to use the AVSQ procedure in still another procedure, we
can again use the OUTPUT command instead of the PRINT command,
like this.

```
TO AVSQ :X :Y
OUTPUT AVERAGE (POWER2 :X) (POWER2 :Y)
END
```

A run of the revised AVSQ procedure is given below.

```
AVSQ 3  4
RESULT: 12.5
```

To have the computer display only the answer, type:

```
PR AVSQ  3  4
```

In summary, the PRINT command displays a value and then "forgets"
it, whereas OUTPUT makes the value available for use elsewhere.

Arithmetic operations can also be used in recursive procedures.
For example, the following problem involves writing a procedure for
raising a number to a nonnegative integer exponent. (There is no
Logo primitive to do this.) Try to write such a procedure on your own
before reading further.

Problem 6-2

Write a procedure for raising any number to a nonnegative integer exponent.

Solution

We have a procedure, **POWER2**, for multiplying a number times itself. We could write similar procedures for cubing any number N, that is N*N*N, or raising a number to the fourth or fifth power. However, it is convenient to have a single procedure for raising any number to any nonnegative integer exponent. Such a procedure, which we call **POWER**, has two variables, the number (:BASE) and the exponent to which the number should be raised (:EXP). If the **POWER** procedure has inputs :BASE and :EXP, then the computer should display 8 when **POWER 2   3** is executed, because $2^3 = 8$.

To write our **POWER** procedure, we observe that a number raised to some exponent can be defined recursively. For example, X^3 can be defined as $X^3 = X*X^2$. Similarly $X^4 = X*X^3$. In general, $X^N = X*X^{N-1}$. Using this equation, let's attempt to write the required procedure. Because $(BASE)^{EXP} = BASE*(BASE)^{EXP-1}$, our first attempt might look like this:

```
TO POWER :BASE :EXP
OUTPUT :BASE * (POWER :BASE :EXP − 1)
END
```

If we execute **POWER 2   3**, we get an error message similar to the following. Why?

```
NO STORAGE LEFT!, IN LINE
  OUTPUT :BASE * (POWER :BASE :EXP − 1)
AT LEVEL 56 OF POWER
```

Theoretically this procedure will run forever, because the exponent can be decreased by 1 indefinitely. Because we assume the exponent is a nonnegative integer, decreasing the exponent by 1 should eventually result in an exponent of 0. At this point we need to tell the computer what POWER :BASE 0 is. Because $X^0 = 1$ when $X \neq 0$, we need to insert the following line in the POWER procedure:

IF :EXP = 0 OUTPUT 1

The edited procedure follows.

```
TO POWER :BASE :EXP
IF :EXP = 0 OUTPUT 1
OUTPUT :BASE * (POWER :BASE :EXP − 1)
END
```

Here's what the POWER procedure might look like with various inputs.

```
POWER 2  3
RESULT:  8
```

```
POWER 3  20
RESULT:  3.48678E9
```

```
POWER 0.7  40
RESULT:  6.36674N7
```

```
POWER 2  60
NO STORAGE LEFT! IN LINE
  OUTPUT :BASE * (POWER :BASE :EXP−1)
AT LEVEL 56 OF POWER
```

Why is the error message given when POWER 2 60 is executed? To answer this question we examine what happens when POWER 2 3 is executed. POWER 2 3 is defined as 2 * (POWER 2 2), POWER 2 2 as 2 * (POWER 2 1), and POWER 2 1 as 2 * (POWER 2 0). Now POWER 2 0 outputs 1 and returns control to the calling procedure, POWER 2 1. Consequently POWER 2 1, which was defined as 2 * (POWER 2 0), outputs the value 2 * 1 or 2 to the calling procedure POWER 2 2. POWER 2 2, defined as 2 * (POWER 2 1), outputs the value 2 * 2 or 4 to the calling procedure POWER 2 3. Finally, POWER 2 3, which was defined as 2 * (POWER 2 2), outputs 2 * 4 or 8. You may want to use the TRACE feature of Logo to follow the execution of

POWER 2 3. You may also want to use the telescoping model for recursion to draw a diagram for this procedure. Notice that when POWER 2 3 is executed OUTPUT 2 * (POWER 2 2), OUTPUT 2 * (POWER 2 1) and OUTPUT 2 * (POWER 2 0) are kept in memory while they are "waiting" to be evaluated. When POWER 2 0 is executed, it returns control to POWER 2 1, and OUTPUT 2 * (POWER 2 0) is evaluated. Then POWER 2 2 and finally POWER 2 3 are evaluated. This process of keeping the procedures in computer memory requires a considerable amount of storage space. When POWER 2 60 is executed as on page 244, all the available storage has been used by the time 55 procedures have been called and no storage is left to complete the computation. Therefore, the POWER procedure outputs a value if and only if :EXP < 56.

Notice that if we execute POWER 0 2 we get 0, which is correct, since $0^2 = 0$. However, executing POWER 0 0 gives us 1. (Do you see why?) This is incorrect, since 0^0 is undefined. It is good programming style to make sure that a procedure will work with any input, even when :BASE = 0 and :EXP = 0. To handle this case, we can insert the line IF ALLOF (:BASE = 0) (:EXP = 0) OUTPUT "ERROR as the first line of POWER.

When we stated Problem 6-2, we intended POWER to accept only nonnegative integer inputs for :EXP. If POWER is given a negative or noninteger exponent, it will not work. We leave it to you as an exercise to modify POWER to stop (or perhaps output the word ERROR) if "bad" input is used. (Hint: You will need to use the IF and INTEGER primitives to check whether the exponent is an integer.)

Our next example of arithmetical procedures using recursion involves finding the repeated block of digits that occurs when certain fractions in the form a/b are written as decimals. We assume a and b are positive integers, a < b and b ≠ 0. If a fraction is in **simplest form** (that is, the numerator and the denominator have no common divisors except 1) and the denominator is divisible by some prime other than 2 and 5, the decimal representation of the fraction will contain a repeated block of digits. (A positive integer greater than 1 is a **prime** if it is not divisible by any positive integer except 1 and

simplest form

prime

itself. For example, the first ten primes are 2, 3, 5, 7, 11, 13, 17, 19, 23, and 29.)

Consider the following division.

$$
\begin{array}{r}
0.142857 \\
7{\overline{\smash{\big)}\,1.000000}} \\
\underline{7} \\
30 \\
\underline{28} \\
20 \\
\underline{14} \\
60 \\
\underline{56} \\
40 \\
\underline{35} \\
50 \\
\underline{49} \\
1
\end{array}
$$

repeating decimal
repetend

terminating decimal

If this division is continued, the pattern of numbers after the decimal point repeats. Thus, the quotient is 0.142857142857. . . . A decimal of this type is called a **repeating decimal,** and the repeating block of digits is called the **repetend.** In the decimal representation of 1/7, we say that the length of the repetend is 6 because a six digit block (142857) repeats. If a/b is a fraction in simplest form that does not represent a **terminating decimal,** (a decimal that can be written with only a finite number of digits to the right of the decimal point) and $a < b$, then the decimal representation of a/b is repeating and the length of the repetend is at most $b-1$. This is because the possible remainders upon division by b are 1, 2, 3, 4, . . . , $b-1$. (We assumed that a/b does not represent a terminating decimal and therefore 0 is not a possible remainder.) After b divisions, there are b remainders, which cannot all be different because there are only $b-1$ possible different nonzero remainders. Thus, after b divisions, at least one remainder must appear twice. When this happens, a block of digits in the quotient repeats.

In fractions with large denominators, the repetend may be very long. The repetend cannot always be found on the computer by dividing the numerator by the denominator because Logo gives only six digits of the decimal representation. Our problem then is to write a procedure that prints the digits in the repetend of any positive fraction less than 1 that can be written as a repeating decimal.

Problem 6-3

Write a procedure that will take as inputs the numerator and denominator of a positive fraction that is less than one and is in simplest form. If the fraction can be represented as a repeating decimal, have the procedure output the digits in the quotient until the repetend can be determined.

Solution

In the division of 1 by 7 given above, the first digit in the decimal representation, 0, is the quotient when 1 is divided by 7. This digit can be found using the Logo primitive **QUOTIENT** with inputs 1 and 7. The second step in the division process is the division of 10 by 7. Here the quotient is 1 and the remainder is 3. (The quotient 1 is recorded as a digit in the decimal representation.) These two results can be obtained from **QUOTIENT 10 7** and **REMAINDER 10 7** respectively, as indicated in the following diagram.

$$
\begin{array}{r}
0\ .\,①\quad \leftarrow \text{QUOTIENT 10 7} \\
7\overline{)\,1\ .\ 0\ \ 0} \\
7 \\
\hline
③\quad \leftarrow \text{REMAINDER 10 7}
\end{array}
$$

The next division, $30 \div 7$, or $3 * 10 \div 7$, yields the quotient 4, which is recorded as the next digit in the decimal expansion. Using the **QUOTIENT** and **REMAINDER** primitives, 4 can be obtained by

executing QUOTIENT 3*10   7 or QUOTIENT (REMAINDER 10 7) *
10 7, as indicated in the diagram.

$$0.\ 1\ \textcircled{4} \leftarrow \text{QUOTIENT (REMAINDER 10}\ \ 7) * 10\ \ 7$$

$$7\ \overline{)\ 1.\ 0\ 0}$$

$$\underline{7}$$

$$\textcircled{3\ \ 0} \leftarrow \text{(REMAINDER 10}\ \ 7) * 10$$

$$\underline{2\ \ 8}$$

$$2$$

In general, if any digit is obtained by QUOTIENT :A :B, it seems
that the digit following QUOTIENT :A :B should be QUOTIENT
(REMAINDER :A :B)*10 :B. Our first attempt to write a procedure
REPETEND1 with inputs :A and :B for the numerator and denominator of a fraction :A/:B might therefore look like this:

TO REPETEND1 :A :B
PRINT QUOTIENT :A :B
REPETEND1 (REMAINDER :A :B)*10 :B
END

When executed, this procedure prints a never ending sequence
of digits that are displayed on the screen so quickly that they cannot
be recorded. It would be useful to edit the procedure so that the digits
could be printed horizontally. This can be accomplished by using the

PRINT1

primitive PRINT1 instead of PRINT. **PRINT1** takes one input and does
not move the cursor to a new line after printing its input. Edit the
REPETEND1 procedure to replace PRINT with PRINT1 and then execute REPETEND1 1 7.

In its present form, REPETEND1 must be stopped with CTRL-G.
It would be useful to edit the procedure so that it stops after a given
number of steps. Because the number of digits in the repetend cannot
be greater than the denominator :B of the fraction :A/:B in simplest
form, the procedure needs to call itself only :B times (once to record
the digit 0 before the decimal point and :B − 1 times for the number
of digits after the decimal point). If the procedure calls itself :B + 1
times rather than :B times, we will see at least one digit being repeated.

To make the procedure call itself :B + 1 times, we use a counter :N in the title. Each time the procedure calls itself, we increase the counter by 1. If we start with :N = 1 and stop when :N = :B + 1, the procedure will call itself :B + 1 times. Thus, if we edit the REPETEND1 procedure by inserting the line IF :N = :B + 1 STOP in an appropriate place, we should obtain a display of the required :B + 1 digits. The edited procedure follows.

```
TO REPETEND1 :A :B :N
PRINT1 QUOTIENT :A :B
IF :N = :B + 1 STOP
REPETEND1 (REMAINDER :A :B)*10  :B  :N + 1
END
```

Notice that the REPETEND1 procedure will work only if the initial conditions that the fraction is less than one, in simplest form and can be represented as a repeating decimal, are satisfied. Thus REPETEND1 3 3 1, REPETEND1 5 3 1, and REPETEND1 2 5 1 do not give meaningful outputs. As in the case of the POWER procedure, it is possible to edit the REPETEND1 procedure so that an error message such as BAD INPUTS TO REPETEND1 will be printed if inappropriate inputs are used. Two executions of the REPETEND1 procedure are given below.

```
REPETEND1 1 7 1
01428571?
```

```
REPETEND1 1 13 1
00769230769230?
```

Remark: Notice that there is a question mark following the digits that REPETEND1 prints. This question mark is the Logo prompt. It appears here because we used a PRINT1 statement in the REPETEND1 procedure and the cursor therefore did not move to the next line when the procedure ended. To avoid this, we could replace the line IF :N = :B + 1 STOP in the REPETEND1 procedure by the line IF :N = :B + 1 PRINT [ ] STOP. This modification will cause the cursor to move down one line before stopping.

Notice that the repetend in the decimal expansion of 1/7 is 142857 and is therefore of length $7 - 1$, or 6. However, in the decimal expansion of 1/13, the repetend is 076923 and is therefore of length 6 rather than $13 - 1$ or 12.

Finally, we write a new **REPETEND** procedure that takes two inputs :A and :B and calls **REPETEND1** :A :B 1 so that :N does not have to be input manually each time. The **REPETEND** procedure is given below.

```
TO REPETEND :A :B
REPETEND1 :A :B   1
END
```

Summary of Commands

PRINT1   Takes one input and does not move the cursor to a new line after printing the input.

Problem Set 6-2

In the following problems you may use any of the procedures previously developed.

1. (a) Write a procedure for finding the average of three numbers.

    (b) Use the procedure developed in part (a) to write another procedure for finding the average of the squares of three numbers.

2. Write a procedure for finding the absolute value of the difference of the squares of two numbers. (You may need to review the ABS procedure described in Chapter 5.)

3. Execute POWER 2 (-3). What is the reason for the message displayed?

4. We have seen that OUTPUT causes a procedure in which it appears to stop. Why does the procedure POWER 2   3 not stop after OUTPUT 2 * (POWER 2   2) is executed?

5. Write a procedure for raising a nonzero number to any negative integer exponent.

6. Write a single procedure for raising a given number to any integral exponent (positive, negative, or 0). An appropriate message should be displayed if the computation is impossible.

7. (a) Suppose A and B are two positive numbers such that A + B = 1. Write a procedure with inputs :A and :B for finding the value of the expression (:A + 1/:A) + (:B + 1/:B).

   (b) Use the procedure in (a) to make a conjecture concerning the least value the expression can have.

8. If N is a positive integer, N! (called **N-factorial**) is defined as the product of all the integers from 1 through N. For example, 3! = 1 * 2 * 3, and 4! = 1 * 2 * 3 * 4. Notice that 3! = 1 * 2 * 3 = (1 * 2) * 3 = 2! * 3, 4! = 1 * 2 * 3 * 4 = (1 * 2 * 3) * 4 = 3! * 4, and in general, N! = (N − 1)! * N. Use the fact that 1! = 1 to write a procedure for computing N! for a given positive integer N.

N-factorial

9. We have used the REMAINDER primitive with positive integers as inputs. If REMAINDER − 10   3 is executed, Logo responds with an answer of − 1. However, in mathematics, remainders must be less than the divisor and greater than or equal to 0. Because − 10 = − 4 * 3 + 2, the remainder when − 10 is divided by 3 is actually 2. In general, when a is divided by b, where a and b are integers such that b > 0, we can find integers q and r such that a = q * b + r, where 0 ⩽ r < b. The integer r is called the remainder. Write a procedure called REMAINDER1 that accepts any integers :A and :B (where :B ≠ 0) as inputs and outputs the remainder when :A is divided by :B.

6-3 More Recursive Procedures Involving Arithmetic

Take any positive integer. If it is even, divide it by 2. If the result is even, continue by dividing it by 2. If at any point (including the first given number) the result is odd, multiply it by 3 and add 1. This will give an even result, and the dividing process can then be continued. The process should be stopped any time a 1 is obtained. For example, suppose we start with 6. Six is even, so we divide it by 2 and obtain 3. Because 3 is odd, we multiply 3 by 3 and add 1 to obtain $3*3 + 1$, or 10. Next we divide 10 by 2 and obtain 5. We multiply 5 by 3 and add 1 to obtain 16, then divide 16 by 2 and obtain 8. Continuing the process, we divide the result by 2 to obtain 4, then 2, and finally 1, where the process stops.

Now consider a second process in which we again start with any positive integer. This time, rather than adding 1 to a multiple of 3, we subtract 1. Below we show the results of two inputs, 6 and 7, when the first process is used and then when the second process is used.

6	7		6	7
3	22		3	20
10	11		8	10
5	34		4	5
16	17		2	14
8	52		1	7
4	26			20
2	13			10
1	40			5
	20			.
	10			.
	5			.
	16			
	8			
	4			
	2			
	1			

First Process   Second Process

Notice that the second process, although similar to the first, does not always produce 1. When the input is 7, the results 7, 20, 10, 5, and 14 repeat themselves. Does the first process always reach 1 regardless of the initial input? The answer is not obvious. The results may steadily increase (due to multiplication by 3), so it is conceivable that for some initial input, the results increase indefinitely; or, as in the second process, the outputs may repeat themselves.

If we want to experiment with the first process to find out whether it eventually reaches 1 for different inputs, it would be far too time-consuming to do so with pencil and paper. Instead, we can write a Logo procedure called PROCESS that simulates this process. We need to incorporate the following into the procedure:

If :N is even, divide :N by 2; otherwise multiply :N by 3 and add 1.

An integer is even if it is divisible by 2, or, equivalently, if :N/2 is equal to the integral part of :N/2. Using the Logo primitives INTEGER, IF, and ELSE, we can therefore write our direction as shown below:

IF :N/2 = INTEGER :N/2 PROCESS :N/2 ELSE PROCESS :N * 3 + 1

We need a STOP statement to complete our procedure. If :N = 1, we want to stop the process. To accomplish this, we need the following line.

IF :N = 1 STOP

The complete PROCESS procedure follows.

```
TO PROCESS :N
PRINT :N
IF :N = 1 STOP
IF :N/2 = INTEGER :N/2 PROCESS :N/2 ELSE PROCESS :N * 3 + 1
END
```

Run the procedure for several different inputs. Notice that the conditional statement IF :N/2 = INTEGER :N/2 PROCESS :N/2 ELSE PROCESS :N*3 + 1 can be replaced by IF REMAINDER :N 2 = 0 PROCESS :N/2 ELSE PROCESS :N*3 + 1.

Arithmetic and Geometric Sequences

Recursion is useful in generating sequences and finding their sums. Two common types of sequences are arithmetic sequences and geometric sequences. If each successive term in a sequence is obtained from the previous term by the addition of a fixed number, the sequence is called an **arithmetic sequence** and the fixed number is called the **difference.** For example, the sequence 1, 4, 7, 10, 13, . . . is an arithmetic sequence with difference 3. If each successive term of a sequence is obtained from the previous term by multiplication by a fixed number called the **ratio,** the sequence is called a **geometric sequence.** For example, the sequence 1, 2, 4, 8, 16, 32, . . . is a geometric sequence with ratio 2.

arithmetic sequence

difference

ratio

geometric sequence

Problem 6-4

Write a procedure that prints successive terms of an arithmetic sequence whose first term is :TERM and whose difference is :DIFF.

Solution

In an arithmetic sequence whose first term is :TERM, we need only to add the difference :DIFF to each term to obtain the next term. Our procedure, called ASEQ (for Arithmetic Sequence), should have two inputs, :TERM and :DIFF. Thus the title line of the procedure becomes the following:

```
TO ASEQ :TERM :DIFF
```

To obtain the next term in the sequence, we add :DIFF to the previous value of :TERM. This can be achieved by using a recursive call with inputs :TERM + :DIFF and :DIFF, that is, ASEQ :TERM + :DIFF :DIFF. In this way, each successive term in the sequence becomes the first input in a new call of ASEQ. Because we want a display of the terms, we need to instruct the computer to print the first input for each recursive call—that is, PRINT :TERM. The ASEQ procedure follows:

```
TO ASEQ :TERM :DIFF
PRINT :TERM
ASEQ :TERM + :DIFF  :DIFF
END
```

If we execute **ASEQ** for any given inputs, we notice that the column of successive terms runs by so fast that it is difficult to record the passing numbers. It is possible to slow down the printing of the terms by inserting the following **WAIT** procedure.

```
TO WAIT :N
IF :N = 0 STOP
WAIT :N - 1
END
```

The **WAIT** procedure makes the computer count backwards without performing any other action, thus causing the computer to pause in the main procedure. If we edit the **ASEQ** procedure by inserting the WAIT procedure, the user will have time to see each term in the sequence as it is printed. The edited **ASEQ** procedure follows.

```
TO ASEQ :TERM :DIFF
PRINT :TERM
WAIT 40
ASEQ :TERM + :DIFF :DIFF
END
```

In the problem set at the end of this section you will be asked to edit the **ASEQ** procedure again to make it print :N terms.

The Fibonacci Sequence

A sequence with many interesting properties and applications is the **Fibonacci sequence,** named for Leonardo of Pisa (also called Fibonacci). In the year 1202, Fibonacci introduced the following sequence:

Fibonacci sequence

1, 1, 2, 3, 5, 8, 13, 21, 34, 55, 89, . . .

The first two terms of the Fibonacci sequence are 1, 1. Each succeeding term is the sum of the two terms immediately before it. Thus, $2 = 1 + 1, 3 = 1 + 2, 5 = 2 + 3, 8 = 3 + 5$, and so on. The sequence does not have to start with 1, 1; we could start with any two numbers. We would still create each new term by adding the two previous terms.

For example, if we start with -2 and 3, we obtain a Fibonacci sequence that looks like this:

$-2, 3, 1, 4, 5, 9, 14, 23, \ldots$

Patterns involving the Fibonacci sequence are found in nature, for example in sunflowers and daisy florets, pineapples, and the shells of some mollusks.

Problem 6-5

Write a procedure called FIB that outputs the first :N terms of a Fibonacci sequence whose first two terms are :A and :B.

Solution

To write the general procedure, consider first the sequence 2, 3, 5, 8, 13, 21, 34. Each number after the first two is created from a pair of numbers preceding it. Concentrate on the pairs that create the numbers in the sequence:

First pair   2,3

Second pair   3,5

Third pair   5,8

Fourth pair   8,13

In general, if :A, :B is any pair, the next pair is :B,   :A + :B. Also notice that the first number in the first pair is the first number in the sequence. The first number in the second pair is the second number in the sequence; the first number in the third pair is the third number in the sequence; and so on. In general, the first number in the Nth pair is the Nth number in the sequence. Thus, to create a procedure that prints the first :N terms of a Fibonacci sequence, we need to call the procedure :N times and print the first number in the current pair each time. The current pair :A, :B must then be replaced by the pair :B,   :A + :B. Calling the procedure exactly :N times can be accomplished by putting a variable :N in the title to serve as a counter. :N can be reduced by 1 each time the procedure is called, until :N = 1.

Then the procedure can be stopped by inserting a **STOP** statement. The procedure, along with runs resulting from several outputs, follows.

```
TO FIB :A :B :N
PRINT :A
IF :N = 1 STOP
FIB :B :A + :B :N − 1
END
```

(a)	FIB 1 1 6	(b)	FIB − 2 2 9	(c)	FIB 1 4 7
	1		− 2		1
	1		2		4
	2		0		5
	3		2		9
	5		2		14
	8		4		23
			6		37
			10		
			16		

As an exercise, edit the **FIB** procedure so that it prints only the Nth term in a given Fibonacci sequence. Also try to write a procedure that finds the sum of the first :N terms of any Fibonacci sequence.

Determining Whether a Number is Prime

In the next example we write a procedure that checks to see whether a number is prime or composite. A positive integer, N greater than 1, is prime if it is not divisible by any positive integer except 1 and itself. If N is divisible by some positive integer other than 1 and N, it is called **composite.** To determine if a number N is prime, it is sufficient to check whether N is divisible by all the primes less than or equal to $\sqrt{N}$. A proof of this can be found in the Mathematical Aside that follows. Thus, to find out whether 101 is prime, we need only to check whether it is divisible by all the primes less than or equal to $\sqrt{101}$, that is, 2, 3, 5, and 7. The next greater prime, 11, is greater than $\sqrt{101}$ because $11^2 = 121 > 101$; therefore, 11 need not be checked.

composite

Mathematical Aside

Suppose N is a positive integer greater than 1 and has no prime factors less than or equal to $\sqrt{N}$. The assumption that N is not a prime causes a contradiction. If N were not a prime, it could be written as a product of two or more primes. Because N is not divisible by any prime less than or equal to $\sqrt{N}$, it follows that all the prime factors of N must be greater than $\sqrt{N}$. Consequently, the product of two prime factors of N is greater than $\sqrt{N} * \sqrt{N}$, or N, which implies that N itself is greater than N. This does not make sense; therefore, our assumption that N is not a prime must be false. This shows that if a positive integer N that is greater than 1 has no prime factor less than or equal to N, then $\sqrt{N}$ is prime.

When writing a procedure called **CHECK** to determine whether a number is prime, it is simpler to determine whether N is divisible by all the positive integers less than or equal to $\sqrt{N}$ rather than by primes only. (If we wanted to test for divisibility by prime divisors only, we would first have to have a procedure to check whether a divisor is a prime.)

The procedure **CHECK** needs two variables; :N, the number to be checked, and :D, a possible divisor of :N. We need only to check whether :N is divisible by numbers less than or equal to **SQRT :N**. For example, **SQRT 127** outputs RESULT: 11.2694; therefore, the greatest integer less than or equal to **SQRT 127** is 11. This can be determined in Logo by computing **INTEGER (SQRT 127)**. In general, the greatest value of :D to be checked as a possible divisor of :N is **INTEGER (SQRT :N)**. Thus, for that value of :D we need to check whether :N/:D is an integer. Expressed in Logo, :N/:D is an integer if and only if :N/:D = **INTEGER (:N/:D)**, or equivalently if and only if **REMAINDER :N :D = 0**. If :N/:D is not an integer, we check to see whether :N/(:D − 1) is an integer, and we continue checking with the values of divisors decreased by 1. If for some value of :D other than 1, :N/:D is an integer, we want the computer to print the word COMPOSITE. If :N/:D is not an integer for all values of :D greater than 1 and less than or equal to **INTEGER (SQRT :N)**, we eventually reach the value 1 for :D. When :D = 1, we know that :N is prime; we then want the computer to print PRIME and stop. Remembering that the value of :D must be input as **INTEGER (SQRT :N)**, we may write our procedure as follows:

```
TO CHECK :N :D
IF :D = 1 PRINT "PRIME STOP
IF REMAINDER :N :D = 0 PRINT "COMPOSITE STOP
CHECK :N :D - 1
END
```

Below are several runs of the **CHECK** procedure.

```
CHECK 101 INTEGER (SQRT 101)
PRIME
```

```
CHECK 407 INTEGER (SQRT 407)
COMPOSITE
```

```
CHECK 1 INTEGER (SQRT 1)
PRIME
```

Because 1 is not a prime (why?), we need to edit the **CHECK** procedure so that it will print the message **NEITHER PRIME NOR COMPOSITE** when 1 is input for :N. We can do that as follows:

```
TO CHECK :N :D
IF :N = 1 PRINT [NEITHER PRIME NOR COMPOSITE] STOP
IF :D = 1 PRINT "PRIME STOP
IF REMAINDER :N :D = 0 PRINT "COMPOSITE STOP
CHECK :N :D - 1
END
```

Notice that our **CHECK** procedure is somewhat awkward; it requires two inputs, one for the number to be checked and another for the first value of the divisor. It would be more convenient to have a procedure that requires only the number to be checked as input. We might call such a procedure **PRIME :N**. This procedure could call the **CHECK** procedure with two inputs, :N and **INTEGER (SQRT :N)**. Here is the new procedure, along with an example of its execution.

```
TO PRIME :N
CHECK :N INTEGER (SQRT :N)
END
```

```
PRIME 1007
COMPOSITE
```

By definition, a prime number must be positive. For that reason, the PRIME procedure was not designed to accept integers less than 1. It is possible to edit the procedure so that it will print an appropriate error message if a value less than 1 is input for :N. This is left as an exercise.

Finding the LCM of Two Positive Integers

Our last example in this section involves writing a procedure to find the least common multiple (LCM) of two positive integers. The least positive multiple that two positive integers have in common is called the **least common multiple (LCM)** of the numbers.

least common multiple (LCM)

Consider, for example, the LCM(144,360). One way to find the LCM is to look at multiples of 144 and pick the least positive one that is also a multiple of 360. Four multiples of 144 are shown below.

$$2 * 144 = 288$$
$$3 * 144 = 432$$
$$4 * 144 = 576$$
$$5 * 144 = 720$$

Because 720 is the least positive multiple of 144 that is also a multiple of 360, LCM(144,360) = 720.

This example gives us a hint for writing a procedure that will find the LCM of any two positive integers :A and :B. We can look at consecutive multiples of :A and pick the least positive number that is also a multiple of :B. A multiple of :A can be designated by :N*:A, where :N takes values of consecutive positive integers starting with 1. The least positive value of :N*:A that is also a multiple of :B is the least common multiple of :A and :B. Therefore we want our procedure to output the value of :N*:A when the desired multiple is found.

Saying that :N*:A is a multiple of :B is equivalent to saying that :N*:A is divisible by :B, that is, that the remainder when :N*:A is divided by :B is 0. Using the Logo primitive REMAINDER, we can write this as (REMAINDER :N*:A :B) = 0.

Our procedure, which we call LCM1, needs three inputs, :A, :B, and :N for a counter. When the procedure calls itself, the counter should be increased by 1. The procedure looks like this:

```
TO LCM1 :A :B :N
IF (REMAINDER :N*:A  :B) = 0 OUTPUT :N*:A
LCM1 :A  :B  :N + 1
END
```

Remark: We use the OUTPUT primitive so that the value can be passed to another procedure.

To find the LCM(100,360), we execute **LCM1 100 360 1**.

```
LCM1 100 360 1
RESULT: 1800
```

Notice that the LCM1 procedure requires an input 1 for :N. We can avoid this by writing another procedure called **LCM**, which has only :A and :B as inputs and calls **LCM1 :A :B 1**. The new procedure is shown below.

```
TO LCM :A :B
LCM1 :A :B 1
END
```

Problem Set 6-3

1. Write a GSEQ procedure that prints successive terms of a geometric sequence whose first term is :TERM and whose ratio is :RATIO.

2. Edit the ASEQ and GSEQ procedures so that

   (a) each procedure prints only a given number of terms.

   (b) each procedure will stop when the absolute value of the term is less than a given number.

3. Write a procedure that outputs the Nth term of any geometric sequence and then stops.

4. Use the procedure that you developed in the preceding problem to write a procedure for raising any number to an integer exponent greater than 0.

5. If the PRINT statement in the final version of the FIB procedure is replaced by OUTPUT, will the procedure display the same result as the original with the same inputs? Check your answer on the computer.

6. Consider the following FIB1 procedure and predict the outcome when FIB1 1 1 5 is executed.

    ```
    TO FIB1 :A :B :N
    IF :N = 1 STOP
    PRINT :A
    FIB1 :B :A + :B :N − 1
    END
    ```

7. Edit the FIB procedure so that it prints only the Nth term of the sequence.

8. Consider the sequence 1/1, 2/1, 3/2, 5/3, 8/5, 13/8, . . . in which each term is formed by finding the ratio of a Fibonacci number and its predecessor in the sequence 1, 1, 2, 3, 5, 8, 13, 21, ... Write procedures that print out

    (a) a list of N values of these ratios for any N.

    (b) only the Nth ratio for any N.

9. The following SUMASEQ procedure finds the sum of the first :N terms of an arithmetic sequence whose first term is :TERM and whose difference is :DIFF.

    ```
    TO SUMASEQ :TERM :DIFF :N
    SUMASEQ1 :TERM :DIFF 0 :N
    END
    ```

    ```
    TO SUMASEQ1 :TERM :DIFF :SUM :N
    IF :N = 0 PRINT :SUM STOP
    SUMASEQ1 :TERM+:DIFF  :DIFF  :SUM+:TERM  :N−1
    END
    ```

    Study the SUMASEQ1 and SUMASEQ procedures and then do following problems.

    (a) Use the SUMASEQ procedure to find the sum of the first 100 positive integers.

(b) Write a **SUMGSEQ** procedure to find the sum of the first :N terms of a geometric sequence with the first term :TERM and ratio :RATIO.

(c) Write a **SUMFIB** procedure to find the sum of the first :N terms of a Fibonacci sequence with first two terms :A and :B.

(d) Write a **SUMSQ** procedure to find the sum of the first :N squares, that is, the sum $1^2 + 2^2 + 3^2 + \ldots + :N^2$.

10. Edit the **CHECK** procedure introduced in this section by changing the **PRINT** statements to **OUTPUT** statements. Is the **STOP** command in each of those lines still necessary? Why or why not?

11. Edit the **PRIME** and **CHECK** procedures so that an appropriate error message is printed when a value less than 1 or a noninteger is input for :N.

12. For a given integer :N greater than 1, write a procedure that will output the least prime that divides :N.

13. Write a Logo procedure to find the LCM of any three positive numbers.

6-4 Random Numbers

In Logo it is possible to simulate various random phenomena by using the primitive **RANDOM**, which was introduced in Chapter 3. As you may recall, **RANDOM** takes a positive number N as an input and outputs an integer between 0 and N − 1 inclusive. (If the input is not an integer, the input is rounded before **RANDOM** acts on it.) For example, **RANDOM 10** picks at random and outputs an integer between 0 and 9 inclusive, while **RANDOM 2** outputs 0 or 1. If we execute **RANDOM 10**, obtain the output 8, and we execute **RANDOM 10** again, we may obtain a number different from 8. (The probability of obtaining a second eight is 1/10.)

Coin-Tossing Simulation

Our first application of the RANDOM command is a computer simulation of a coin-tossing experiment. Suppose we want to write a procedure that takes the number of tosses of a coin as input and outputs the number of heads obtained. If we let 1 designate a head and 0 a tail, then we would like to know the number of 1's obtained after the simulated tosses are completed.

Let's try a simpler version of the problem first. We can write a procedure that prints 0 or 1 each time a simulated tossing of a coin is performed and then count the number of 1's on the screen ourselves. We call this procedure EXPERIMENT. We let :N designate the number of tosses; in other words, EXPERIMENT should be repeated :N times. Thus EXPERIMENT :N should call EXPERIMENT :N − 1 until :N = 0, when the process should stop. The 0 or 1 outputs are obtained by using RANDOM 2.

One possible EXPERIMENT procedure is given below.

```
TO EXPERIMENT :N
IF :N = 0 STOP
PRINT RANDOM 2
EXPERIMENT :N − 1
END
```

In this form, the experiment is repeated :N times, but the procedure does not record the number of 1's obtained.

One way to record the number of 1's is to edit EXPERIMENT to have another variable, :K, which counts the 1's. The value of :K should be increased by 1 if and only if 1 is output by RANDOM 2. If the procedure is EXPERIMENT :N :K, the recursive call should be to EXPERIMENT :N − 1 :K + 1 if 1 is output by RANDOM 2 and to EXPERIMENT :N − 1 :K if 0 is output. This can be accomplished by using the TEST command. We want the computer to test whether RANDOM 2 = 1; then, if the condition is true, we want :K + 1 to be substituted for :K, which can be done by calling EXPERIMENT :N − 1 :K + 1. If the condition is false, we do not want to change the current value of :K; therefore, we want the procedure to call EXPERIMENT :N − 1 :K. This scheme can be written in Logo as follows:

```
TEST (RANDOM 2) = 1
IFTRUE EXPERIMENT :N − 1 :K + 1
IFFALSE EXPERIMENT :N − 1 :K
```

We also want to stop the procedure when **EXPERIMENT** is repeated :N times. When the procedure stops, we want it to output the number of 1's. If we start the procedure with :K = 0, the current value of :K gives the number of 1's output by :N repeated executions of **RANDOM** 2. Thus, immediately after the title line, we need the following line.

```
IF :N = 0 PRINT :K STOP
```

The complete edited **EXPERIMENT** procedure follows.

```
TO EXPERIMENT :N :K
IF :N = 0 PRINT :K STOP
TEST (RANDOM 2) = 1
IFTRUE EXPERIMENT :N − 1 :K + 1
IFFALSE EXPERIMENT :N − 1 :K
END
```

To simulate tossing a coin 100 times and to record the number of heads, we execute **EXPERIMENT 100 0**. We should expect an output of approximately 50.

It is possible to eliminate the typing of 0 for :K by defining a new procedure, **TOSSES**, with only one variable :N. We do this by calling the already defined **EXPERIMENT** with inputs :N and 0. The procedure follows:

```
TO TOSSES :N
EXPERIMENT :N  0
END
```

An alternate approach, similar to the one used to write **POWER**, can also be used to write a procedure for recording the number of heads when a coin is tossed :N times. We'll call this new procedure **NUM**. Suppose **NUM** :N counts the number of 1's when **RANDOM 2** is repeated :N times. It is possible to define **NUM** :N in terms of **NUM** :N − 1. Because **NUM** :N equals the number of 1's accumulated after :N tosses, it also equals the number of 1's accumulated after

:N − 1 tosses plus RANDOM 2, that is, (NUM :N − 1) + RANDOM 2. To complete the definition of NUM :N we need to know the value of NUM for :N = 0. That value is 0. Consequently, we have the following NUM procedure:

```
TO NUM :N
IF :N = 0 OUTPUT 0
OUTPUT (NUM :N–1) + RANDOM  2
END
```

Execute NUM for :N = 60 and for :N = 100. Then execute TOSSES 100. TOSSES 100 outputs an integer close to 50, but NUM 100 produces an error message similar to the following:

```
NO STORAGE LEFT!, IN LINE
  OUTPUT (NUM :N − 1) + RANDOM 2
AT LEVEL 67 OF NUM
```

Why is this error message given in the NUM procedure but not in the TOSSES procedure?

The Use of the RANDOM Primitive in Turtle Graphics

The RANDOM primitive can also be used in turtle graphics. Let's start exploring these uses by writing a procedure for a random turtle walk. The following procedure, called RANDOM.WALK with inputs :ANGLE and :DIS causes the turtle to turn right a random number of degrees between 0 and :ANGLE − 1 inclusive, and then to move forward a random number of steps between 0 and :DIS − 1 inclusive, and finally to repeat this process.

```
TO RANDOM.WALK :ANGLE :DIS
RT (RANDOM :ANGLE)
FD (RANDOM :DIS)
RANDOM.WALK :ANGLE :DIS
END
```

Execute RANDOM.WALK 360 30. Then try RANDOM.WALK with some other inputs.

Sometimes it is desirable to obtain negative as well as non-negative outputs from RANDOM. Consider RANDOM 5. The possible outputs are 0, 1, 2, 3, and 4. If we want to obtain a negative output using RANDOM 5, it would be sufficient to subtract from RANDOM 5 a number greater than the greatest possible output of RANDOM 5. Because the greatest possible output of RANDOM 5 is 4, (RANDOM 5) − 5 always outputs a negative number. (Do you see why parentheses are needed?) In fact, the only possible outputs of (RANDOM 5) − 5 are −5, −4, −3, −2, and −1. Do you see how to output the numbers −5, −4, −3, −2, −1, 0, 1, 2, 3, 4, 5?

If we want to use the RANDOM primitive to output positive as well as negative numbers, we could use (RANDOM 11) − 5. The possible outputs would be all the integers between −5 and 5 inclusive. In general, (RANDOM 2*:X + 1) − :X outputs an integer between − :X and :X inclusive.

The RANDOM primitive can be used to create various designs other than random walks. For example, we could use RANDOM to put small circles around the screen at random. In writing such a procedure it would be helpful to have another procedure that places the turtle at a random position on the screen. Then we could use this procedure and the CIR procedure shown below to write a procedure called BUBBLES that places circles on the screen at random. Try to write such a procedure before reading further.

```
TO CIR
HT
REPEAT 10 [FD 5 RT 36]
END
```

BUBBLES could be written using a recursive procedure that draws the circles, starting each circle at a random point on the screen. If SET is a procedure that moves the turtle to a random position on the screen, then BUBBLES should call SET, draw a circle using the CIR procedure, and finally call itself to repeat the process indefinitely. Thus the BUBBLES procedure would look like this:

```
TO BUBBLES
FULLSCREEN
SET
CIR
BUBBLES
END
```

Our remaining task is to write the **SET** procedure. To make sure that all the circles are drawn on the screen, we want to move the turtle only to points with coordinates that are not too large or too small. One possibility is to restrict the x- and y-coordinates to values between −100 and 100. This can be achieved by using the **SETXY** command with both inputs equal to (**RANDOM 201**) − 100. To keep the turtle from leaving a trace when it moves to a new position, we use the **PENUP (PU)** command. The complete **SET** procedure is given below.

```
TO SET
PU
SETXY (RANDOM 201) – 100   (RANDOM 201) – 100
PD
END
```

A design created by a run of **BUBBLES** stopped by CTRL-G is shown in Figure 6-1.

Figure 6-1

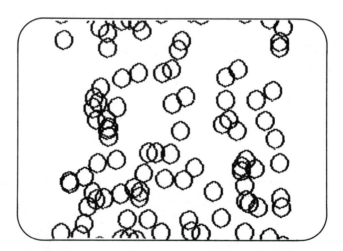

Problem Set 6-4

1. Write a procedure that simulates rolling a die and records the number of sixes when a die is rolled a given number of times.

2. Write a procedure that will record the number of times a negative output is obtained when (RANDOM 2*:X+1) − :X is executed N times. Run the procedure for several values of :X and :N.

3. Write a version of the RANDOM.WALK procedure in which the turtle stops whenever it is 1 turtle step away from the boundary of a rectangle with center at home and with dimensions 240 by 160 turtle steps.

4. Consider the following POLY-type procedures.

```
TO RANPOLY :S :A
IF (RANDOM 5) = 0 THEN PU ELSE PD
FD :S RT :A
RANPOLY :S :A
END
```

```
TO RANPOLY1 :S :A
IF (RANDOM 5) = 0 THEN PU ELSE PD
FD :S RT :A
IF HEADING = 0 STOP
RANPOLY1 :S :A
END
```

Assuming that the turtle has initial heading 0, what do you expect the outcome of the following to be?

(a) RANPOLY 80 120
(b) RANPOLY1 80 120
(c) RANPOLY 80 144
(d) RANPOLY1 80 144

5. Write a version of the POLY procedure from Chapter 4 in which both the angle and the side are incremented by some random number.

6. Edit BUBBLES so that it stops after 20 circles are drawn.

7. Write a procedure similar to the BUBBLES procedure that draws circles of random radius not greater than 15.

8. Write a procedure similar to the BUBBLES procedure that puts variable size nine-pointed stars at random on the screen.

*6-5 Mathematics of the POLY Procedure

Recall the POLY procedure introduced in Section 4-1. (For easier reference, we will use the variables :S and :A instead of :SIDE and :ANGLE.)

```
TO POLY :S :A
FD :S RT :A
POLY :S :A
END
```

A figure drawn by POLY eventually repeats itself. After the POLY procedure begins to repeat, we could stop it by executing CTRL-G or by introducing a STOP statement. The edited POLY procedure shown below always stops the procedure if the turtle's initial heading is 0 and the angle input is an integer.

```
TO POLY :S :A
FD :S RT :A
IF HEADING = 0 STOP
POLY :S :A
END
```

POLY appears to be a simple recursive procedure, but this is not necessarily the case. Execute each of the following and see how many outcomes you can predict.

(a) POLY 50   60   (b) POLY 50 120
(c) POLY 50   72   (d) POLY 2   2
(e) POLY 80 144   (f) POLY 70 135
(g) POLY 60 180   (h) POLY 60 160
(i) POLY 50 100   (j) POLY 50 101
(k) POLY 50 102   (l) POLY 50 103

The outputs in (a) − (d) do not cross themselves. Can you predict which inputs produce polygons and which do not?

Some POLY figures, for example POLY 50 100, have many sides. (How many?) However, POLY 50 101 produces a figure that appears to have many more sides than the figure produced by POLY 50 100. In fact, the figure produced by POLY 50 101 has so many sides that when it is executed it may seem that the turtle will never stop. The final result for **POLY 50 101** looks like an automobile tire. The result of **POLY 50 102** also looks like a tire; however, it probably has fewer sides than the result of **POLY 50 101** because the turtle seems to take less time to draw the figure. To explore why it takes the turtle so long to stop when **POLY 50 101** is executed, we attempt to find a way to predict the number of sides of a figure generated by the **POLY** procedure. We assume that the angle input is a positive integer.

Problem 6-6

Determine a method for predicting the number of sides of a figure generated by the **POLY** procedure with any input for :S and a positive integer input for :A.

Solution

If :S is the length of a side and :A is the measure of the turning angle, where :A > 0, we are to predict the number of sides of the figure drawn by **POLY** :S :A.

Does :S have an effect on the number of sides? For example, how are **POLY 40 144** and **POLY 70 144** related? To find out, execute the two procedures.

We find that all figures generated by **POLY** with the same angle input are **similar**—that is, they have the same shape. Thus the length of the side does not determine the number of sides. However, the angle input does affect the number of sides, so our problem becomes one of finding the number of sides of a **POLY** figure if we are given the angle input.

similar

If N is the number of sides of a **POLY** figure, then N is both the number of turns required to draw the figure and the number of vertices of the figure. Because the turtle turns A degrees at a time, its total turning must be N * A when it completes the figure drawn by **POLY**. Because the turtle ends up with the same heading it started with, it follows from the Total Turtle Trip Theorem given in Chapter 3 that the total turning must be some multiple of 360, that is,

K * 360, where K is some positive integer. Consequently, we have the following:

$$N * A = K * 360 \quad \text{or} \quad N = \frac{K * 360}{A}$$

Unfortunately, we do not know the value of K, so the above expression for N is not a solution. What information do we have about K? Because we do not want the turtle to redraw any part of the figure drawn by the **POLY** procedure, K * 360 must be the least positive multiple of 360 that is equal to N * A. Because N * A = K * 360, K * 360 must be a multiple of A. Consequently, K * 360 is the least positive multiple that A and 360 have in common. The least positive multiple that two positive integers have in common is the least common multiple (LCM) of the numbers, which we discussed earlier in Section 6-3. Thus we have:

$$N * A = \text{LCM (A, 360)} \quad \text{or} \quad N = \frac{\text{LCM (A, 360)}}{A}$$

This last expression gives us the solution to our problem. To find the number of sides of a figure drawn by **POLY** with a positive input :A, we need only to find the **LCM (:A, 360)** and divide it by :A.

We have seen that if :A = 101, the figure drawn by **POLY** has so many sides that it is virtually impossible to identify them. However, the exact number of sides is given by **LCM(101,360)/101**. Using the **LCM** procedure from Section 6-3, we obtain 36360 for **LCM(101, 360)**. Consequently, LCM(101,360)/101 = 36360/101, or 360 and the figure has 360 sides.

Are there other values for :A that produce figures with 360 sides? Try to answer this question before reading further.

A figure produced by **POLY** has 360 sides if and only if **LCM(:A,360)** /:A = 360, or, equivalently, **LCM(:A,360) = :A*360**. Notice that LCM(101,360) = 101 * 360. The LCM of two numbers is not always equal to the product of the numbers, however. For example, LCM(90,360) = 360, not 90*360. On the other hand, LCM(4,9) = 4*9, and LCM(5,9) = 5*9.

What happens if :A is a negative integer? For example, how is the number of sides of **POLY** 50 (− 135) related to the number of sides of

POLY 50 135? Why? Can you predict the number of sides for non-integer inputs for :A? For example, can you predict the number of sides in each of the following?

(a) POLY 20 22.5

(b) POLY 20 14.4

(c) POLY 50 720/11

(d) POLY 50 144.1

Finding the Number of Different POLY Figures with a Given Number of Sides

In Problem 6-6 we determined a method for predicting the number of sides of a figure drawn by the POLY procedure for a given angle input, :A. Conversely, suppose we want to create a POLY figure with a given number of sides. How can we determine the possible turning angle inputs? For example, suppose the number of sides we want is 5. We have already seen two POLY figures with five sides: a pentagon, for which :A = 72, and a five-pointed star, for which :A = 144. Are there other POLY figures with five sides and different shapes?

Problem 6-7

How many different shapes of POLY figures are possible with a given number of sides?

Solution

Because POLY figures have sides of equal measure and angles of equal measure, it seems that with 3 sides we should get exactly one POLY figure—an equilateral triangle, which is obtained for an angle input of 120. With 4 sides it seems obvious that the only possible POLY figure is a square, which is obtained if :A = 90. With five sides we have seen two POLY figures: a pentagon with :A = 72 and a five-pointed star with :A = 144. To determine whether there are other figures with five sides, we need to know the possible angle inputs. We have seen in Problem 6-6 that if N is the number of sides,

N * A = K * 360 where K is a positive integer. Thus, 5 * A = K * 360, or A = K * 360/5. Because K is a positive integer, we can substitute the values 1, 2, 3, 4, 5... for K and obtain the following:

K	A
1	1 * 360/5 or 72
2	2 * 360/5 or 144
3	3 * 360/5 or 216
4	4 * 360/5 or 288
5	5 * 360/5 or 360
6	6 * 360/5 or 1 * 360/5 + 5 * 360/5 or 72 + 360
7	7 * 360/5 or 2 * 360/5 + 5 * 360/5 or 144 + 360
.	.
.	.
.	.

Notice that for K = 5, the value of A is 360, which results in the same turns as for A = 0. For K = 6 we get A = 72 + 360, the same result as for turning by 72. Thus it seems that values of K greater than or equal to 5 do not generate new **POLY** figures. However, the values K = 1, 2, 3, 4 give four different angles, so it seems that they should generate four different **POLY** figures. Check this on the computer.

Surprisingly, there are only two different **POLY** figures possible with five sides, as shown in Figure 6.2.

Figure 6-2

(a)   (b)

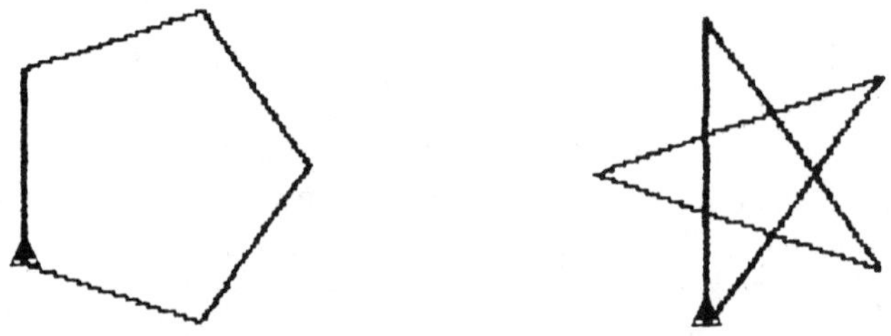

POLY 50 72   POLY 80 144

(c)

(d)

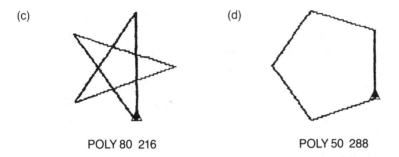

POLY 80 216   POLY 50 288

POLY 50 72 is the same as POLY 50 288 except that the turtle turns to the right in POLY 50 72 and to the left in POLY 50 288. A similar relationship holds for POLY 80 144 and POLY 80 216. Why is this true? Observe that the sum of 72 and 288 is 360. Similarly, 144 + 216 = 360. Thus the sum of the measures of the angles is 360, or one of the angles is 360 minus the other. However, turning RT (360 − 72) is equivalent to turning LT 72. (Why?)

To understand why this phenomenon occurs for any number of sides, notice first that 3 * 360/5 and (5 − 3) * 360/5 (or 360 − 3*360/5) produce POLY figures with the same shape. In general, angle inputs K * 360/N and (N − K)*360/N (or 360 − K*360/N) produce the POLY figures with the same shape. Thus we see that POLY figures occur in pairs.

Now let's apply what we just learned to predict the number of different POLY figures with 10 sides. We have 10*A = K*360, or A = K*360/10. For K = 1 we obtain A = 360/10. Executing POLY 40 36, we obtain a regular polygon with 10 sides. Next let K = 2. Then A = 2*360/10, or 72. If we execute POLY 40 72, we obtain a pentagon rather than a ten-sided figure as we might have expected. Why did this happen?

Notice that 2*360/10 reduces to 1*360/5, which corresponds to N = 5 (rather than N = 10), giving us a pentagon. Thus, in order to obtain POLY figures of 10 sides, we want the 10 in the denominator of K*360/10 not to be reduced with K. Therefore we should substitute only those values of K such that K/10 does not reduce, that is, numbers that have no factors in common with 10. By this rule the allowed values of K are 1, 3, 7, and 9. Because, as we demonstrated, POLY figures occur in pairs (K = 1 and K = 9 produce POLY figures with the same shape, as do K = 3 and K = 7), there are two POLY figures with 10 sides.

To find the number of **POLY** figures possible with N sides, we introduce the concept of relatively prime numbers. Two positive inte-

relatively prime

gers are **relatively prime** if they have no common factors other than 1. For example, 9 and 10 are relatively prime, but 8 and 10 are not relatively prime because they have a common factor of 2. Using this terminology, the allowed values for K in K*360/10 (the turning angle input for 10-sided figures) are those that are relatively prime to 10 and less than 10. The number of **POLY** figures with 10 sides can therefore be expressed as half of the number of positive integers less than 10 that are relatively prime with 10. In general, we have the following answer to our problem:

The number of different **POLY** figures with N sides is half the number of positive integers less than N that are relatively prime to N.

Try to write a procedure that finds the number of positive integers less than N that are relatively prime to N. This and related problems are investigated in the problem set.

rational

Remark: The number of different **POLY** figures with N sides includes those with rational noninteger angle inputs. (A number is **rational** if it can be expressed as a ratio of two integers.) For example, the angle inputs 4 * 360/7, 2 * 360/7 and 3 * 360/7 produce the three different **POLY** figures with 7 sides.

Problem Set 6-5

1. Which inputs for :A in **POLY** produce polygons and which do not?

2. Without using the computer, predict the number of sides generated by the **POLY** procedure for each of the following values of :A.

(a) 5   (b) 30   (c) 80   (d) 31   (e) 17

(f) 100   (g) 104   (h) 160   (i) 162   (j) 121

3. Use the **POLYCOUNT** procedure below to check your predictions from Problem 2.

```
TO POLYCOUNT :S :A
DRAW
NUM1 :S :A 1
END

TO NUM1 :S :A :N
FD :S RT :A
IF HEADING = 0 PRINT :N STOP
NUM1 :S :A :N+1
END
```

4. Find the number of sides of a **POLY** figure if :A is −104 degrees.

5. (a) Find the number of different **POLY** figures with the following numbers of sides:

     (i) 17   (ii) 31   (iii) 20

   (b) Use the **POLY** procedure to draw all the **POLY** figures with the following number of sides:

     (i) 11   (ii) 20

6. The following procedure for finding the greatest common divisor (GCD) of two nonnegative integers :A and :B, where :A>:B, makes use of a method called the **Euclidean Algorithm.** Type this procedure into your computer and then answer the following questions.

Euclidean Algorithm

```
TO GCD :A :B
IF :B = 0 OUTPUT :A
OUTPUT GCD :B (REMAINDER :A :B)
END
```

   (a) The **GCD** procedure above is based on the assumption that :A > :B. Run **GCD 18 12** and **GCD 12 18**. Explain why both give a correct result.

   (b) Use the **GCD** procedure to write a procedure that finds the number of positive integers that are less than :N and relatively prime to :N, where :N is a positive integer.

(c) Write a procedure that finds the number of different POLY figures with :N sides.

(d) How many different POLY figures are there with 360 sides?

7. Use the fact that LCM(A,B)*GCD(A,B) = A*B and the GCD procedure from Problem 6 to write a procedure for finding the LCM of any two nonnegative integers.

☆8. (a) Find an expression for the number of sides N of POLY for the turning angle input :A/:B, where :A and :B are positive integers and the fraction is in simplest form.

(b) Use the expression developed in part (a) to find the number of sides of POLY for the following angle inputs:

(i) 22.5   (ii) 14.4   (iii) 720/11   (iv) 144.1

Solution to the Preliminary Problem

Understanding the Problem

The problem is to write a recursive procedure that can be used to draw squares inscribed in squares, as shown in Figure 6-3.

Figure 6-3

After the first and largest square is drawn, the second square can be obtained by joining the midpoints of the sides of the first square. Then we obtain the third square by joining the midpoints of the sides of the second square, and so on to draw all the squares in the design.

Devising a Plan

We know how to write a **SQUARE** procedure to draw a square of any size :S. Once the first square is drawn, how can we draw the next square? If square ABCD in Figure 6-4 is drawn with the turtle beginning and ending at point A with heading 0, then to get the turtle ready to draw the next square, we need to get it to point E and facing point F. Because **AE** = :S/2 and angle BEF is 45 degrees (why?), we may use the following instructions:

FD :S/2 RT 45

Figure 6-4

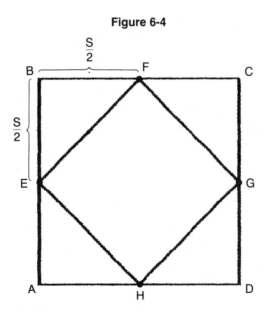

Now the turtle is ready to draw the second square. Before it draws the square, however, we need to know the size of the side of this square. Applying the Pythagorean Theorem to triangle EBF in Figure 6-4, we have:

$$EF^2 = \left(\frac{S}{2}\right)^2 + \left(\frac{S}{2}\right)^2 \quad \text{or} \quad EF^2 = \frac{S^2}{2} \quad \text{or} \quad EF = \frac{S}{\sqrt{2}}$$

In general, the side of any square (starting from the second largest) equals the length of a side of the next larger square divided by $\sqrt{2}$. We call our procedure **NESTEDSQS** and utilize recursion by calling **NESTEDSQS** with an input equal to the current input divided by $\sqrt{2}$. If we want the procedure to stop when the squares get too small, we may include a line in the **NESTEDSQS** procedure to stop when the side length is less than, say, 10.

Carrying Out the Plan

The steps explained above can be combined into the following NESTEDSQS procedure:

```
TO NESTEDSQS :S
IF :S < 10 STOP
SQUARE :S
FD :S/2 RT 45
NESTEDSQS :S/SQRT 2
END
```

Looking Back

We could take a slightly different approach to the problem by drawing the smallest square first and then progressively drawing larger squares.

The problem can be generalized to figures other than squares. For example, we could start with a rectangle and then join its sides to obtain the second figure, and so on.

Chapter 6 Problem Set

1. (a) Write a procedure that will calculate the value of :X^3 + 3 * :X + 6 for a given input :X.

   (b) Write a procedure that will print out all the values of :X^3 + 3 * :X + 6 for all the integral values of :X from 1 through a given number :N.

2. The following sequence starts with the numbers 1, 1, 1. Each successive term is the sum of the previous three terms. Thus, the first few terms of the sequence are 1, 1, 1, 3, 5, 9, 17, 31, ...

   (a) Write a procedure to print the first n terms of the sequence.

   (b) Write a procedure to find the nth term of the sequence.

   (c) Write a procedure to find the sum of the first n terms of the sequence.

3. The following **FIB2** procedure uses the recursive definition of the Fibonacci sequence:

   ```
   TO FIB2 :A :B :N
   IF :N = 1 OUTPUT :A
   IF :N = 2 OUTPUT :B
   OUTPUT (FIB2 :A :B :N – 1) + (FIB2 :A :B :N – 2)
   END
   ```

   Run FIB2 1 1 4 and FIB2 1 1 15. What do you observe? Explain the reason for what happened.

4. Write a procedure that outputs at random an integer less than a given integer B and greater than or equal to another integer A.

5. (a) Write a procedure that evaluates how frequently a given sum is obtained when the experiment of rolling two dice is repeated a given number of times.

   (b) Use your procedure from (a) to find out which sum occurs most frequently.

6. The following procedure, **DPOLY**, is a type of **POLY** procedure in which each time the turtle turns twice as much as in the previous turn. Run the procedure for several inputs. Why does the procedure stop so quickly?

   ```
   TO DPOLY :S :A
   FD :S RT :A
   DPOLY :S :A*2
   END
   ```

7. For any integer input, :A, edit the **DPOLY** procedure of problem 6 so that it will not stop. (Hint: for any integer angle :A, RT :A is equivalent to **RT (REMAINDER :A   360)**.)

8. Run the following **HPOLY** procedure for several different inputs and compare the results with the outcomes of **DPOLY** for corresponding inputs. What do you notice? Why?

    ```
    TO HPOLY :S :A
    FD :S RT :A
    HPOLY :S HEADING
    END
    ```

9. Write a procedure that draws a variable size circle and a square inscribed in that circle.

☆10. Write recursive procedures with **STOP** statements that draw the following figures. In (a) and (b) the triangles are equilateral. In (b) the figures inside the triangles are squares. In (c) the triangle is equilateral and each segment drawn is perpendicular to one of the sides of the triangle.

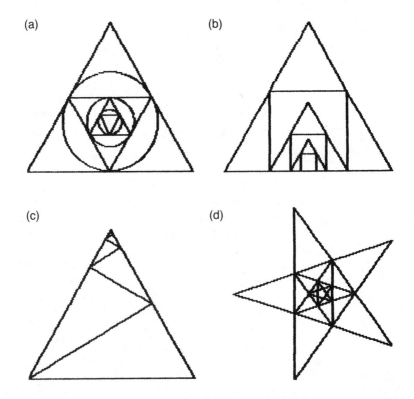

(a)   (b)

(c)   (d)

☆☆11. Logo includes several trigonometric functions as primitives. Among them are SIN, COS, and ATAN, which stand for sine, cosine, and arctangents respectively. Both SIN and COS take one input as an angle in degrees. They output the sine and cosine, respectively. ATAN takes two numeric inputs and outputs an angle whose tangent is the first input divided by the second input. The angle is expressed in degrees between 0 and 360. Use these commands as needed to draw the sun figure shown below.

SIN
COS
ATAN

7

New Vocabulary in Chapter 7

Terms	Primitives	Shape Editor Commands and Procedures
simulation p. 287	READCHARACTER (RC) p. 306	SETUP p. 317
algorithm p. 288		MAKESHAPE p. 317
animation p. 303	RC? p. 307	U p. 318
character buffer p. 305	CLEARINPUT p. 308	D p. 318
queue p. 305	PADDLE(0) p. 326	← p. 318
Logo Shape Editor p. 317	PADDLE(1) p. 326	→ p. 318
		CTRL-P p. 318
		CTRL-N p. 318
		CTRL-C p. 318
		CTRL-G p. 318
		SAVESHAPES p. 318
		INITSHAPES p. 319
		SETSHAPE p. 319
		SIZE p. 319

Preliminary Problem

Write a set of procedures to draw a figure similar to the one shown above.

7

Applications of Turtle Graphics

Introduction

This chapter uses the Logo commands introduced in previous chapters to investigate several new topics. In the first several sections we do some experiments in which the turtle imitates simple animal-like behaviors. The next sections examine procedures that can be used in games and simulations. In the last sections we show how to develop Logo games and use the Logo Shape Editor to enhance games.

7-1 Radio Transmitter Simulation

In this section we pose several problems that can be solved with the help of the turtle by using a Logo simulation. A **simulation** is a program that allows the computer to imitate some kind of behavior. In this chapter the simulations deal with the behavior of robots and animals.

simulation

Suppose we want to program a robot to find a small stationary radio transmitter in a very large room. A device will be installed in the robot to allow it to detect whether a radio signal from the transmitter is becoming stronger or weaker and in this way to detect if the robot is getting closer or farther from the radio.

Developing an Algorithm

algorithm

Our first step is to develop a set of instructions for the robot to follow in finding the radio transmitter. A general set of instructions for accomplishing a task is often called an **algorithm,** after the ninth-century Arabian mathematician Al-Khowarizmi. Once we have these instructions, we can model the robot's behavior by translating the algorithm into Logo procedures so that the turtle can simulate the robot's searching method.

Suppose the robot starts at a reference point and moves one unit forward from this point. If the robot is closer to the transmitter than it was before the step, the robot assumes that its path is good; it resets the reference point to the new location and then repeats the algorithm. However, if the robot is farther from the transmitter than before, it moves back to the old reference point, turns right one degree, and then repeats the algorithm. In this manner, the robot searches for a position that brings it closer to the transmitter than it was previously. If each reference point brings the robot closer to its destination than the previous reference point, the robot should eventually find the radio.

What would the robot's path to the transmitter look like? Would it take a long time for the robot to reach the transmitter, or would the algorithm lead the robot there almost immediately? These are the kind of questions that the manufacturer of the robot might want to answer before actually building the robot. Answering these questions without the computer might require a great deal of time or special insight. A simulation, however, checks the algorithm and quickly shows us how the robot behaves.

We use the words "closer" and "farther" in the proposed algorithm. What should these words mean to the robot? Both refer to the robot's distance from the radio. The proposed algorithm compares two distances: the distance from the reference point to the transmitter (the old distance) and the distance from the robot to the transmitter after it has moved forward from the reference point (the new distance). The robot stores these two distances, :OLDISTANCE and :NEWDISTANCE. If :NEWDISTANCE is less than :OLDISTANCE, the robot is closer to the radio transmitter; otherwise it is farther away.

We write a procedure called CLOSER? that makes this comparison. The CLOSER? procedure, shown below, compares the global variables (defined using MAKE statements) :NEWDISTANCE and :OLDISTANCE and outputs TRUE if the turtle is closer to the transmitter after making a step and FALSE otherwise.

```
TO CLOSER?
IF :NEWDISTANCE < :OLDISTANCE OUTPUT "TRUE ELSE OUTPUT
    "FALSE
END
```

Remark: The CLOSER? procedure outputs TRUE only if the turtle is closer to the radio than it was before the move. Notice that it is possible (although unlikely) that the turtle will not be able to find a closer position. In this case the algorithm will not allow the turtle to reach the transmitter.

Using the DISTANCE Procedure

We now consider how to simulate the robot's transmitter-sensing device. We want this device to compute the distance from the robot to the radio based on the signal strength. We store the x- and y-coordinates of the radio as the global variables :XRAD and :YRAD respectively. In the simulation we allow the turtle to use coordinates to calculate the distance from the robot to the transmitter. To find the distance from the turtle to the radio, we use the DISTANCE procedure of Chapter 5, shown below for easy reference.

```
TO DISTANCE :X1 :Y1 :X2 :Y2
OUTPUT SQRT((:X1 − :X2)*(:X1 − :X2) + (:Y1 − :Y2)*(:Y1 − :Y2))
END
```

Once the coordinates of the turtle and the radio are determined, the distance between the turtle and the radio can be determined by calling DISTANCE XCOR YCOR :XRAD :YRAD.

Incorporating the Algorithm

Finally, we are ready to incorporate the planned algorithm into a procedure called **SEARCH**. A step-by-step outline of the way the procedure works follows.

Search Procedure Outline

1. Compute the distance from the reference point to the radio.

2. Move forward one unit from the reference point.

3. Compute the new distance from the turtle to the radio.

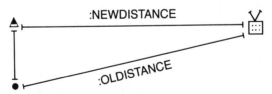

4. If :NEWDISTANCE<:OLDISTANCE, the new location becomes the reference point; that is, we **MAKE** "OLDISTANCE :NEWDISTANCE, and the process starts anew.

5. If :NEWDISTANCE>:OLDISTANCE, the turtle returns to the old
    reference point (back one unit), turns right one degree, and starts
    the process again to search for a better (closer) reference point.

This outline can be translated into a Logo procedure, as follows:

```
TO SEARCH
FD 1
MAKE "NEWDISTANCE DISTANCE XCOR YCOR :XRAD :YRAD
IF CLOSER? MAKE "OLDISTANCE :NEWDISTANCE ELSE BK 1 RT 1
SEARCH
END
```

Debugging the Search Algorithm

In our Logo simulation, CLOSER? and DISTANCE output data to
SEARCH, the main procedure. However, the SEARCH procedure contains several bugs. First, when Logo executes DISTANCE, it responds
with an error message because :XRAD and :YRAD have not been defined.
When SEARCH is executed, there is also a bug because :OLDISTANCE
is undefined in CLOSER?.

One option for debugging SEARCH is to introduce variables in
the title line, such as SEARCH :XRAD :YRAD, and then compute the
value of :OLDISTANCE in the first line of SEARCH. This is inefficient
because the DISTANCE procedure is called twice in each pass through
SEARCH. A better solution is to create a new procedure called
STARTUP1 in which :XRAD, :YRAD, and :OLDISTANCE are defined as
global variables with MAKE statements. For example, if the coordinates of the radio are (20,30), then the STARTUP1 procedure would
appear as shown on page 292.

```
TO STARTUP1
MAKE "XRAD 20
MAKE "YRAD 30
MAKE "OLDISTANCE DISTANCE XCOR YCOR :XRAD :YRAD
SEARCH
END
```

If we execute the simulation for the values of :XRAD and :YRAD given in STARTUP1 and with a turtle at home with heading of 0, the path of the search is shown in Figure 7-1.

Figure 7-1

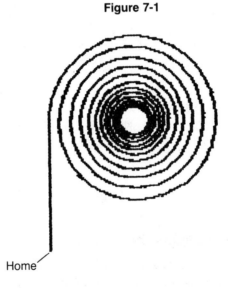

Home

At present, the SEARCH procedure does not stop until a CTRL-G is typed. Therefore, we modify SEARCH to stop the turtle automatically when it is within ten units of the radio by adding the line IF :NEWDISTANCE<10 STOP after the line MAKE "NEWDISTANCE DISTANCE XCOR YCOR :XRAD :YRAD.

Improving the Search Algorithm

How could we change the algorithm to allow the turtle to reach the radio transmitter faster? In Figure 7-1, the turtle's path is somewhat circular. This seems to be the result of the RT 1 statement in SEARCH. We experiment with this part of the procedure to see what happens if we turn the turtle right by an angle other than one degree when a closer reference point is not discovered.

By experimentation, we find that an improvement to the algorithm is a substitution of **RT 30** in place of **RT 1**. This modification to the **SEARCH** procedure creates the path shown in Figure 7-2.

Figure 7-2

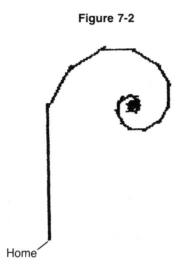

Home

Although this path is the shortest and fastest path to the radio so far, it would be wrong to conclude that there is no shorter and faster path that can be obtained using this algorithm. Experiment with other angles to try to find an angle that seems to create the fastest and shortest path to the radio.

Problem Set 7-1

1. Varying the angle in the **SEARCH** procedure caused a variation in the turtle's path. What angle do you think produces the shortest path possible for this algorithm? Does this angle produce the shortest path even if the radio is moved to another location?

2. Is the turtle capable of finding the radio regardless of where the radio is placed and regardless of the angle used in the **SEARCH** procedure?

3. Edit the procedures in this section to place the turtle and radio on the screen at random positions and give the turtle a random angle to use in searching for the radio.

4. (a) Assume that the radio transmitter rolls along the y-axis at the same speed that the robot moves. How can you simulate this new situation by adding exactly one line to the **SEARCH** procedure?

   (b) After making the modification in (a), execute the simulation. Can the robot find the radio now? Why or why not?

7-2 Fox-and-Hare Simulation

A second simulation involves two animals moving simultaneously. One animal, the fox, chases the second animal, the hare. The fox runs directly towards the hare and the hare runs directly away from the fox. Initially, let us assume that both animals run at the same rate. The problem is to simulate these two interacting animals using only one turtle. We can use the solution to this problem as a basis for investigating other simulations in which more than two animals interact.

Developing the Chase Algorithm

Assume that the fox starts at a point F and the hare starts at a point H. The turtle first plays the role of the fox by putting its pen up, moving to point F, and taking one step toward the hare with the pen down to mark the path. The turtle then plays the hare by putting its pen up, moving to point H, putting its pen down, and taking one step away from the fox. This process is repeated until the user stops the chase. The chase algorithm is outlined below.

1. The turtle moves to point F to simulate the fox.

●
H

F

2. The turtle points towards the hare and moves forward, marking the path. The turtle's new position is now the fox's new position, F.

3. The turtle moves to point H with its pen up to simulate the hare.

4. The turtle points away from the fox and moves forward, marking the path. The turtle's new position is the hare's new position, H.

5. The process is repeated.

Developing the CHASE Procedure

We first write a CHASE procedure that incorporates the concept of the two-role turtle.

```
TO CHASE
BE.THE.FOX
BE.THE.HARE
CHASE
END
```

The procedures BE.THE.FOX and BE.THE.HARE do the actual moving of the turtle. To do the moving, we assign coordinate values to points

F and H. We call the coordinates of the fox :XFOX and :YFOX and the coordinates of the hare :XHARE and :YHARE. As in the last section, these variables will be global. The procedure BE.THE.FOX moves the turtle to point F(:XFOX, :YFOX), points the turtle toward the hare, moves the turtle forward one unit, and records this new position as F. The last step is necessary because the turtle later returns to this new point to play the role of the fox again. The procedure BE.THE.HARE does essentially the same thing as BE.THE.FOX except that BE.THE.HARE moves the turtle to H(:XHARE, :YHARE) and moves it one step away from the fox. We assume that for the hare to move away from the fox, the animals must have the same heading.

```
TO BE.THE.FOX
PU
SETXY :XFOX :YFOX
SETHEADING TOWARDS :XHARE :YHARE
PD
FD 1
MAKE "XFOX XCOR
MAKE "YFOX YCOR
END


TO BE.THE.HARE
PU
SETXY :XHARE :YHARE
PD
FD 1
MAKE "XHARE XCOR
MAKE "YHARE YCOR
END
```

Before beginning the simulation, we create a procedure called STARTUP2 that sets initial values for the global variables :XFOX, :YFOX, :XHARE, and :YHARE.

```
TO STARTUP2
MAKE "XFOX 0
MAKE "YFOX 0
MAKE "XHARE 30
MAKE "YHARE 30
CHASE
END
```

If you test this simulation, you may find that the fox cannot catch the hare if they are initially set more than one unit apart. For example, if the fox starts at (0,0) and the hare at (30,30), a portion of their paths looks like Figure 7-3.

Figure 7-3

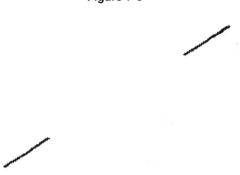

This procedure must be stopped by CTRL-G. As an exercise, design a procedure for stopping **CHASE** without the use of CTRL-G.

Further Explorations

Variations of **BE.THE.FOX** and **BE.THE.HARE** create more interesting results. For example, if the hare maintains a 90-degree bearing relative to the fox instead of a 180-degree bearing, thus exposing its side to the fox, the paths appear as in Figure 7-4.

Figure 7-4

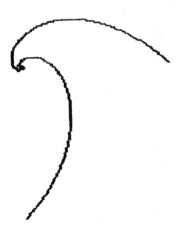

If we now modify the fox's speed to be one quarter of the hare's speed, the paths form spirals, as shown in Figure 7-5.

Figure 7-5

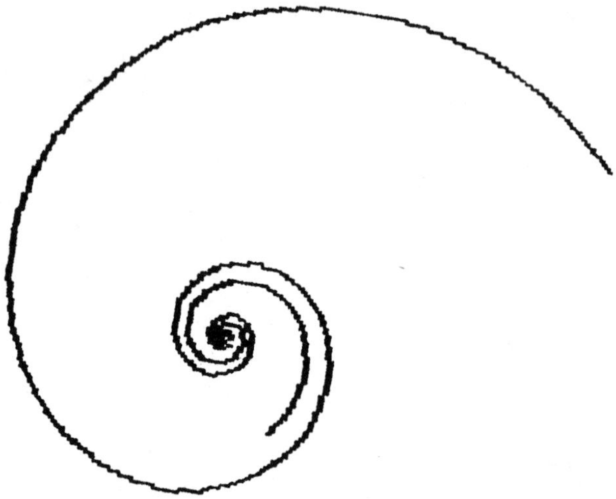

Further explorations reveal other interesting paths involving the two animals. We pose questions about the effects of variations of the chase algorithm in the problem set.

Problem Set 7-2

1. (a) Modify the **BE.THE.HARE** procedure so that the hare sets an entirely random heading each time it moves.

    (b) Now can the fox catch the hare?

    (c) Can the fox catch the hare if the hare moves at twice the speed of the fox?

2. (a) Edit **BE.THE.HARE** back to its original form. Now, modify **BE.THE.FOX** to move forward two units rather than one and keep a heading 45 to the right of the hare rather than a direct heading.

    (b) What happens to the two paths now?

3. Modify the procedures in this section to stop the **CHASE** proce-
    dure when the fox is within a distance of 5 units from the hare.

7-3 Four-Bugs Simulation

The four-bugs problem is a well-known mathematical problem that
can be simulated using Logo. Four bugs are located at the four vertices
of a square—one bug at each vertex—as shown in Figure 7-6.

Figure 7-6

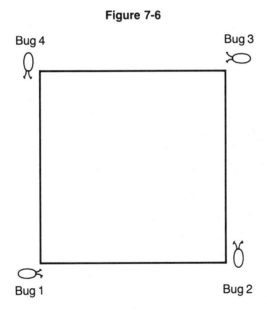

Bug 1 is attracted to Bug 2, Bug 2 to Bug 3, Bug 3 to Bug 4, and
Bug 4 to Bug 1. Bug 1 begins by taking a step in the direction of Bug
2. Bug 2 in turn takes a step toward Bug 3. Bug 3 and Bug 4 behave
similarly. When it is Bug 1's turn to move again, it adjusts its heading
to point toward Bug 2's new position. The problem is to simulate the
paths of the four bugs. Do you think any of the bugs will ever reach
each other? A computer simulation can be used to investigate this
question.

Developing the Interact Procedure

In this simulation the turtle plays four roles, but the concept is basically the same as that of the previous two-animal (fox and hare) simulation. The main procedure here is comparable to the **CHASE** procedure in that simulation. It instructs the turtle to play four roles.

```
TO INTERACT
BE.BUG1
BE.BUG2
BE.BUG3
BE.BUG4
INTERACT
END
```

The **INTERACT** procedure must be recursive because after each of the four bugs has taken a step in the direction of the bug it is chasing, the procedure must be repeated to continue the chase. The procedures called by **INTERACT** are **BE.BUG1**, **BE.BUG2**, **BE.BUG3**, and **BE.BUG4**. These procedures are basically alike. For example, **BE.BUG1** lifts the pen up, moves the turtle to the current position of Bug 1, sets the turtle's heading towards Bug 2, and moves forward one unit with the pen down to mark Bug 1's path. Because Bug 1's location has changed, its new postion must be saved in order for the turtle to return to this point. We call Bug 1's x- and y-coordinates :X1 and :Y1, respectively; Bug 2's coordinates are :X2 and :Y2, and so on. The coordinates of the bugs are stored as global variables. **BE.BUG1** can now be written as follows:

```
TO BE.BUG1
PU
SETXY :X1 :Y1
PD
SETHEADING TOWARDS :X2 :Y2
FD 1
MAKE "X1 XCOR
MAKE "Y1 YCOR
END
```

We define the other bug procedures similarly.

```
TO BE.BUG2
PU
SETXY :X2 :Y2
PD
SETHEADING TOWARDS :X3 :Y3
FD 1
MAKE "X2 XCOR
MAKE "Y2 YCOR
END


TO BE.BUG3
PU
SETXY :X3 :Y3
PD
SETHEADING TOWARDS :X4 :Y4
FD 1
MAKE "X3 XCOR
MAKE "Y3 YCOR
END


TO BE.BUG4
PU
SETXY :X4 :Y4
PD
SETHEADING TOWARDS :X1 :Y1
FD 1
MAKE "X4 XCOR
MAKE "Y4 YCOR
END
```

We now have five procedures: one procedure to tell the turtle in which order to interact, and four other procedures to tell the turtle how to interact. A **STARTUP3** procedure is necessary to set initial values for the global x- and y-coordinates of the four bugs and to call **INTERACT** to begin the simulation. If we choose the lengths of the sides of the square on which the bugs begin to be 100 units, the STARTUP3 procedure may appear as shown below.

```
TO STARTUP3
MAKE "X1 0
MAKE "Y1 0
MAKE "X2 100
MAKE "Y2 0
MAKE "X3 100
MAKE "Y3 100
MAKE "X4 0
MAKE "Y4 100
INTERACT
END
```

We are now ready to execute the simulation. The paths generated by the four bugs are shown in Figure 7-7. To stop the simulation, we type CTRL-G.

Figure 7-7

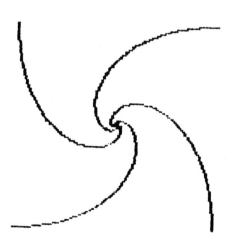

This simulation seems to indicate that each bug not only finds its friend but in fact meets all the other bugs. Where do these four bugs meet? To investigate where the bugs meet, we allow the simulation to run for some time and print the x- and y-coordinates of the turtle using the **XCOR** and **YCOR** primitives. If we do not abort the simulation too early, we find that the four bugs meet at the point

(50,50) or at least extremely close to this point. Notice that this point is the center of the square (point where diagonals cross) on which the four bugs started. This is not a proof that the four bugs always meet at the center of the square on which they start, but it is evidence that they probably meet in the center. Different size squares can be used to explore whether this is always true.

Problem Set 7-3

1. (a) Modify the four-bugs simulation so that Bug 2 heads for the upper right vertex of the square regardless of Bug 3's location.

    (b) How many bugs (other than Bug 2) are affected by Bug 2's new path?

    (c) Do the four bugs still meet? If so, where? If not, why not?

2. Rewrite the procedures in this section to have the bugs start on the vertices of a rectangle with randomly chosen side lengths between 50 and 100.

☆3. (a) Create a simulation for three bugs located at the vertices of an equilateral triangle.

    (b) Do the three bugs meet? If so, where?

☆4. (a) Create a simulation for six bugs located at the vertices of a regular hexagon.

    (b) Where do the six bugs meet? Is this the center of the hexagon?

7-4 Animation

In this section we discuss simple animation of the turtle, review some important Logo commands and principles, and introduce several new ones. **Animation** is the state in which the turtle is constantly in motion.   **animation**

To demonstrate the simplest form of animation, try the following procedure on your computer.

```
TO ANIMATE
FD 1
ANIMATE
END
```

In Logo, the turtle stops after executing a command and awaits the next command. We wish to create a set of procedures that keeps the turtle constantly in motion, as the **ANIMATE** procedure does, but also allows the user to interact with the moving turtle. To avoid interruption of the turtle's motion, we would like to be able to type in commands to the turtle as it moves. To communicate with a constantly moving turtle, certain keys can be made to represent certain commands. For example, we could designate the R key to mean **RIGHT** 10 and the L key to mean **LEFT 10**. Then, when R or L is pushed, the turtle turns right 10 degrees or left 10 degrees without any apparent stop in motion. If any other key is pushed, the **ANIMATE** procedure continues without turtle reaction.

Our first step is to modify the **ANIMATE** procedure to call a second procedure that causes the turtle to take action if the R or L key has been pressed. We call this second procedure **CHECK**. The edited **ANIMATE** procedure is given below.

```
TO ANIMATE
FD 1
CHECK
ANIMATE
END
```

The **CHECK** procedure in turn calls a third procedure, **READKEY**, which returns to **CHECK** the key that was pressed. **CHECK** then determines if this key was an R or an L.

```
TO CHECK
MAKE "KEYPRESSED READKEY
IF :KEYPRESSED = "R RT 10 STOP
IF :KEYPRESSED = "L LT 10 STOP
END
```

Notice the use of STOP on the third and fourth lines of CHECK. When the correct key is found, the procedure stops without further unnecessary searching. For example, if R is the correct key, the line IF :KEYPRESSED = "R RT 10 STOP is executed, and the procedure ends. There is no need to check whether the key was an L because the procedure has already discovered that an R was pressed. In a procedure with many IF statements, the use of STOP saves time by avoiding unnecessary checks. With only two items to check, the use of STOP is not really necessary, but we include it as a good programming technique.

Developing the READKEY Procedure

The READKEY procedure must use an OUTPUT statement to return the value or name of the pressed key to the CHECK procedure. READKEY must also output something to CHECK even when a key has not been pressed. If READKEY fails to output, there is an error in line MAKE "KEYPRESSED READKEY because KEYPRESSED has no value to take. Thus, if a key has been pressed, READKEY should output that key, and if no key has been pressed, READKEY should output a blank character to avoid an error in CHECK. Before actually writing the READKEY procedure, we must introduce the concept of the character buffer and the Logo commands RC? and READCHARACTER.

The **character buffer** is a section of computer memory that stores characters entered from the keyboard until the computer is ready to use them. For example, if we begin typing while a procedure is being executed, that text does not appear on the screen immediately. Instead, the characters are stored in the buffer until the procedure is done and the computer is ready to accept text. At that point, the computer begins emptying the buffer character by character in the order in which the characters were entered. To better understand this, we can represent the buffer by a structure known as a **queue**. Assume that

character buffer

queue

we wish to type DRAW, so we enter the characters D,R,A,W into the buffer. First D goes in the queue, as shown in Figure 7-8.

Figure 7-8

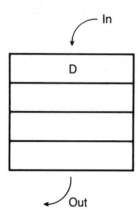

The characters R, A, and W follow D in the way shown as in Figure 7-9. Each character enters at the top of the queue and pushes the preceding one further down.

Figure 7-9

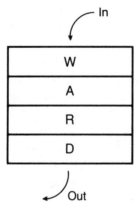

When the computer is ready to read from the buffer, it first reads D, the first character entered. Then it reads the R, followed by A and then finally by W.

READCHARACTER (RC)

The Logo primitives READCHARACTER and RC? are directly related to the buffer. The **READCHARACTER (RC)** command simply outputs the first character in the buffer; it waits for a character to be entered into the buffer if the buffer is empty. The **RC?** command outputs TRUE if there is at least one character in the buffer, that is, if one or more keys have been pressed and FALSE otherwise.

RC?

Using RC, we now write a READKEY procedure to output the first character in the buffer to the CHECK procedure.

TO READKEY
OUTPUT RC
END

Unfortunately, there is a problem in this procedure. If no keys have been pressed and the buffer is empty, the RC command stops the procedure and waits until a key is pressed. This in turn stops the turtle. Since we intended READKEY to output a blank character if no key had been pressed, we must make a slight modification to make READKEY work correctly.

TO READKEY
IF RC? OUTPUT RC ELSE OUTPUT [   ]
END

The statement OUTPUT [   ] outputs a blank character if no key has been pressed.

Stopping the ANIMATE Procedure

We can now execute ANIMATE, preferably with the pen up, and use R and L to control the turtle. Since we have not included any stopping conditions in the ANIMATE procedure, CTRL-G is required to stop it. It would be more convenient if we could stop the procedure automatically by typing s instead. Try to modify the procedure to produce this result before you read further.

To make the stop modification, we edit the CHECK procedure to determine whether s was pressed. We also must decide what is to be done if s is pressed. One possibility is to write IF :KEYPRESSED = "S STOP. We insert this line in the CHECK procedure and execute ANIMATE. Unfortunately, we find that pressing s does not stop the procedure!

The reason our stop modification did not work is that since CHECK was called by ANIMATE, CHECK is obligated to return to the ANIMATE procedure when CHECK is stopped. However, the next line in ANI-MATE is the recursive call that starts the procedure again. We therefore need to free the CHECK procedure from its obligation to return to ANIMATE. The TOPLEVEL primitive will do this; it aborts the current procedure as well as all calling procedures. Whereas STOP stops only the current procedure and returns control to the calling procedure, TOPLEVEL stops everything. The edited CHECK procedure looks like this:

```
TO CHECK
MAKE "KEYPRESSED READKEY
IF :KEYPRESSED = "R RT 10 STOP
IF :KEYPRESSED = "L LT 10 STOP
IF :KEYPRESSED = "S TOPLEVEL
END
```

Controlling the Turtle in ANIMATE

We now execute ANIMATE again and experiment with controlling the turtle. Quickly typing R many times or using R with the REPEAT feature for a few seconds (pressing R and the REPT key simultaneously on the Apple II +, or keeping the R key down on the Apple IIe or IIc) may make the turtle fail to respond to a typed L or S because the buffer may be full of R's. We can avoid this problem by using the **CLEARINPUT** command, which clears the buffer entirely. If we overuse this command, however, the buffer will always be empty, and the turtle will again appear unresponsive. We can clear the buffer occasionally by adding the following line to CHECK.

CLEARINPUT

```
IF (RANDOM 10) = 1 CLEARINPUT
```

Such a statement clears the buffer on approximately one out of every ten passes through CHECK.

Modifying the CHECK Procedure

Other features may be added to the CHECK procedure. For example, we can make keys represent other commands, such as U for PENUP, D for PENDOWN, and B for PENCOLOR 5 (Blue). Next, suppose we want the turtle to move 1 step when 1 is typed, 5 steps when 2 is typed, and 10 steps when 3 is typed. To do this, we must modify both **ANIMATE** and **CHECK**. The statement FD 1 in the **ANIMATE** procedure must be replaced by FD :SPEED, where :SPEED is a global variable taking the values 1, 5, or 10. The edited procedure is given below.

```
TO ANIMATE
FD :SPEED
CHECK
ANIMATE
END
```

The **CHECK** procedure must also be modified as follows:

```
TO CHECK
IF (RANDOM 10) = 1 CLEARINPUT
MAKE "KEYPRESSED READKEY
IF :KEYPRESSED = "R RT 10 STOP
IF :KEYPRESSED = "L LT 10 STOP
IF :KEYPRESSED = "S TOPLEVEL
IF :KEYPRESSED = "1 MAKE "SPEED 1 STOP
IF :KEYPRESSED = "2 MAKE "SPEED 5 STOP
IF :KEYPRESSED = "3 MAKE "SPEED 10
END
```

Finally, a **STARTUP4** procedure is necessary to set an initial value for :SPEED.

```
TO STARTUP4
MAKE "SPEED 1
ANIMATE
END
```

Instead of a three-speed turtle, we could have created a nine-speed turtle in which the keys 1 through 9 represent values of :SPEED from 1 to 9.

Track Games

We now incorporate our animation procedures into a game in which the turtle simulates a car that is to be driven around a narrow circular track. This game might have applications, for example, in improving the manipulative skills of young children. Using an **RCIRCLE** procedure similar to the one in Chapter 3, we draw two circles with centers at the origin (home). We give the smaller circle a radius of thirty units and the larger circle a radius of fifty units. These two concentric circles create a track of width 20 units, as shown in Figure 7-10.

Figure 7-10

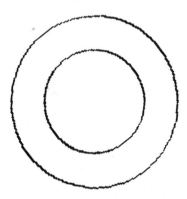

Now we edit the **STARTUP4** procedure as shown below to draw the track and set the car on the track. Because every point on the inner part of the track is 30 units from the origin and every point on the outer part of the track is 50 units from the origin, the point ($-40,0$) is definitely on the track.

```
TO STARTUP4
DRAW PU  SETXY  − 30 0  PD
RCIRCLE 30
PU  SETXY  − 50 0  PD
RCIRCLE 50
PU  SETXY  − 40 0
MAKE "SPEED 1
ANIMATE
END
```

```
TO RCIRCLE :RADIUS
REPEAT 360 [FD :RADIUS*3.14159/180  RT 1]
END
```

Next, we edit the **ANIMATE** procedure to check whether the car has gone off the track, in which case a procedure named **OFF.TRACK** will be called to print YOU WENT OFF THE TRACK and terminate the game. If the car's distance from the origin is less than or equal to 30 units or greater than or equal to 50 units, we know that it is no longer between the two concentric circles that form the track and therefore has gone off the track. A **DISTANCE.ORIGIN** procedure that calls the **DISTANCE** procedure of Chapter 5 to output the turtle's distance from the origin is given below.

```
TO DISTANCE.ORIGIN
OUTPUT DISTANCE XCOR   YCOR   0   0
END
```

ALLOF (DISTANCE.ORIGIN>30)(DISTANCE.ORIGIN<50) outputs TRUE if the car's position is between the circles and FALSE otherwise. We now add this statement to **ANIMATE**, as follows:

```
TO ANIMATE
FD :SPEED
CHECK
IF NOT (ALLOF (DISTANCE.ORIGIN>30) (DISTANCE.ORIGIN<50))
  OFF.TRACK
ANIMATE
END
```

Since **NOT FALSE** is equivalent to **TRUE** and **NOT TRUE** is equivalent to **FALSE**, the statement NOT (ALLOF (DISTANCE.ORIGIN>30) (DISTANCE.ORIGIN<50)) outputs TRUE if the car has gone off the track. The **OFF.TRACK** procedure, which is called if the car goes off the track, is given below.

```
TO OFF.TRACK
PRINT [YOU WENT OFF THE TRACK]
TOPLEVEL
END
```

Remark: Without the **TOPLEVEL** command, **OFF.TRACK** would be forced to return to **ANIMATE** after printing its message.

Our choice for the shape of the track is a good one because it makes it easy to find out whether the car is on the track. A track like the one in Figure 7-11 may be more interesting, but it is also much more difficult to check if the car is off the track.

Figure 7-11

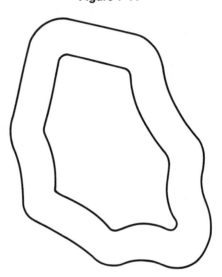

Testing a triangular track like the one in Figure 7-12 would also be difficult because points on the track are not a fixed distance from any given point.

Figure 7-12

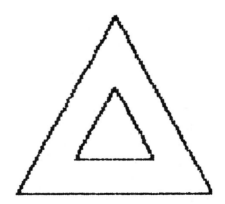

Summary of Commands	
READCHARACTER (RC)	Takes no inputs. Outputs the first character in the character buffer and waits for a character to be entered into the buffer if the buffer is empty.
RC?	Takes no inputs. Outputs TRUE if the buffer is not empty and FALSE if the buffer is empty.
CLEARINPUT	Takes no inputs. Clears the character buffer.

Problem Set 7-4

1. Try adding at least five new features to the **CHECK** procedure.

2. Using the procedures for animation, create a game in which the user guides the turtle into a randomly placed circle. When the turtle is inside the circle, the game should stop and print a message such as YOU MADE IT.

3. Modify the track game to make it impossible for the car to leave the track. When the car reaches the edge of the track, the procedure should move it slightly to place it back on the track.

4. Recall the fox-hare simulation in Section 7-2. Create a set of procedures in which the user controls one of the two turtles and the computer guides the other.

5. Recall the four-bugs simulation in Section 7-3. Combine this simulation with the procedures for animation so that one of the four bugs is controlled by the user.

7-5 Creating a Game

In the last section we introduced animation and an application of it in a game. In this section we introduce and develop procedures for a strategy game using animation, the Secret Point Game. In our game, the computer randomly selects a secret point on the screen. The user controls the animated turtle with the R and L keys. After each move the turtle makes, the computer prints CLOSER or FARTHER to indicate whether the turtle has moved closer to or farther from the secret point. The object of the game is to bring the turtle within 5 units of the secret point. This game requires the player to devise strategies to find the point, given only the information CLOSER or FARTHER.

Using the concepts of animation introduced in the previous section, we begin writing this game with a main **ANIMATE** procedure followed by **CHECK** and **READKEY**, as follows:

```
TO ANIMATE
FD 1
CHECK
ANIMATE
END
```

```
TO CHECK
MAKE "KEYPRESSED READKEY
IF :KEYPRESSED = "R RT 10 STOP
IF :KEYPRESSED = "L LT 10 STOP
END
```

```
TO READKEY
IF RC? OUTPUT RC ELSE OUTPUT [ ]
END
```

We also need a procedure called **COMPARE** that prints the message CLOSER or FARTHER based on the comparison between the turtle's old distance from the secret point and the turtle's new distance from the point. If :NEWDISTANCE<:OLDISTANCE, the computer should print CLOSER, otherwise, it should print FARTHER. Since the **COMPARE** procedure needs to compare :NEWDISTANCE, the distance after the turtle's move, with :OLDISTANCE, the distance before the move, we must make sure that we have both values available for the **COMPARE** procedure. Since it is inefficient to call the **DISTANCE** procedure twice, once before and once after the move, we give the command MAKE "OLDISTANCE :NEWDISTANCE after the two distances have been compared. We must initialize :OLDISTANCE in a **STARTUP5** procedure so that :OLDISTANCE has a value the first time **COMPARE** is executed. The **STARTUP5** procedure also sets random values for the coordinates of the secret point, which we denote by the global vari-

ables :XSEC and :YSEC. These random values will be created by a
RANDOMCOORDINATE procedure. The modified ANIMATE procedure,
the COMPARE procedure, and the STARTUP5 procedure follow.

```
TO ANIMATE
FD 1
COMPARE
CHECK
ANIMATE
END
```

```
TO COMPARE
MAKE "NEWDISTANCE DISTANCE XCOR YCOR :XSEC :YSEC
IF :NEWDISTANCE<:OLDISTANCE PRINT [CLOSER] ELSE PRINT
   [FARTHER]
MAKE "OLDISTANCE :NEWDISTANCE
END
```

```
TO STARTUP5
MAKE "XSEC RANDOMCOORDINATE
MAKE "YSEC RANDOMCOORDINATE
MAKE "OLDISTANCE DISTANCE XCOR YCOR :XSEC :YSEC
ANIMATE
END
```

We now write the RANDOMCOORDINATE procedure to establish
random values for :XSEC and :YSEC. For the sake of simplicity, we
decide that :XSEC and :YSEC will take random values between -50
and 50. Recall from Section 4 of Chapter 6 that random numbers
from $-$:X to :X are generated by the statement (RANDOM 2*:X + 1) $-$:X.
Numbers from -50 to 50 are therefore generated by the statement
(RANDOM 101) -50. The RANDOMCOORDINATE procedure below
outputs values for :XSEC and :YSEC.

```
TO RANDOMCOORDINATE
OUTPUT (RANDOM 101) - 50
END
```

This game is supposed to stop when the turtle is within 5 units
of the secret point. By adding the line IF :NEWDISTANCE<5 TOPLEVEL
to the COMPARE procedure we can stop both the COMPARE procedure

and the calling **ANIMATE** procedure when the turtle is within five units of the secret point. We can improve our game further by adding a procedure called **MESSAGE**, which is called by **COMPARE** when the secret point is found.

```
TO COMPARE
MAKE "NEWDISTANCE DISTANCE XCOR YCOR :XSEC :YSEC
IF :NEWDISTANCE<5 MESSAGE
IF :NEWDISTANCE<:OLDISTANCE PRINT [CLOSER] ELSE PRINT
  [FARTHER]
MAKE "OLDISTANCE :NEWDISTANCE
END

TO MESSAGE
PRINT [YOU FOUND ME!]
TOPLEVEL
END
```

The game is now complete and ready to be tested. We leave strategies and further modifications to this game as exercises.

In all the animated games presented so far in this chapter there has been a common format that we can generalize. All the games include the basic animation procedures **ANIMATE**, **READKEY**, and **CHECK**. The **CHECK** procedure can be easily modified to perform a variety of functions when different keys are pressed, thus adding interesting features to the games. Most of these games also have a stopping condition that stops the game when the player has either failed or succeeded. The track game stopped when the car went off the track, and the Secret Point Game stopped when the player guided the turtle to within 5 units of the secret point.

Problem Set 7-5

1. Describe a simple strategy for the player to use in the Secret Point Game that always leads the turtle to the secret point. How many such strategies can you find?

2. Modify the Secret Point Game so that the computer counts the number of steps taken by the animated turtle in its search for the point. This number should be printed at the end of the game.

3. Create a game in which the computer displays a random number R, between 25 and 100, and then sets the animated turtle in motion along a straight line. The player pushes the s key when he believes that the turtle has travelled approximately R steps. The game should then print a message such as GOOD TRY or YOU WERE WAY OFF, based on the player's judgment of the length of the turtle's path.

7-6 The Turtle Takes On New Shapes

In the last two sections we introduced animation and animated games. In these games, the turtle often simulated another object, such as a car. The car itself, however, was only imaginary, since the object on the track was actually the turtle. In this section we demonstrate the use of the **Logo Shape Editor,** which allows us to create new shapes for the turtle to make games more realistic. We first transform the turtle into a square. Later in the section we design a car that can be used instead of the triangular turtle in the track game presented in Section 7-4.

Logo Shape Editor

Using the Shape Editor

To use the Shape Editor, you will need the Logo Utilities disk supplied with Krell or Terrapin Logo. We begin by reading in the SHAPE.EDIT file from the Utilities Disk by typing READ "SHAPE.EDIT and then typing the Shape Editor procedure **SETUP.** Now we must decide on a name for our first shape. Since the shape will be a square, we call our first shape SQUARE. We now use the **MAKESHAPE** procedure to begin the shape. MAKESHAPE must be followed by the name of the shape as shown below.

SETUP

MAKESHAPE

MAKESHAPE "SQUARE

Now the Shape Editor is ready to have us define the first shape. We do this by using designated keys to draw small line segments on the screen. These segments make up the new shape. On page 318 is a list of commands that can be used in defining a shape.

U	Puts the pen up.
D	Puts the pen down.
←	Moves to the left and draws a segment if the pen is down.
→	Moves to the right and draws a segment if the pen is down.
CTRL-P	Moves up and draws a segment if the pen is down.
CTRL-N	Moves down and draws a segment if the pen is down.

Now, to draw a square, we could use the keystrokes below.

→ → → → → CTRL-P CTRL-P CTRL-P CTRL-P CTRL-P ←
← ← ← ← CTRL-N CTRL-N CTRL-N CTRL-N CTRL-N

CTRL-C
CTRL-G

When we are satisfied with the new shape, we type CTRL-C to exit the Shape Editor and define the shape. CTRL-G can be used to abort the shape. We may now use the **MAKESHAPE** procedure again to define a second shape, or we can save the current shape with the procedure **SAVESHAPES**.

SAVESHAPES

Using SAVESHAPES

The SAVESHAPES procedure saves all the shapes created since SETUP was typed. We must give SAVESHAPES the name of a file under which it saves the shapes. For the example given above, we use the name BOXES.

SAVESHAPES "BOXES

Now the Shape Editor asks us to insert an initialized Logo disk into the disk drive. The shapes will be stored on this disk. Once the shapes are saved on the disk, we are asked to return the Utilities Disk to the drive and press RETURN. After a few moments, we are back in Logo. If we catalog the disk on which the shape or shapes are stored, we see that two new files were created, BOXES.SHAPES and BOXES.AUX.LOGO. The BOXES.SHAPES file stores the actual shape, while BOXES.AUX.LOGO contains a variety of Shape Editor procedures. To verify that these files contain our new shape, type GOODBYE and then the following series of commands.

```
READ "BOXES.AUX
INITSHAPES
SETSHAPE :SQUARE
```

The square should now appear on the screen in place of the turtle. The **INITSHAPES** command loads the actual shapes into the computer's memory. It can only be used after a shape file such as BOXES.AUX is loaded. If we had defined a hexagon-shaped object at the time we defined the box, we could also type SETSHAPE :HEXAGON. **SETSHAPE** can take any name that we defined when we saved the BOXES file.

INITSHAPES

SETSHAPE

Using SETSHAPE

Now suppose we experiment with the box that replaced the turtle. We soon find that the box behaves just like the turtle except that it does not seem to respond to commands like RT 45 or LT 10. In fact, user-defined shapes can be displayed only at angles of 0, 90, 180, and 270 degrees. These shapes will draw all figures exactly the way the turtle would draw them even though the shape does not appear to take the appropriate heading. To get the turtle back on the screen, we type SETSHAPE 0. The square-shaped turtle can be brought back by typing SETSHAPE :SQUARE.

Using SIZE

Another command that can be used in the Shape Editor, or at any time after a shape file such as BOXES.AUX is loaded, is **SIZE**. SIZE takes a positive integer such as 1, 2, or 3 as input and changes the size of the current shape according to that number. For example, try typing SIZE 2 and SIZE 5 for the square and the turtle, respectively. The SIZE command can be used in many applications, but it is especially useful for defining a shape in the Shape Editor. If we type SIZE 4 before beginning the segments of our shape, the segments will be

SIZE

be drawn four times their normal size. This allows us to draw a large, detailed shape with great precision. We can later shrink it down to SIZE 1 (the normal size) or any other size. When a shape is being created in the Shape Editor, the keys 1 through 9 can be used as a shorthand for SIZE 1 through SIZE 9. Thus, for example, typing 4 in the Shape Editor is equivalent to typing SIZE 4.

We now demonstrate the use of the SIZE procedure as we define our car. We clear memory using GOODBYE and load SHAPE.EDIT again. Now we type SETUP followed by SIZE 4. After typing the procedure MAKESHAPE "CAR, we can begin drawing the segments of the car in Figure 7-13.

Figure 7-13

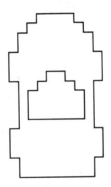

The following keystrokes define the car:

→ → → → → CTRL-P CTRL-P → CTRL-P CTRL-P CTRL-P ← CTRL-P CTRL-P
CTRL-P CTRL-P CTRL-P → CTRL-P CTRL-P CTRL-P ← CTRL-P CTRL-P ← CTRL-P
← CTRL-P ← ← ← ← CTRL-N ← CTRL-N ← CTRL-N CTRL-N ← CTRL-N
CTRL-N CTRL-N → CTRL-N CTRL-N CTRL-N CTRL-N CTRL-N ← CTRL-N CTRL-N
CTRL-N → CTRL-N CTRL-N → → → U ← ← CTRL-P CTRL-P CTRL-P CTRL-P
CTRL-P CTRL-P CTRL-P D CTRL-P CTRL-P CTRL-P → CTRL-P → CTRL-P → →
CTRL-N → CTRL-N → CTRL-N CTRL-N CTRL-N ← ← ← ← ← ← CTRL-C

The final CTRL-C defines the shape, which we can now store by typing SAVESHAPES "CAR. The shape is stored as SIZE 1 even if we defined it with SIZE 4.

We now edit the STARTUP4 procedure from Section 7-4 to read in the car-shaped turtle as follows.

```
TO STARTUP4
READ "CAR.AUX
INITSHAPES
SETSHAPE :CAR
MAKE "SPEED 1
PU
SETXY  -40 0
ANIMATE
END
```

The SIZE procedure is available to us now because we have loaded in CAR.AUX. For a different effect, we can modify the OFF.TRACK procedure of the track game to contain the following line:

REPEAT 5 [SIZE 1   SIZE 2   SIZE 3   SIZE 2]

This line enlarges and contracts the car when it leaves the track to indicate to the player that the game is over.

Summary of Shape Editor Commands

U	Puts the pen up.
D	Puts the pen down.
←	Moves to the left and draws a segment if the pen is down.
→	Moves to the right and draws a segment if the pen is down.
CTRL-P	Moves up and draws a segment if the pen is down.
CTRL-N	Moves down and draws a segment if the pen is down.
CTRL-C	Exits the editor and defines the shape.
CTRL-G	Exits the editor without defining the shape.
1...9	Specifies SIZE in the Shape Editor; for example, typing 5 is equivalent to typing SIZE 5.

Problem Set 7-6

1. Draw a few shapes on paper, then enter them into the computer using the Shape Editor and save all the shapes in one file.

2. Create two shapes in the Shape Editor, a fox and a hare, to be used in the fox-hare simulation and modify that simulation to load in these two shapes automatically.

3. Create a bug shape in the Shape Editor to be used in the four-bugs simulation and modify that simulation to load in the shape automatically.

4. Create a game and a shape in which the player flies an airplane through a tunnel (the tunnel can be represented by two parallel lines). The game should end if the airplane touches the tunnel.

Solution to the Preliminary Problem

Understanding the Problem

The problem is to write a set of procedures that draw a design similar to the one in Figure 7-14.

Figure 7-14

Devising a Plan

This design is similar to the design produced by the four-bugs simulation. We can think of this design as a five-bugs simulation in which each bug begins on the vertex of a regular pentagon. The lines in the design of Figure 7-14 are created by keeping the pen down throughout the simulation.

To solve the problem, we must know the coordinates of the five vertices of the pentagon on which the five bugs are to begin. There are several ways of finding these points. We could plot the pentagon on graph paper and approximate the coordinates of each point; we could use geometry to find the points; or we could have the turtle move along the pentagon and record the coordinates of each of the vertices using **MAKE** statements. We use this last method, since it involves the least computation. We call the first point on the pentagon (X1,Y1) and the fifth point (X5,Y5). Recall that the angle in which the turtle turns as it draws a regular pentagon is 360/5 degrees.

The following procedure finds and stores the five points on a pentagon with side length 100 units.

```
TO STARTUP6
MAKE "ANGLE (360/5)
MAKE "SIDE 100
MAKE "X1 XCOR
MAKE "Y1 YCOR
FD :SIDE
MAKE "X2 XCOR
MAKE "Y2 YCOR
RT :ANGLE
FD :SIDE
MAKE "X3 XCOR
MAKE "Y3 YCOR
RT :ANGLE
FD :SIDE
MAKE "X4 XCOR
MAKE "Y4 YCOR
RT :ANGLE
FD :SIDE
MAKE "X5 XCOR
MAKE "Y5 YCOR
RT :ANGLE
FD :SIDE
END
```

To avoid forcing the turtle off the screen, we need to set the turtle initially at the point $(-50, -50)$.

The other procedures needed to create this design are **BE.BUG1**, **BE.BUG2**, **BE.BUG3**, **BE.BUG4**, **BE.BUG5**, and **INTERACT**. These procedures are much like those in the four-bugs simulation of Section 7-3 except that now we always keep the pen down.

Carrying Out the Plan

To carry out the plan, we must remember the order in which the procedures are called. First, a modified version of **STARTUP6** is called to move the turtle to point $(-50, -50)$, store the five points of the pentagon, and call **INTERACT**, which in turn repeatedly calls the five **BE.BUG** procedures. A complete listing follows.

```
TO STARTUP6
MAKE "ANGLE ( 360 / 5 )
MAKE "SIDE 100
PU
SETXY ( -50) ( -50)
PD
MAKE "X1 XCOR
MAKE "Y1 YCOR
FD :SIDE
MAKE "X2 XCOR
MAKE "Y2 YCOR
RT :ANGLE
FD :SIDE
MAKE "X3 XCOR
MAKE "Y3 YCOR
RT :ANGLE
FD :SIDE
MAKE "X4 XCOR
MAKE "Y4 YCOR
RT :ANGLE
FD :SIDE
MAKE "X5 XCOR
MAKE "Y5 YCOR
RT :ANGLE
FD :SIDE
INTERACT
END
```

```
TO INTERACT
BE.BUG1
BE.BUG2
BE.BUG3
BE.BUG4
BE.BUG5
INTERACT
END

TO BE.BUG1
SETXY :X1 :Y1
SETHEADING TOWARDS :X2 :Y2
FD 5
MAKE "X1 XCOR
MAKE "Y1 YCOR
END

TO BE.BUG2
SETXY :X2 :Y2
SETHEADING TOWARDS :X3 :Y3
FD 5
MAKE "X2 XCOR
MAKE "Y2 YCOR
END

TO BE.BUG3
SETXY :X3 :Y3
SETHEADING TOWARDS :X4 :Y4
FD 5
MAKE "X3 XCOR
MAKE "Y3 YCOR
END

TO BE.BUG4
SETXY :X4 :Y4
SETHEADING TOWARDS :X5 :Y5
FD 5
MAKE "X4 XCOR
MAKE "Y4 YCOR
END
```

```
TO BE.BUG5
SETXY :X5 :Y5
SETHEADING TOWARDS :X1 :Y1
FD 5
MAKE "X5 XCOR
MAKE "Y5 YCOR
END
```

Looking Back

In this chapter we have examined simulations in which two or more turtles interact with one another. We also found out how to control turtles manually via keyboard input in the section on animation. Some interesting related projects are given below.

1. Keep the pen down in the **BE.BUG** procedures of the multibug simulations and examine the created designs.

2. Modify the five-bugs simulation so that two bugs are independently controlled through the keyboard.

3. If paddles are available, make the modification in problem 2 using paddles. The **PADDLE(0)** command returns a value from 0 to 255 depending on the position of the paddle. Multiplying this value by 360/255 gives a value between 0 and 360. One of the bugs can be controlled with the aid of the following statement:

PADDLE(0)

MAKE "HEADING1 (PADDLE(0))*360/255

PADDLE(1)

BUG.1's heading would then be set to HEADING1. The **PADDLE(1)** command takes input from the second paddle and can be used to control the second bug.

Summary of Commands

PADDLE(0)   Takes no inputs. Outputs an integer value from 0 to 255 depending on the position of the first paddle.

PADDLE(1)   Takes no inputs. Outputs an integer value from 0 to 255 depending on the position of the second paddle.

Chapter 7 Problem Set

1. A robot is trying to find a single object in a large open space. After the robot makes each move, a special device tells it whether the object is **NORTH** or **SOUTH** of the robot and then whether it is **EAST** or **WEST**. The robot must find the object by using this information alone.

   (a) Develop and outline an algorithm for the robot to use.

   (b) Incorporate the algorithm from (a) into a Logo simulation to find out whether your algorithm will work.

   (c) Describe the path that the robot takes when using the simulation in (b) to find the object.

2. Can you improve the algorithm in Problem 1 to lead the robot to the object on a shorter and faster path?

3. (a) Modify the fox-and-hare simulation of Section 7-2 so that the fox keeps a bearing 45 degrees to the left of the hare and the hare moves in a circle of radius 50. Both animals should move at the same speed.

   (b) Can the fox catch the hare?

4. Using the concept of the four-bugs problem in Section 7-3, create a simulation involving three bugs that are placed at random points on the screen.

5. (a) Create a simulation of three whimsical bugs, initially located on the vertices of an equilateral triangle, that choose their preferences randomly. For example, at one moment Bug 1 might chase Bug 2, while at the next it might go for Bug 3. The bugs should decide their preferences using the **RANDOM** statement, but no bug should be attracted to itself!

   (b) Do the three bugs still meet?

6. Create an animated game in which the player controls one turtle using the R and L keys and two other turtles chase the player's turtle. The two chasing turtles should move at two-thirds the speed of the player's turtle. If the player's turtle starts at the origin, the chasing turtles should be initially placed at the points (50,0) and (−50,0).

7. Using the Shape Editor, create the shape of a robot. Modify the radio transmitter simulation so that the robot is loaded in every time the simulation is executed.

CHAPTER

8

New Vocabulary in Chapter 8

Terms		Primitives	
empty word	p. 333	NUMBER?	p. 333
palindrome	p. 338	WORD?	p. 333
list	p. 344	WORD	p. 333
empty list	p. 344	FIRST	p. 336
		LAST	p. 336
		BUTFIRST (BF)	p. 336
		BUTLAST (BL)	p. 336
		CURSOR	p. 338
		LIST?	p. 344
		FPUT	p. 346
		LPUT	p. 346
		LIST	p. 346
		SENTENCE (SE)	p. 347
		REQUEST	p. 348

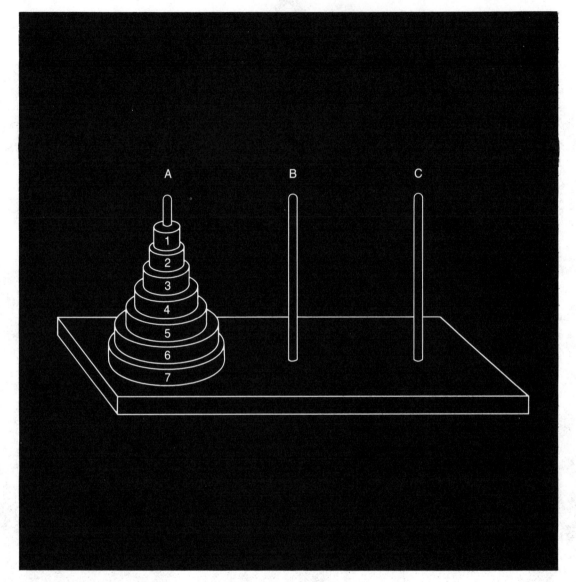

Preliminary Problem

Write a procedure to tell how to move all the disks from Peg A to Peg C in the Tower of Hanoi puzzle pictured above. The rules of the puzzle are to seek the minimal number of moves, to move no more than one disk at a time, and never to place a larger disk on a smaller one.

8

An Introduction to List Processing

Introduction

The list-processing capabilities of Logo make it possible to manipulate words and sentences with the computer. List-processing is the manipulation of lists and words to perform useful tasks. It makes it possible for users to add commands to their procedures so that other users can understand how to run the procedures. List-processing can also be used to compare, edit, and manipulate the user's writing. This chapter applies list-processing to three types of computer data: numbers, words, and lists.

8-1 Words and Numbers

Logo words, as first defined in Chapter 4, are considered to be any strings of printable characters except the right and left square brackets. A space may not be used as a character in a word because a space signals the end of a word. To indicate a word to the computer, a double quotation mark, ", precedes the string of characters. The following strings of characters would all be considered words by the computer if they were preceded by double quotation marks.

R2D2

*?>

ONE.WORD

If any of the strings of characters above is not preceded by a double quotation mark, Logo does not recognize it as a word. Try each of the following and compare the results. Why do you think each part gives the result that it does?

(a) PRINT "R2D2

(b) PRINT "R2D2"

(c) PRINT " "R2D2

(d) PRINT R2D2

(e) PRINT "R2 "D2

(f) PR "R2 D2

(g) PR "1984

(h) PR 1984

(i) PR "19+84

(j) PR "19 + 84

From the preceding investigation, we see that if a double quotation mark is used on the right, as in (b), the right-hand mark is treated as if it were just another character in the string. The same is true if a second double quotation mark is added immediately following the first one, as in (c). If no quotation mark is used at the beginning, as in (d), Logo does not treat the characters as a word. Instead, it examines its procedure library to see if there is a procedure with that name. If there is no such procedure, Logo responds with the appropriate error message.

In (e), because **PRINT** expects only one input, the computer prints R2 and then proceeds to the rest of the line, namely, "D2. It recognizes that "D2 is a word, but because there are no other Logo operations that need inputs, it does not know what to do with this word and therefore prints the following:

RESULT: D2

The results of (g) and (h) may be somewhat surprising because they are the same. Logo does not seem to recognize the difference between numbers and words. In fact, in MIT Logo (Terrapin/Krell versions), it is appropriate to think of numbers as words, just as though they were preceded by a double quotation mark. In (i), the plus sign is treated just like any other character in the word "19+84, and the computer prints 19+84. Finally, in (j), the sum 103 is printed because "19 + 84 is no longer treated as a word. The space after 19 indicates the end of the word "19, and the plus indicates that there is an addition to be carried out.

Whenever there is any doubt about whether something is a number or a word, the primitives **NUMBER?** and **WORD?** can be used, respectively, to decide. NUMBER? takes one input and outputs TRUE if the input is a number and FALSE if the input is not a number. WORD? takes one input and outputs TRUE if the input is a word and FALSE if the input is not a word.

NUMBER?
WORD?

A special word that is often useful in Logo is the **empty word,** a word composed of no characters. It is designated by a double quotation mark with nothing following it. For example, try the following and observe the result.

empty word

PRINT "HELLO
PRINT "
PRINT "THERE

The result of using PRINT with an empty word as input is a blank line, as seen below because PRINT prints its input and executes a carriage return. In the case of the empty word, there is nothing to print so it just executes a carriage return.

HELLO

THERE

Operating on Words and Numbers

Logo contains several primitives that can be used to manipulate numbers and words. One such primitive is **WORD.** Type the following and observe the result.

WORD

WORD "DOG "HOUSE

As you saw, the computer responds with the following line.

RESULT: DOGHOUSE

The primitive **WORD** takes two words as inputs and outputs the combination as one word. Compare the preceding result with the output obtained by typing the following:

PRINT WORD "DOG "HOUSE

Observe that in this case the output of **WORD** provides input for **PRINT**, so that the word DOGHOUSE is printed. What do you think would happen if we executed the following?

PRINT WORD "BROWN "DOG "HOUSE

In this case, when the computer looks for the input to **PRINT**, it reads **WORD**. **WORD** directs the computer to look for **WORD**'s own input. When the computer looks for inputs to **WORD**, it reads "**BROWN** and "**DOG**. Those inputs are used by **WORD** to form **BROWNDOG**. **PRINT**, in turn, uses "**BROWNDOG** as input and prints BROWNDOG. Once that is accomplished, the computer reads the word "**HOUSE**. Not having been given instruction about what to do with this word, it outputs RESULT: HOUSE.

Fortunately, in Logo, more than two inputs can be given to the primitive **WORD**. If **WORD** is enclosed in parentheses along with any inputs, the inputs are combined into a single word. For example, this is a way of combining three inputs into a single word.

PR (WORD "BROWN "DOG "HOUSE   )

Notice the space between the last character in the third input and the right parenthesis. This space is necessary to make the primitive **WORD** function correctly with more than two inputs. Explore what happens if the space is omitted, as in the following:

PR (WORD "BROWN "DOG "HOUSE)

Why does the computer treat this line differently than the one in the preceding example? If a space is not placed before the right parenthesis, Logo thinks that the symbol) is a character in the word

"HOUSE) and treats it as such. Remember that in order to end a word, you must type a space or, if at the end of a line, press RETURN.

We demonstrated the use of parentheses to allow more inputs with such Logo primitives as ANYOF, ALLOF, and PRINT. For example, when we execute (PR "R2 "D2), we obtain this output:

R2 D2

If instead of PRINT we use the primitive PRINT1, introduced in Chapter 6, then the words "R2 and "D2 are printed next to each other on the same line, with no intervening space, like this:

R2D2

Recall that the primitive PRINT1 works like PRINT except it does not start a new line after printing its input, and it doesn't print a space between words. Investigate whether (PRINT1 "R2 "D2) and PRINT WORD "R2 "D2 produce the same result. Predict the results of each of the following and check your answers.

(a) PRINT "GOOD PRINT "MORNING

(b) PRINT1 "GOOD PRINT1 "MORNING

(c) (PRINT "GOOD "MORNING)

(d) (PRINT1 "GOOD "MORNING)

(e) PRINT1 "GOOD PRINT "MORNING

Sometimes it is useful to be able to print words on a line with a desired number of spaces between them. This can be done using single quotes, as shown below. (Another way to develop columns is to use the primitive CURSOR, discussed later.) Consider the following line, which could be used to make two column headings:

PRINT1 " 'COLUMN ONE' PRINT " '   COLUMN TWO'

(It should be noted that in Terrapin-Logo Version 2.0, when a procedure is saved and later recalled, single quotes in the procedure may be deleted. This may cause difficulties with the use of single quotes.) The use of single quotes is fairly rare, and we mention it only to make readers aware of its availability in Logo. It is easy to encounter difficulty with single quotes. For example, type the following:

PRINT " 'WHAT'S UP DOC'

Could you have predicted the result?

Other Logo commands that operate on words are FIRST, LAST, BUTFIRST (BF), and BUTLAST (BL). To explore these primitives, try each of the following lines, along with some of your own.

(a) PR FIRST "ALPHABET

(b) PR LAST "ALPHABET

(c) PR BUTFIRST "ALPHABET

(d) PR BUTLAST "ALPHABET

(e) PR FIRST FIRST "ALPHABET

(f) PR FIRST BF "ALPHABET

(g) PR FIRST FIRST "A

FIRST
LAST
BUTFIRST (BF)
BUTLAST (BL)

When **FIRST** and **LAST** are used with a word, they output the first or last character of the word, respectively. When **BUTFIRST (BF)** and **BUTLAST (BL)** are used with a word, they output words containing everything but the first or last character of the word, respectively.

Problem 8-1

Devise a procedure to print the following:

```
LOGO
LOG
LO
L
```

Solution

To obtain this type of display with any word that is input, we want the computer to print the complete word, then print the word without the last letter, to keep repeating this process until the empty word is reached, and then to stop. If we call the procedure **TRIANGLE**, shown below, with variable input :**W**, we can stop the procedure with the line **IF :W = " STOP** (Note that the double quotation marks followed by a space denote the empty word.) The **TRIANGLE** procedure with input "**LOGO** prints the desired display. Try the **TRIANGLE** procedure with other inputs.

```
TO TRIANGLE :W
IF :W = "   STOP
PRINT :W
TRIANGLE BUTLAST :W
END
```

Problem 8-2

Write a procedure to produce the display below.

```
L
LO
LOG
LOGO
```

Solution

If we recall the discussion of embedded recursion in Section 4-4 and the procedures **DOWN** and **SUB**, we have the clue needed to write the desired procedure. We need only to edit the **TRIANGLE** procedure in Problem 8-1 to include the line **PRINT :W** after the recursive call instead of before it. The new procedure, which we call **TRIANGLE1**, is given below.

```
TO TRIANGLE1 :W
IF :W = "   STOP
TRIANGLE1 BUTLAST :W
PRINT :W
END
```

As an extension of Problem 8-2, consider how we could obtain each of the displays below.

```
LOGO          O
OGO           GO
GO            OGO
O             LOGO
```

CURSOR

Sometimes it is convenient to start printing on the screen at positions other than the cursor's current location when printing columns. The primitive **CURSOR** allows us to move the cursor to any location on the screen. CURSOR takes two number inputs, namely column number and row number, which tell the computer the location of the point where the cursor is to be moved. Keep in mind that there are 39 columns and 23 rows on the screen. For example, CURSOR 10 20 positions the cursor at the tenth column and the twentieth row on the screen. Position 0 0 is at the upper left corner of the screen. Execute the following to see where the cursor is positioned for printing in each case:

(a) CURSOR 13 12 PRINT "HELLO

(b) CURSOR 0 0 PRINT "HELLO

(c) CURSOR 0 23 PRINT "HELLO

(d) CURSOR 32 20 PRINT "HELLO

(e) CURSOR 52 20 PRINT "HELLO

Creating Palindromes

palindrome

Consider writing a procedure that takes a word such as NO, prints it, reverses the letters, and prints ON next to NO to form the word NOON. A word such as NOON, EVE, WOW, or MADAM, which reads the same backward as forward, is called a **palindrome.** How might we write a procedure that takes any word as input and creates a palindrome from it?

Let us name the procedure PAL and call the variable :W. Because we want to see the result to PAL, we need to use the PRINT primitive. To determine the input for PRINT, consider what we want the procedure to do. We want the input for :W to be printed, and then we want to reverse the letters and print that set of characters next to the characters of :W. To reverse the characters of :W, we need a new procedure called REVERSE. To combine the characters in :W and in REVERSE into one word, we use the primitive WORD as follows. (Parentheses are added for clarity but are not necessary.)

```
WORD (:W) (REVERSE :W)
```

The line above provides input for PRINT. We write the whole PAL procedure as follows.

```
TO PAL :W
PRINT WORD (:W) (REVERSE :W)
END
```

To complete the procedure for a palindrome, we need to write a REVERSE procedure. Because we want REVERSE to give output to the PAL procedure, we need to use the OUTPUT primitive. We want to obtain the next-to-last character of :W and continue this process of obtaining the letters until all have been placed in reverse order. Then the characters have to be assembled into a word and output to the PAL procedure. In the REVERSE procedure, the following line accomplishes what we want:

```
OUTPUT WORD (LAST :W) (REVERSE BUTLAST :W)
```

To stop the procedure, we might use the following line, which outputs the empty word when all letters in the word have been used:

```
IF :W = "   OUTPUT   "
```

Thus, we have the following REVERSE procedure. (Parentheses are not needed but are added for clarity.)

```
TO REVERSE :W
IF :W = "   OUTPUT   "
OUTPUT WORD (LAST :W) (REVERSE BUTLAST :W)
END
```

For example, if we execute REVERSE "SO, the computer goes through the following steps:

1. Because "SO is not equal to the empty word, the next line is executed.

2. OUTPUT WORD (LAST "SO) (REVERSE BUTLAST "SO) is executed as follows:

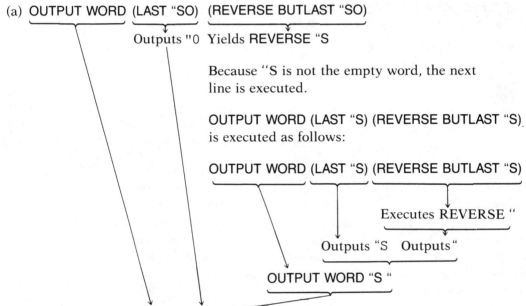

(a) OUTPUT WORD (LAST "SO) (REVERSE BUTLAST "SO)

Outputs "0   Yields REVERSE "S

Because "S is not the empty word, the next line is executed.

OUTPUT WORD (LAST "S) (REVERSE BUTLAST "S) is executed as follows:

OUTPUT WORD (LAST "S) (REVERSE BUTLAST "S)

Executes REVERSE "

Outputs "S   Outputs "

OUTPUT WORD "S "

(b) Now we have OUTPUT WORD "0 "S which yields 0S.

The following are examples of the PAL procedure.

(a) PAL "NO
   NOON

(b) PAL "AN
   ANNA

(c) PAL 1234
   12344321

(d) PAL "TO
   TOOT

Summary of Commands

NUMBER?	Takes one input and outputs TRUE if that input is a number; FALSE otherwise.
WORD?	Takes one input and outputs TRUE if that input is a word; FALSE otherwise.
WORD	Takes two inputs (may take more if parentheses are used) and outputs one word composed of the inputs.
FIRST	Takes one input and outputs the first element of that input. (If the input is a word, then the output is the first character in the word.)
LAST	Takes one input and outputs the last element of that input. (If the input is a word, then the output is the last character in the word.)
BUTFIRST (BF)	Takes one input and outputs all but the first item of the input. (If the input is a word, then the output is all but the first character of the word.)
BUTLAST (BL)	Takes one input and outputs all but the last item of the input. (If the input is a word, then the output is all but the last character of the word.)
CURSOR	Takes two inputs, namely column number and row number, and positions the cursor there. Column numbers range from 0 to 39, and row numbers range from 0 to 23.

Problem Set 8-1

1. Predict the results of each of the following. Then use the computer to check your predictions.

    (a) PRINT 2+3

    (b) PRINT 5*3+1

    (c) PRINT 2

    (d) PRINT "2

    (e) PRINT 6 + 8

    (f) PRINT "6+8

    (g) PRINT 6<8

    (h) PRINT (6+8)

    (i) (PRINT 6+8)

    (j) (PRINT 6 + 8)

    (k) (PRINT 6 "+ 8)

    (l) PRINT "6<8

2. Determine the result of executing each of the following. Tell why each has the output that it does.

   (a) PRINT "WHY
   (b) PRINT "WHY.NOT
   (c) PRINT"WHY
   (d) PR "WHY
   (e) PRINT "WHY "NOT
   (f) PR ("WHY "NOT)
   (g) PR ("WHY "NOT)
   (h) PR "WHY NOT
   (i) PR "WHY PR "NOT
   (j) PRINT1 "WHY "NOT
   (k) (PR "WHY "NOT)
   (l) (PRINT1 "WHY " ' ' "NOT)

3. Predict the results of executing each of the following.

   (a) WORD? "3
   (b) NUMBER? "2
   (c) NUMBER? 2
   (d) NUMBER? "3 + 2
   (e) NUMBER? "3 + 2
   (f) WORD? "3 + A
   (g) WORD? "3 + A

4. Predict the result of executing each of the following and check your answers on the computer.

   (a) FIRST "LOGO
   (b) PR FIRST "LOGO
   (c) PR BF "LOGO
   (d) PR BL "LOGO
   (e) PR FIRST BF "LOGO
   (f) PR LAST BF "LOGO
   (g) PR FIRST "
   (h) PR WORD "C3 "PO
   (i) PR 67 89
   (j) PR (WORD "HERE "TO "FORE)

5. (a) Predict the outcome of executing SEQUENCE 1 if SEQUENCE and SLOW are defined as follows:

   ```
   TO SEQUENCE :N
   PRINT :N
   SLOW 100
   SEQUENCE :N + 1
   END

   TO SLOW :N
   REPEAT :N [PRINT1 " ]
   END
   ```

   (b) How would the outcome of SEQUENCE 1 be different if SLOW 100 were deleted from the SEQUENCE procedure?

   (c) How would the outcome of SEQUENCE 1 be different if PRINT :N were replaced by PRINT1 :N?

6. Design a procedure (or procedures) to print the natural numbers 1, 2, . . . , 9 and their squares under the column headings **NUMBER** and **SQUARE**.

7. Why does the computer respond as it does when the following is typed?

   PRINT " 'WHAT'S UP DOC'

8. Use the **TRIANGLE** procedure described in this section to write an **INVERTTRIANGLE** procedure that produces the following format:

   ```
   LOGO
   OGO
   GO
   O
   ```

9. Write an **INVERTTRIANGLE1** procedure that uses the **TRIANGLE** procedure to produce the following format:

   ```
   LOGO
   LOG
   LO
   L
   LO
   LOG
   LOGO
   ```

10. Use the **CURSOR** primitive and recursion in a procedure to print X's on the diagonal of the screen from the upper left corner to the lower right corner.

11. Edit the **PAL** procedure to cause it to print a palindrome that is one character shorter than the palindrome it would currently print with the same input; for example, **PAL** "NO would output NON.

☆12. Design a procedure to accept a word as input and to determine whether or not the word is a palindrome. (Hint: Use the **REVERSE** procedure.)

8-2 Lists

list

Just as a string of characters can be considered a word, an ordered collection or string of words, numbers, or other lists can be considered a **list.** "Ordered collection" means only that it matters which item comes first, which item comes second, and so on. Lists may be used as inputs for procedures, as will be seen later in the chapter. A list is indicated in Logo by typing the items composing the list separated by spaces and enclosing them in brackets. For example, the following are lists.

(a) [I AM IN A LIST]

(b) [A B C D]

(c) [A B C D]

(d) [ABCD]

(e) []

(f) [1 2 3]

(g) [A B C [D]]

empty list

Note that [ ] denotes an **empty list,** just as " denoted an empty word. Also notice that [A B C D] and [A B C D   ] are considered to be the same list: The space following the letter D does not matter. Spaces are significant only as separators. They are important in that context, however. For example, in list [ABCD] there is only one item, whereas there are four items in [A B C D].

LIST?

Recall that both "1984 and 1984 denote the same word. Do you think that both [1984] and 1984 represent the same list? If you're not sure, you can use the primitive **LIST?** to determine whether this or any other input is considered to be a list. LIST? takes one input and outputs TRUE if the input is a list and FALSE otherwise. For example, if we execute LIST? 1984, the computer displays FALSE.

PRINT and PRINT1 may also be used in connection with lists. For example, try the following:

(a) PRINT [GOOD MORNING]

(b) PRINT [GOOD   MORNING]

(c) PRINT [1234]

(d) PRINT [1 2 3 4 5]

(e) PRINT [ ]

(f) PRINT1 [HOW] PRINT1 [ARE] PRINT1 [YOU]

(g) PRINT [GOOD MORNING TO YOU]

(h) (PRINT1 [GOOD] [MORNING])

(i) (PRINT [GOOD] [MORNING])

(j) PRINT1 [GOOD] PRINT1 [ ] PRINT1 [MORNING]

Many of the primitives used to manipulate words may also be used to manipulate lists. Consider these examples and their results.

(a) FIRST [WHY NOT]   RESULT: WHY

(b) LAST [WHY NOT]   RESULT: NOT

(c) FIRST [ ]   FIRST DOESN'T LIKE [ ] AS INPUT

(d) BUTFIRST [WHY NOT NOW]   RESULT: [NOT NOW]

(e) BUTLAST [WHY NOT NOW]   RESULT: [WHY NOT]

(f) FIRST BUTLAST [WHY NOT NOW]   RESULT: WHY

(g) BUTLAST FIRST [WHY NOT NOW]   RESULT: WH

(h) FIRST [[WHY] NOT]   RESULT: [WHY]

Now investigate the effect the primitive **PRINT** has on each of the above.

The primitives **FIRST, LAST, BUTFIRST,** and **BUTLAST** are all-purpose selectors. Combinations of them can be used to select any part of a list or word. As an exercise, try to type a line that outputs a specific word in a list. For example, consider the list below.

[NOW IS THE TIME FOR ALL GOOD MEN TO COME TO THE AID OF THEIR COUNTRY.]

What primitives would you use to select GOOD from the list? One possibility is the following:

FIRST BF BF BF BF BF BF [NOW IS THE TIME FOR ALL GOOD MEN TO COME TO THE AID OF THEIR COUNTRY.]

Can you think of other ways to do this? Can you devise instructions to make the computer select the letter W from the sentence above?

Other primitives that can be used with lists include FPUT and LPUT, which are used to combine items into a list. They are particularly useful if we are accumulating information and want it stored as a list.

FPUT

FPUT takes two inputs. The first may be a word or a list, but the second must be a list. FPUT puts its first input in front of its second input; that is, FPUT outputs a list whose first item is the first input and the remainder is its second input. (FPUT is an abbreviation for FirstPUT.) For example, consider the following:

(a) FPUT "S [TOP]   RESULT: [STOP]

(b) FPUT [S] [TOP]   RESULT: [[S] TOP]

(c) FPUT [R E S] [TOP]   RESULT: [[R E S] TOP]

LPUT

LPUT also takes two inputs. It makes its first input become the last item in the list that is its second input. (LPUT is an abbreviation for LastPUT.) For example, consider the following:

(a) LPUT "S [TOP]   RESULT: [TOP S]

(b) LPUT [S] [TOP]   RESULT: [TOP [S]]

(c) LPUT [R E S] [TOP]   RESULT: [TOP [R E S]]

LIST

Just as the primitive **WORD** is used to combine characters into a word, the primitive **LIST** is used to combine items into a list. Normally LIST takes two inputs, but it can be made to take more by using parentheses. Here are some examples involving the primitive LIST, along with their outputs.

(a) LIST "HELLO "THERE   RESULT: [HELLO THERE]

(b) LIST 3+4 "UP   RESULT: [7 UP]

(c) (LIST "PEACE "IN 2000)   RESULT: [PEACE IN 2000]

(d) (LIST 1 2 3)   RESULT: [1 2 3]

Another primitive that allows a list to be formed is **SENTENCE (SE).** SENTENCE normally takes two inputs, but it can also take more if parentheses are used. Examples using SENTENCE and their outputs are shown below.

SENTENCE (SE)

(a) SENTENCE "HELLO "THERE   RESULT: [HELLO THERE]

(b) SENTENCE 3+4 "UP   RESULT: [7 UP]

(c) (SE "PEACE "IN 2000)   RESULT: [PEACE IN 2000]

(d) (SE 1 2 3)   RESULT: [1 2 3]

It appears from these examples that **SENTENCE** and **LIST** perform exactly the same function. That is not the case, however. Consider the following examples and their results.

SE "ZION [NATIONAL PARK]   RESULT: [ZION NATIONAL PARK]

SE [DEVIL'S] [TOWER]   RESULT: [DEVIL'S TOWER]

LIST "ZION [NATIONAL PARK]   RESULT: [ZION [NATIONAL PARK]]

LIST [DEVIL'S] [TOWER]   RESULT: [[DEVIL'S] [TOWER]]

If one of the inputs to **SENTENCE** is a list, **SENTENCE** first breaks the list into the items composing the list and then recombines the items with the rest of the inputs to form the final output list. For example, if [WHY NOT] is an input to **SENTENCE**, then [WHY NOT] will be treated as the words WHY and NOT, as seen in the result below.

(SENTENCE [OH] [WHY NOT] [TONIGHT?])
RESULT: [OH WHY NOT TONIGHT?]

However, if an input to SENTENCE is a list containing a list, then the interior list will not be broken up. Consider the following:

SENTENCE [WHY [NOT]] [TONIGHT?]
RESULT: [WHY [NOT] TONIGHT?]

In general, LIST puts a set of brackets around its inputs, while SENTENCE first strips outside brackets off each input (that is, one level of brackets) and then puts one set of brackets around the result. SENTENCE is more useful than LIST for making simple instructions in interactive procedures, that is, procedures that give instructions to the user and respond to the user's replies. SENTENCE is used this way in the following example.

Writing a Multiplication Procedure

As an example of the use of some of the primitives introduced in this chapter, we write a simple single-digit multiplication procedure called MFACT, which includes instructions to the user.

In our procedure, we have the computer choose two single digits at random to be multiplied. If we denote the two digits by :A and :B, we can use two MAKE statements to set the variables, :A and :B, equal to RANDOM 10, as shown below. (Recall that RANDOM 10 chooses a number between 0 and 9 inclusive. Thus, RANDOM 10 will make :A and :B random single digits.)

MAKE "A RANDOM 10
MAKE "B RANDOM 10

Now we want to have the computer ask the user for the product of :A and :B. This can be accomplished with the following PRINT statement:

PRINT (SE [WHAT IS THE PRODUCT OF] :A "AND :B "?)

REQUEST (RQ)

To enable the user to respond, we need a way to have the computer accept input typed by the user. The primitive REQUEST allows this to happen. **REQUEST (RQ)** accepts an input that the user types and outputs it as a list. Hence, we might let the next line be the following:

MAKE "ANSWER REQUEST

To make the procedure more readable when it is executed, we make the next line blank. We obtain the blank line by using the following statement:

PRINT [ ]

To compare the product of :A and :B to the user's input, we must have that input as a number, not as an item in a list. How can we take a list such as [14], which could appear as the output of REQUEST, and strip the brackets away? There are many ways to do this, but perhaps the easiest is to use the primitive FIRST. FIRST [14] outputs 14.

Next we need a conditional to compare FIRST :ANSWER and :A *:B. If these two numbers are equal, the user should be told that the response was correct. The following conditional produces this.

IF FIRST :ANSWER = :A*:B PRINT [CORRECT!]

If the response is not correct, as determined by NOT FIRST :ANSWER = :A*:B, we would like the computer to print a sentence stating that the user's answer is not correct, showing the correct answer and asking if the user would like another problem. A line to accomplish this follows.

IF NOT FIRST :ANSWER = :A*:B PRINT (SE [SORRY,
    THE ANSWER IS] :A*:B)

Now we need the procedure to ask if another problem is desired. A line to do this follows:

PRINT [WOULD YOU LIKE ANOTHER PROBLEM? TYPE YES OR NO.]

We want the computer to accept the user's typed response, and for readability we use a blank line after the response. The following lines accomplish these aims.

MAKE "ANSWER REQUEST
PRINT [ ]

If the user's response is YES, then MFACT should be called again and the procedure stopped. If the user's response is NO, we might have the computer print a closing message and stop. If the user types neither YES nor NO, we might have the computer print yet another message. Lines to accomplish these last three instructions follow.

```
IF :ANSWER = [YES] MFACT STOP
IF :ANSWER = [NO] PRINT [THANK YOU FOR PLAYING.] STOP
PRINT [YOU DIDN'T TYPE YES OR NO.]
PRINT [TYPE MFACT TO PLAY AGAIN.]
```

The complete **MFACT** procedure is shown below.

```
TO MFACT
MAKE "A RANDOM 10
MAKE "B RANDOM 10
PRINT (SE [WHAT IS THE PRODUCT OF ] :A "AND :B "? )
MAKE "ANSWER REQUEST
PRINT [ ]
IF FIRST :ANSWER = :A * :B PRINT [CORRECT!]
IF NOT FIRST :ANSWER = :A*B PRINT ( SE [SORRY,
    THE ANSWER IS ] :A*:B)
PRINT [WOULD YOU LIKE ANOTHER PROBLEM? TYPE YES OR NO.]
MAKE "ANSWER REQUEST
PRINT [ ]
IF :ANSWER = [YES] MFACT STOP
IF :ANSWER = [NO] PRINT [THANK YOU FOR PLAYING.] STOP
PRINT [YOU DIDN'T TYPE YES OR NO.]
PRINT [TYPE MFACT TO PLAY AGAIN.]
END
```

An exploration of drill procedures involving list-processing primitives is given in the problem set for this section.

Using List Processing with Turtle Graphics

The following problems illustrate how list processing can be used to make procedures understandable to others.

Problem 8-3

The slope, M, of a line is a measure of the steepness of the line. The slope of a line containing points (:X1, :Y1) and (:X2,:Y2) is given by M = (:Y2 − :Y1)/(:X2 − :X1). The procedure below finds the slope of a line segment connecting two points with coordinates (:X1, :Y1) and (:X2, :Y2). Edit the procedure to make it allow user input as the procedure is run.

```
TO SLOPE :X1 :Y1 :X2 :Y2
PRINT (:Y2 − :Y1)/(:X2 − :X1)
END
```

Solution

If the user does not know what the SLOPE procedure does, he or she will not learn much by seeing it run. To make the procedure more instructive, we might use NODRAW and CURSOR 0 8 to move the cursor to start the printing towards the middle of the screen for easier reading. Then we might include the following PRINT statements:

```
PRINT [THIS PROGRAM COMPUTES THE SLOPE]
PRINT [OF A LINE GIVEN THE COORDINATES OF TWO POINTS.]
```

Now, instead of typing SLOPE and four values to execute the procedure, we could have the computer ask the user for the coordinates of the desired points, using MAKE statements with the REQUEST primitive to input the coordinates. The following PRINT statements tell the user what to do.

```
PRINT [TYPE THE COORDINATES OF THE FIRST]
PRINT [POINT SEPARATED BY A SPACE, E.G., 20 30]
```

To have the computer accept the user's input, we could type:

```
MAKE "ANS REQUEST
```

Here, :ANS is the user's response. REQUEST waits for the response and outputs it as a list; for example, 20 30 would be output as [20 30]. Because we need responses for both :X1 and :Y1, the next lines in our interactive procedure should be as follows.

```
MAKE "X1 FIRST :ANS
MAKE "Y1 LAST :ANS
```

To make the output on the monitor screen more readable, we follow these lines with another blank line by using PRINT [ ].

Now we need to repeat the process to input :X2 and :Y2. We can do this using the lines below.

```
PRINT [TYPE THE COORDINATES OF THE SECOND]
PRINT [POINT SEPARATED BY A SPACE]
MAKE "ANS REQUEST
MAKE "X2 FIRST :ANS
MAKE "Y2 LAST :ANS
```

Finally, to show what the output of the procedure is, we include the following line.

```
PRINT (:Y2 − :Y1)/(:X2 − :X1)
```

Combining all of these lines, our edited SLOPE procedure looks like the one below:

```
TO SLOPE
NODRAW
CURSOR 0 8
PRINT [THIS PROGRAM COMPUTES THE SLOPE]
PRINT [OF A LINE GIVEN TWO POINTS.]
PRINT [TYPE THE COORDINATES OF THE FIRST ]
PRINT [POINT SEPARATED BY A SPACE, E.G., 20 30]
MAKE "ANS REQUEST
MAKE "X1 FIRST :ANS
MAKE "Y1 LAST :ANS
PRINT [ ]
PRINT [TYPE THE COORDINATES OF THE SECOND ]
PRINT [POINT SEPARATED BY A SPACE.]
MAKE "ANS REQUEST
MAKE "X2 FIRST :ANS
MAKE "Y2 LAST :ANS
PRINT [ ]
PRINT [THE SLOPE OF THE SEGMENT IS]
PRINT (:Y2 − :Y1)/(:X2 − :X1)
END
```

As an exercise, edit **SLOPE** further to include lines that take care of the case where :X1 = :X2 and therefore no slope exists. Also, investigate what happens if characters other than numbers are input in this procedure.

Problem 8-4

Combine the **SLOPE** procedure designed in Problem 8-3 with the **SEGMENT** procedure from Chapter 5 to produce an interactive slope procedure that includes graphics.

Solution

The **SEGMENT** procedure from Section 5-1 is given below.

```
TO SEGMENT :X1 :Y1 :X2 :Y2
PENUP
SETXY :X1 :Y1
PENDOWN
SETXY :X2 :Y2
HT
END
```

All we need to do is to combine the **SLOPE** and **SEGMENT** procedures with the **WAIT** procedure below into one procedure called **SEGSLOPE**.

```
TO WAIT :N
IF :N = 0 STOP
WAIT :N − 1
END
```

The following **PRINT** statement may also be added.

```
PRINT [A PICTURE OF THE SEGMENT IS ABOVE.]
```

The complete **SEGSLOPE** procedure is given below.

```
TO SEGSLOPE
SLOPE
WAIT 200
SEGMENT :X1 :Y1 :X2 :Y2
PRINT [A PICTURE OF THE SEGMENT IS ABOVE.]
END
```

Summary of Commands

LIST?	Takes one input. Outputs TRUE if the input is a list and FALSE otherwise.
FPUT	Takes two inputs, the second of which is a list, and outputs a list consisting of the first input followed by the items of the second input.
LPUT	Takes two inputs, the second of which is a list, and outputs a list consisting of the items of the second input followed by the first input.
LIST	Normally takes two inputs, but may take more if parentheses are used. Outputs a list of the inputs.
SENTENCE (SE)	Normally takes two inputs, but may take more if parentheses are used. Outputs all the inputs as a single list.
REQUEST	Takes no inputs. Waits for an input line to be typed followed by RETURN. Outputs the line as a list.

Problem Set 8-2

1. Predict the output of each of the following lines. Then execute each line to determine whether your answer is correct.

    (a) FIRST [GOOD DAY]
    (b) PR FIRST [GOOD DAY]
    (c) FIRST [A B C D]
    (d) BF [A B C D]
    (e) PR LAST [A B C D]
    (f) PR BL [A B C D]

(g) PR FIRST BF [A B]

(h) PR FIRST [[WHY] NOT]

(i) PR LAST [[WHY] NOT]

(j) PR FIRST [[A] [B]]

(k) PR BF [[A] [B]]

(l) PR BF BF BF [A B C]

(m) PR FIRST [ ]

(n) PR SENTENCE [A LIST] [PLUS A LIST]

(o) PR SE "WORD [PLUS A LIST]

(p) PR SE "TWO "WORDS

(q) PR (SE [MORE THAN] "TWO [INPUTS CAN BE] "USED)

2. Use only the **FIRST** and **BUTFIRST** primitives to print the letter R from each of the following.

(a) [R I C K]

(b) [RICK]

(c) [PROBLEM]

(d) [[R] [I] [C] [K]]

3. (a) Use only the **LAST** and **BUTLAST** primitives to print the letter R from the lists in Problem 2.

(b) Write a procedure called **ELEMENT** that accepts a list and a position number as input and outputs the element in the list in the position number, for example, **ELEMENT** [A B C D] 3 outputs RESULT: C.

4. Predict the output for each of the following and then execute each to check your predictions.

(a) FPUT "A [B C]   (b) FPUT [A] [B C]

(c) FPUT "A "B   (d) FPUT "A [ ]

(e) LPUT "A [B C]   (f) LPUT [A] [B C]

(g) LPUT "A "B   (h) LPUT "A [ ]

5. Write a procedure called **RLIST** to take a list as input and to reverse the items of the list.

6. Write an interactive procedure for single-digit addition, similar to the **MFACT** procedure designed in this section.

7. Edit the **SLOPE** procedure of Problem 8-3 to make the computer print a line stating that no slope exists when :X1 = :X2.

8. Write a procedure to print out each item in a list on a line by itself.

9. Type the following set of procedures on your computer and then execute QUIZ to try the procedures. The set of procedures form an interactive drill program for addition. Edit the procedures to form an interactive drill program for multiplication.

```
TO QUIZ
START.QUIZ
MAKE "PROB 1
MAKE "SCORE 0
GIVE.QUIZ :PROB :TOTAL :SCORE
END
```

```
TO START.QUIZ
CLEARTEXT
PRINT [HELLO, WHAT'S YOUR NAME?]
PRINT (SENTENCE [HELLO] REQUEST )
PRINT [ ]
PRINT [THE FOLLOWING IS A DRILL PROGRAM]
PRINT [THAT PROVIDES PRACTICE ADDING TWO ]
PRINT [NUMBERS.]
PRINT [ ]
PRINT [TO STOP THE PROGRAM PRESS CTRL-G]
REPEAT 3 [PRINT [ ]]
PRINT [HOW MANY PROBLEMS DO YOU WANT?]
MAKE "TOTAL READNUMBER
END
```

```
TO READNUMBER
MAKE "IN FIRST REQUEST
TEST NUMBER? :IN
IFTRUE OUTPUT :IN
IFFALSE PRINT [PLEASE ANSWER WITH A NUMBER]
IFFALSE OUTPUT READNUMBER
END
```

```
TO GIVE.QUIZ :PROB :TOTAL :SCORE
CLEARTEXT
MAKE "NUM1 RANDOM 100
MAKE "NUM2 RANDOM 100
MAKE "ANSWER :NUM1 + :NUM2
PRINT [ ]
PRINT SENTENCE [PROBLEM ] :PROB
PRINT [ ]
PRINT (SENTENCE [HOW MUCH IS ] :NUM1 [ +] :NUM2 )
MAKE "REPLY READNUMBER
TEST :REPLY = :ANSWER
IFTRUE PRINT [GOOD]
IFTRUE MAKE "SCORE :SCORE + 1
IFFALSE PRINT SENTENCE [SORRY, THE ANSWER IS ] :ANSWER
PRINT [ ]
WAIT 200
IF :PROB = :TOTAL ENDING STOP
GIVE.QUIZ (:PROB + 1 ) :TOTAL :SCORE
END


TO WAIT :TIME
IF :TIME = 0 STOP
WAIT :TIME − 1
END


TO ENDING
CLEARTEXT
PRINT SENTENCE [YOUR SCORE IS ] :SCORE
PRINT (SENTENCE [OUT OF ] :TOTAL [PROBLEMS] )
END
```

8-3 Applications in List Processing

In this section, we introduce several projects involving words and lists. The first project is to write a procedure for determining the number of items in a list. To accomplish this, we write a procedure called LENGTH, which has the list :L as input.

Think about what we want the procedure to do. If the list :L is empty, we want the computer to output 0. If the list is not empty, we want the computer to read the first item in the list. We could have the computer output 1, but if there are more items in the list, we do not want an output yet. Next we want the computer to read the second item in the list, if there is one.

The use of BUTFIRST causes the computer to output a list without its first item; that is, the second item in the original list becomes the first item in the new list. Thus, for any input :L, the number of items in :L is one more than in BUTFIRST :L. Hence if LENGTH :L gives the number of items in :L, the number of items in :L can be defined recursively in terms of the number of items in BUTFIRST :L as 1 + LENGTH (BUTFIRST :L). For example, if :L = [MOVIE PARK SCHOOL], we have LENGTH [MOVIE PARK SCHOOL] = 1+ LENGTH [MOVIE PARK]. However, LENGTH [MOVIE PARK] = 1 + LENGTH [MOVIE], and LENGTH [MOVIE] = 1 + LENGTH [ ]. If we define LENGTH to be 0 when its input is [ ], then LENGTH [MOVIE] = 1 + 0, or 1; LENGTH [MOVIE PARK] = 1 + 1, or 2; LENGTH [MOVIE PARK SCHOOL] = 1 + 2, or 3. Drawing on these ideas, we write the following LENGTH procedure:

```
TO LENGTH :L
IF :L = [ ] OUTPUT 0
OUTPUT 1+LENGTH BUTFIRST :L
END
```

This LENGTH procedure can be generalized to find the number of elements in a word as well as in a list. (In Terrapin Logo version 2.0, the primitive COUNT does this.) All we need to do is edit the conditional IF :L = [ ] OUTPUT 0 to include the case in which the input is the empty word. The new procedure, which we call COUNT, is shown here.

```
TO COUNT :L
IF ANYOF (:L = [ ]) (:L = " ) OUTPUT 0
OUTPUT 1 + COUNT BUTFIRST :L
END
```

Picking a Word from a List

Next, let's write a procedure called PICK to choose an item from a list. Obviously, our procedure must have a list, :L, as one input. To have the computer choose an item from the list, we assign a number, :NUMBER, to the item that we want chosen and make that a second input. For example, if we want the second item from the list to be chosen, we might give the computer 2 as the :NUMBER input.

If :NUMBER = 1, we want the computer to output the first item in the list. We can tell the computer this with the following line:

```
IF :NUMBER = 1 OUTPUT FIRST :L
```

Notice that the third item in [A B C D] is the same as the second item in list [B C D]. Thus, if :NUMBER is not 1, we want to execute PICK again with the first input being :NUMBER − 1 and the second being a list of all items in the original list except the first. The following line will accomplish this.

```
OUTPUT PICK (:NUMBER − 1)(BF :L)
```

With this the statement, we can call PICK recursively until each item is identified with a number. The complete PICK procedure is given below.

```
TO PICK :NUMBER :L
IF :NUMBER = 1 OUTPUT FIRST :L
OUTPUT PICK (:NUMBER − 1)(BF :L)
END
```

Here is a telescoping model of the **PICK** procedure.

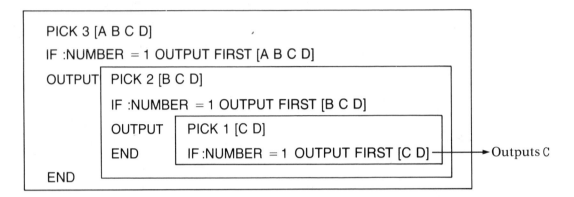

Remark: In Terrapin Logo version 2.0, the primitive **ITEM** does the same thing as **PICK**.

Picking a Word at Random from a List

At this time, we do not know how to choose an item at random from a list. However, we do know both how to choose an item from a list when we know the number of its position and how to choose a number at random using the primitive **RANDOM**. The **PICKRANDOM** procedure that we now write combines these two techniques.

First we must know how many items are in our list, :L. The **LENGTH** procedure we wrote earlier can find the length of a list. Now we can choose the number of a word at random using **RANDOM** (1 + **LENGTH** :L). (Do you see why 1 is added to **LENGTH** :L?) Finally, we can use the **PICK** procedure with inputs (1 + **RANDOM LENGTH** :L) and :L. The **PICKRANDOM** procedure follows.

```
TO PICKRANDOM :L
OUTPUT PICK (1 + RANDOM LENGTH :L) :L
END
```

Constructing Sentences

Our next project is to write a procedure, SENTENCE1, for constructing simple grammatical sentences in which the first word, an article,
is followed by an adjective, a noun, a verb, and an adverb, all chosen
at random from lists of words for each part of speech. To write this
procedure, we first need a procedure called STARTUP in which we
teach the computer the possible words for each part of speech. Next
we go to the nodraw mode and set the cursor where we want the
printing of the sentence to begin. We choose CURSOR 0 8 as the place
to start the sentence. Finally, our procedure needs to print the sentence. This can be accomplished by using the PRINT primitive. We
also need to write procedures that choose each of the parts of speech
for our sentence from the list of possible words for that part of speech.
We call these procedures ARTICLE, ADJECTIVE, NOUN, VERB, and
ADVERB. The PRINT statement using these procedures could be as
shown here:

```
PRINT (SENTENCE ARTICLE ADJECTIVE NOUN VERB ADVERB )
```

Our complete SENTENCE1 procedure looks like this:

```
TO SENTENCE1
STARTUP
NODRAW
CURSOR 0 8
PRINT (SENTENCE ARTICLE ADJECTIVE NOUN VERB ADVERB )
END
```

Now we need to write the STARTUP procedure. For this procedure
we need to provide the computer with a list of words to use for each
part of speech. For example, the list of articles could be [A THE]. To
provide the lists of words for the parts of speech, we use MAKE statements with the variables :ARTICLELIST, :ADJECTIVELIST, :NOUNLIST,
:VERBLIST, and :ADVERBLIST. (Observe that a variable can be used
to name a list as well as a number.) If the lists assigned to these
variables are, respectively, [A THE], [LARGE SMALL PLUMP SKINNY],

[GRIZZLY BOBCAT TIGER [SWEAT HOG] RABBIT], [RUNS JUMPS SWIMS WALKS], and [QUICKLY SLOWLY QUIETLY LOUDLY], the STARTUP procedure looks like this.

```
TO STARTUP
MAKE "ARTICLELIST [A THE]
MAKE "ADJECTIVELIST [LARGE SMALL PLUMP SKINNY]
MAKE "NOUNLIST [GRIZZLY BOBCAT TIGER [SWEAT HOG] RABBIT]
MAKE "VERBLIST [RUNS JUMPS SWIMS WALKS]
MAKE "ADVERBLIST [QUICKLY SLOWLY QUIETLY LOUDLY]
END
```

Next we need to write the ARTICLE, ADJECTIVE, NOUN, VERB, and ADVERB procedures for choosing the parts of speech from the respective lists. For example, the procedure called ARTICLE should output a word from :ARTICLELIST. Because we do not wish to choose a specific word from the list, we choose our word with the PICKRANDOM procedure, which chooses a word from the list at random. The procedure called ARTICLE follows.

```
TO ARTICLE
OUTPUT PICKRANDOM :ARTICLELIST
END
```

In a similar manner we write procedures for choosing the rest of the parts of speech.

```
TO ADJECTIVE
OUTPUT PICKRANDOM :ADJECTIVELIST
END
```

```
TO NOUN
OUTPUT PICKRANDOM :NOUNLIST
END
```

```
TO VERB
OUTPUT PICKRANDOM :VERBLIST
END
```

```
TO ADVERB
OUTPUT PICKRANDOM :ADVERBLIST
END
```

Now, if we execute **SENTENCE1**, an output such as the following may be obtained.

```
A SKINNY TIGER RUNS SLOWLY
```

Run this procedure several times and compare the results.

The Fibonacci Sequence

Our final project is to rewrite the procedure from Chapter 6 for producing Fibonacci numbers, using list-processing primitives. Recall that a Fibonacci sequence of numbers is formed by starting with two numbers and adding them to obtain a third number, adding the second and third numbers to obtain a fourth number, and so on.

We may enter the first two numbers of the sequence as items in a list. The list becomes the input to the variable :**NUMBERS**. To obtain the third term of the sequence, we must add the first and second terms, and so on; in general, to find the nth term, we must add the $(n-1)$ and $(n-2)$ terms.

To translate this process into a Logo procedure involving list-processing primitives, we write a procedure called **FIBONACCI** that accepts a list called :**NUMBERS** containing two numbers as input. Suppose the first input is [5 7]. The first term in the sequence, then, is 5; the second term is 7; the third term is $5+7$, or 12; the fourth term is $7+12$, or 19, and so on. Thus, the sequence appears as 5, 7, 12, 19, 31, ...

The successive numbers in the sequence can be thought of as the first items in the following lists.

[5 7]

[7 12]

[12 19]

[19 31]

•

•

•

Observe that the second item in every list after the first list is the sum of the numbers in the previous list. For example, 19 = 7 + 12. Thus, we can compute each successive term in the sequence, which we call :NEXT, as follows:

MAKE "NEXT ((FIRST :NUMBERS) + (LAST :NUMBERS))

We want the FIBONACCI procedure to print the first term in the successive lists. This can be accomplished using PRINT FIRST :NUMBERS and making the procedure recursive. The input has to change for each recursive call; the new input becomes a list consisting of LAST :NUMBERS and :NEXT. How may we combine these inputs into a list? One way is to use SENTENCE and the MAKE statement, as in this example:

MAKE "NUMBERS (SENTENCE LAST :NUMBERS :NEXT)

To complete the procedure, we use the recursive call FIBONACCI :NUMBERS, as shown below.

```
TO FIBONACCI :NUMBERS
MAKE "NEXT ((FIRST :NUMBERS) + (LAST :NUMBERS))
PRINT FIRST :NUMBERS
MAKE "NUMBERS (SENTENCE LAST :NUMBERS :NEXT)
FIBONACCI :NUMBERS
END
```

If you execute this procedure using FIBONACCI [1 1], it is impossible to see what is happening because the results are printed too fast. Several things can be done to change this. One way to do this is to include the line PAUSE in the procedure immediately after the PRINT statement. Once we have seen the output, we would have to type CONTINUE (CO) to continue the execution of the procedure. Another alternative is to use the WAIT procedure shown below.

```
TO WAIT :N
IF :N=0 STOP
WAIT :N-1
END
```

We include the line **WAIT 50** in the edited **FIBONACCI** procedure shown below.

```
TO FIBONACCI :NUMBERS
MAKE "NEXT ((FIRST :NUMBERS) + (LAST :NUMBERS))
PRINT FIRST :NUMBERS
WAIT 50
MAKE "NUMBERS (SENTENCE LAST :NUMBERS :NEXT)
FIBONACCI :NUMBERS
END
```

Yet another extension is to have **FIBONACCI** output the results in a list. If this is done, then other procedures can be written to make use of this list.

Problem Set 8-3

1. It is often said that predicting the weather is a random process. Using the list [FAIR RAIN SNOW SLEET HAIL SUNNY CLOUDY], write a procedure to output a prediction for the weather.

2. Write a procedure to print a letter in which the computer chooses to address the letter to your mother, cousin, aunt, or friend; chooses the body of the letter to ask to borrow either money or a car; and chooses the closing from the following: Sincerely, Love, Fondly, or Thanks. All choices should be made at random.

3. Edit the **FIBONACCI** procedure given in this section to make it stop after n terms are printed.

4. Write a procedure called **VOWEL?** to determine whether or not an input letter is a vowel.

5. Write a procedure called **ORDER**, which accepts a number from 1 to 26 inclusive and outputs the corresponding letter of the alphabet.

6. Documentation tells what a procedure or a line in a procedure does. To add documentation to a procedure, simply type a semicolon followed by whatever comments you wish. Logo takes no action on material typed after a semicolon. Here is an example:

```
TO SQUARE :S
;THIS PROCEDURE DRAWS A VARIABLE SIDE SQUARE.
;:S STANDS FOR THE LENGTH OF A SIDE.
REPEAT 4 [FORWARD :S RIGHT 90] ;THIS LINE
    ACTUALLY DRAWS THE SQUARE.
END
```

Write documentation for the FIBONACCI procedure.

Solution to the Preliminary Problem

Understanding the Problem

In the Tower of Hanoi puzzle in Figure 8-1, we are to write a procedure to tell how to move the disks from Peg A to Peg C. The rules are that no more than one disk can be moved at a time and no disk can be placed upon a smaller disk. We are also required to use the minimum number of moves.

Figure 8-1

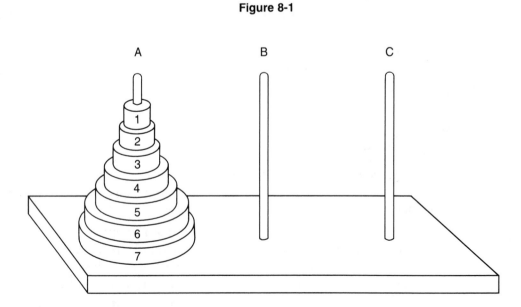

Devising a Plan

Consider Figure 8-2. If the top six disks could be moved to Peg B somehow, then the seventh disk could be moved to Peg C. After that, the problem becomes one of moving the six disks on Peg B to Peg C. Thus, if we knew how to move six disks to another peg, we could move all of the original seven disks.

Figure 8-2

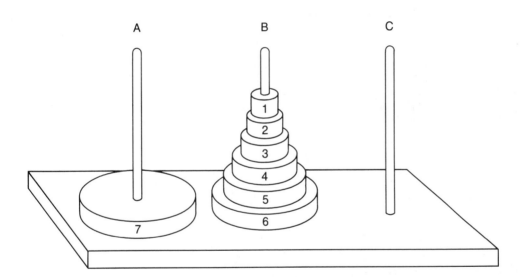

Similarly, the problem of moving six disks can be reduced to a problem of moving five disks. If the top five disks could be moved to Peg A, then the sixth disk could be moved to Peg C—and so on. In other words, we have a recursive series of moves that continues until all moves are completed and the puzzle is finished.

To help in writing the procedure, we use the strategy of solving a simpler problem. Consider the three-disk puzzle pictured in Figure 8-3(a) on page 368. Suppose we want to move these three disks from

Peg A, the beginning peg, to Peg C, the ending peg. The necessary moves are pictured in Figure 8-3(b)–(h) and summarized following the figure.

Figure 8-3

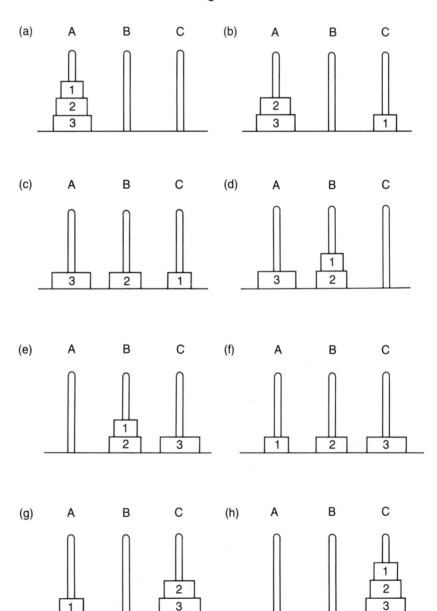

(a)   All disks on Peg A.

(b)   Move disk 1 from Peg A to Peg C.

(c)   Move disk 2 from Peg A to Peg B.

(d)   Move disk 1 from Peg C to Peg B.

(e)   Move disk 3 from Peg A to Peg C.

(f)   Move disk 1 from Peg B to Peg A.

(g)   Move disk 2 from Peg B to Peg C.

(h)   Move disk 1 from Peg A to Peg C.

By looking at the series of disk moves, we see the pattern 1213121. The top two disks are moved until they are placed on Peg B, the alternate peg; then disk 3 is moved to the ending peg, Peg C; and the series of moves with disks 1 and 2 is repeated until the disks are placed in order on Peg C. The process involved may bring to mind the "winding" and "unwinding" of embedded recursion previously discussed in Chapter 4.

We want our procedure, which we call TOWER, to move all disks except the bottom one from the beginning peg to the alternate peg and move the bottom disk to the ending peg. The process is then repeated but with the original starting peg becoming the alternate peg and the original alternate peg becoming the starting peg. With this approach, we need input for the number of disks (:NUMBER) and for each of the three pegs (:BEGINNING, :ALTERNATE, and :ENDING). If the pegs are labeled as shown in Figure 8-3, we can enter them as input lists [A], [B], and [C] when the procedure is executed.

Our title line will be as follows:

TO TOWER :NUMBER :BEGINNING :ALTERNATE :ENDING

The first moves can be determined by calling the TOWER procedure with one less disk, that is, :NUMBER − 1, and keeping the beginning peg the same but making the ending peg be the alternate peg. (Recall that we first wanted the 1 and 2 disks to go to Peg B, as in Figure 8-3(d).)

The final moves can be determined by calling the **TOWER** procedure with one less disk, that is, :NUMBER − 1, but starting the moves from the alternate peg and making the ending peg be the ending peg. (Recall that, as shown in Figure 8-3, we wanted the 1 and 2 disks to be moved from Peg B to Peg C at the end.) Thus, our procedure might look like this:

```
TO TOWER :NUMBER :BEGINNING :ALTERNATE :ENDING
TOWER :NUMBER − 1 :BEGINNING :ENDING :ALTERNATE
TOWER :NUMBER − 1 :ALTERNATE :BEGINNING :ENDING
END
```

This **TOWER** procedure has two problems: It contains no **STOP** statement, and it contains no directions showing how to make the moves. To correct the first problem, we must decide when we want the recursive "winding" to stop. We want the procedure to stop winding when there are no disks left to move from Peg A, that is, when :NUMBER = 0. Hence, we need the line **IF :NUMBER = 0 STOP.** Trial and error should convince you that this line should come immediately after the title line in the procedure.

To rewrite the procedure to give directions for moving the disks, we need to use some list-processing commands. We need the computer to tell us not only the number of the disk to move but also the names of the pegs we are moving the disk from and to. For example, a line of directions might look like this:

```
MOVE DISK____FROM PEG____TO PEG____
```

where the first blank is :NUMBER; the second blank, :BEGINNING, is the name of the peg where the move starts; and the last blank, :END-ING, is the name of the peg where the move ends. We can place the phrases MOVE DISK, FROM PEG, TO PEG with the inputs :NUMBER, :BEGINNING, and :ENDING in lists in a print statement and use the primitive **SENTENCE** to combine them, as follows:

```
PRINT (SENTENCE [MOVE DISK] :NUMBER
    [FROM PEG] :BEGINNING [TO PEG] :ENDING )
```

This line should fit between the recursive calls to TOWER (Why?), giving us the procedure below.

```
TO TOWER :NUMBER :BEGINNING :ALTERNATE :ENDING
IF :NUMBER = 0 STOP
TOWER :NUMBER – 1 :BEGINNING :ENDING :ALTERNATE
PRINT (SENTENCE [MOVE DISK] :NUMBER
    [FROM PEG] :BEGINNING [TO PEG] :ENDING )
TOWER :NUMBER – 1 :ALTERNATE :BEGINNING :ENDING
END
```

Carrying Out the Plan

If we execute TOWER 7 [A] [B] [C], we may not like the results. The series of moves is listed, but the lines flash on the monitor screen and scroll off so rapidly as to be unreadable. There are several ways to rectify this. One is to use PAUSE immediately following the PRINT statement. If this route is taken, the user must type CONTINUE (CO) to have the procedure continue execution after each move is listed. An alternative is to use the WAIT procedure given earlier in this chapter after the PRINT statement or to use the READCHARACTER primitive introduced in Chapter 7 to stop and wait for the user to press a key before continuing with the procedure. Readers may decide which method is best.

Looking Back

A variation of this procedure is to have the computer count the number of moves necessary to complete the puzzle. The original Tower of Hanoi puzzle supposedly contained 64 disks. Could you actually make the moves if there were 64 disks?

Chapter 8 Problem Set

1. Predict the output of each of the following lines. Then execute the lines to check your results.

   (a) PRINT "DRAGONS

   (b) PRINT "56778

   (c) PRINT "DUNGEONS AND DRAGONS

   (d) PRINT "DUNGEONS "AND "DRAGONS

   (e) PRINT " 27 + 13

   (f) PRINT "27 + 13

   (g) PRINT [DRAGONS]

   (h) PRINT [DUNGEONS AND DRAGONS]

   (i) PRINT [DUNGEONS] "AND "DRAGONS

   (j) PRINT DUNGEONS AND DRAGONS

   (k) PRINT SE "DUNGEONS AND DRAGONS

   (l) PRINT SE "DUNGEONS "AND "DRAGONS

   (m) PRINT (SE [DUNGEONS] [AND] [DRAGONS])

   (n) PRINT LIST "DUNGEONS "AND "DRAGONS

   (o) PRINT LIST "DUNGEONS "AND [DRAGONS]

   (p) PRINT FIRST BUTLAST [DRAGONS]

   (q) PRINT FIRST BUTLAST "DRAGONS

   (r) PRINT LAST BUTFIRST [DUNGEONS AND DRAGONS]

2. (a) Write a procedure to instruct the computer to accept **D** as an abbreviation for **DRAW**.

   (b) Write a procedure to instruct the computer to accept **F** as an abreviation for **FIRST**.

3. Write an interactive procedure that is similar to the **MFACT** procedure written in this section but involves single-digit subtractions.

4. Use the **POLY** procedure from Chapter 4 to write a procedure that asks the user which polygon to draw. That is, the computer should ask the user how many sides are desired and the length of the side. Have the procedure draw the polygon, given these inputs.

5. Write a procedure called **TRIANGLE.L**, which takes a list such as [THIS IS A LIST] as input and outputs the following format:

```
THIS IS A LIST
IS A LIST
A LIST
LIST
```

6. (a) Write a program in which the computer chooses a number at random between 1 and 1000 inclusive and the user tries to guess the number. After each guess, the computer should tell the user whether the guess is too high, too low, or correct.

   ☆ (b) What is the minimum number of guesses that the user needs to make in order to ensure the correct answer?

7. Write a procedure that takes any word as input and, as output, states whether the word starts with a vowel or not.

8. Write a procedure called **ROTATE**, which takes a list as input and outputs a list with the first item last and the remaining items in the list in the same order.

Games and Answers Disk Appendix

Using the Games Portion of the Disk

The disk contains six games written in the Logo language and solutions to selected problems in this book. The next two sections of this appendix deal with using the games and modifying the games.

Using the Games

The games on this disk are intended to be entertaining, but they also demonstrate some of the powerful properties of Logo. Several of the games are very useful for learning about distances in "turtle steps," turning angles, and the turtle graphics features of Logo. Logo games are discussed in Chapter 7 of this book. After reading the book through Chapter 7 and studying the games procedures, you could attempt to write similar games.

You should make a copy of the Games and Answers Disk as soon as possible. The original Games and Answers Disk should then be kept in a safe place; only a copy of the disk should actually be used. This precaution will protect you against the potential disaster of losing or changing the only copy of your Games and Answers Disk. Please note, however, that copying this disk for any reason other than creating a backup copy for the disk's owner is a violation of copyright laws.

There are several ways of copying a disk. One way is to use the Logo commands READ and SAVE as discussed in Chapter 2. A faster way is to use the COPYA program supplied on the Apple System Master Disk. Complete instructions for this program can be found on pages 38–40 of the Apple DOS Manual. (If you have a IIc or newer IIe, use the ProDOS System Utilities disk to make the copies. See your user's manual for instructions.) There are subtle differences between the two copying methods that are important to users who wish to modify the games. These differences will be discussed in the section on modifications.

For instructions on how to use the games on the Games and Answers Disk, insert it into the disk drive (Drive 1 if you have two drives) and turn on the computer. Type I for instructions. When a menu of options is displayed, select option 1 for complete instructions. If you desire specific instructions on how to load Logo, load a game, or start a game, select one of the other options. The complete instructions include all of these more specific instructions. Note that the instructions on the disk cannot be used after Logo has been loaded.

If you do not wish to use the instructions on the disk, you can refer to the following brief explanation of how to use the disk:

1. Insert the Logo Language Disk into the disk drive and turn on the power. After a few moments you will be welcomed to Logo. If you are using an Apple IIe or Apple IIc, make sure the CAPS LOCK key is down.

2. Remove the Logo Language Disk from the disk drive and insert the Games and Answers Disk in its place.

3. Type the word **CATALOG** and press the RETURN key. You will see a listing of the contents of the disk. Games are indicated by a * at the left. The other files are not games.

4. Select one of the six games (they are described below) and load that game by typing **READ "GAMENAME** and pressing the RETURN key, where **GAMENAME** is the name of the game you wish to play. Do *not* include the .**LOGO** prefix as part of the name when you use the **READ** command. Notice that the name of the game is preceded by one double quotation mark.

5. Once you have typed **READ** followed by a quotation mark and the name of your game, the disk will spin for some time and a listing of all of the game's components will be printed. When you see the Logo prompt (the question mark symbol) again, type the word **START** and press the RETURN key. Instructions for the game will then be displayed and the game will begin.

6. If you wish to stop the game before it is over, type Q. You will then be asked if you wish to play the same game again. If you choose not to play again, type N as a response to the question.

The game will be erased from memory, and you will be returned to Logo.

7. If you wish to play another game, repeat the process beginning with step 3.

The six games on this disk are DARTGAME, SKETCH, CHASE, CHAMELEON, GOLF, and LANDER. Below is a description and instructions for playing each game. Similar instructions are displayed on the computer screen prior to playing the games.

DARTGAME

This is a computerized game of darts and a good introduction to turtle distances and turning angles. A target is drawn at the center of the screen. You will get three darts, one at a time, to "throw" at the target. Each dart will appear at a random position along the bottom of the screen.

Aim the dart at the center of the target by using the R and L keys. The R key turns the dart (turtle) right 10 degrees (**RT 10**); the L key turns it left 10 degrees (**LT 10**). When the dart has been aimed, press the F (for fire) key. Type the word **DART** and the number of turtle steps the dart is to be thrown. For example, **DART 120** throws the dart 120 steps.

You will receive extra points for good throws. When you are out of darts, the total score will be given.

SKETCH

This program allows you to investigate the powerful features of turtle graphics without any knowledge of Logo. It is useful in demonstrating turtle graphics and can be used creatively to draw pictures.

You control the turtle with a variety of commands. The designs you create can be saved on disk and reproduced on the screen. Below is a list of the sketching commands. They are also displayed at the bottom of the screen as you sketch.

L	Turns the turtle left 10 degrees.
R	Turns the turtle right 10 degrees.
P	Lets you change the pen color.

U   Pulls the pen up so you can move the turtle without drawing.

D   Puts the pen down to continue drawing.

F   "Freezes" the turtle.

T   "Thaws" the turtle.

H   Home (moves the turtle to the center of the screen).

C   Clears the screen.

S   Saves your picture on a disk.

G   Gets a saved picture from a disk and displays it on the screen.

0 to 9 Adjusts the turtle's speed. 9 is the fastest.

Q   Quit sketching.

When you save a picture on a disk, it is saved with the filename **STEADY**. When you get a saved picture, it's the one in this file. If you wish to save your picture in a more permanent file or to save more than one picture, read about the **READPICT** and **SAVEPICT** commands described in the book.

When you wish to change the pen color, type P. You will then be asked to type the name of the color you want. The colors are black, white, blue, green, violet, and orange.

When you start, the turtle will be "frozen." Type T to "thaw" it and begin sketching.

CHASE

This game is included because its design is specifically discussed in Chapter 7. In this game you control a rabbit, which is chased by a fox. Both are represented by blinking turtle symbols; both leave "tracks" to help you see the directions they are moving.

Use the R and L keys to turn the rabbit. The R key turns it right 15 degrees (**RT 15**); the L key turns it left 15 degrees (**LT 15**). The rabbit may not cross the boundaries of the screen.

A running indication of the amount of time left will appear at the bottom of the screen. If the rabbit hasn't been caught when the time runs out, you've won!

CHAMELEON

In this game you control a hungry chameleon that moves in a straight line up the center of the screen.

Use the R and L keys to change the direction of the chameleon's head. The R key turns the head right 15 degrees (**RT 15**), and the L key turns the head left 15 degrees (**LT 15**). Flies (represented by stars) will appear one at a time at random locations.

The F key "fires" the chameleon's tongue. You must hit the fly with the very tip of the chameleon's tongue. Help the chameleon eat as many flies as possible before the clock at the bottom of the screen runs out.

GOLF

This game, like the DARTGAME, helps you learn to judge turning angles and distances in "turtle steps." It also demonstrates the use of randomness in games. Both the golf hole and the slammer club incorporate a certain degree of randomness.

In this game, a hole is drawn at a random location. The object is to put the golf ball in the hole in as few shots as possible. For each shot you will first be asked the direction. Type **POINT**, the direction (turtle direction 0-360), and RETURN. Next you will be asked which club you want to use. Type one of the following and RETURN:

SLAMMER	Hits the ball 100 or more steps.
WOOD	Hits the ball 100 steps.
IRON	Hits the ball 50 steps.
CHIPPER	Hits the ball 20 steps.
PUTTER	Hits the ball 5 steps.

LANDER

This is an especially entertaining game that demonstrates Logo's power in stimulating physical phenomena. It lets you attempt to land a rocket on a rocky planet.

The lander's heading is controlled by the R and L keys. The R key turns the lander right 15 degrees (**RT 15**), while the L key turns it left

15 degrees (LT 15). You can apply thrust to move in the direction the lander is pointing by typing 1, 2, 3, 4, or 5. 1 is just a little thrust, while 5 is a very powerful thrust. Remember that gravity is always trying to pull you toward the bottom of the screen. The lander can cross either edge of the screen, but if it goes off the top you will be lost in space.

If the rocket begins moving too fast, type E for emergency assistance. The rocket will freeze for a moment before the force of gravity begins pulling it downwards again.

Modifications (For Advanced Users)

Locked Files

Names of all games are preceded by an asterisk (*) in the catalog of the Games and Answers Disk. The * symbol allows users to identify the games easily, but it serves another purpose as well. The * indicates that the file is locked. A locked file can be read into memory and used like any other file but cannot be erased by a command such as ERASEFILE and cannot be written over (that is, it cannot be modified and then saved under the same name). To modify a locked file, you must unlock the file before saving the modified version or else save the modified file under a new name. If we wished to modify CHAMELEON, for example, we could make the modifications, unlock CHAMELEON with the Logo command DOS [UNLOCK CHAMELEON.LOGO], save the new version of CHAMELEON with SAVE "CHAMELEON, and finally relock the file with DOS [LOCK CHAMELEON.LOGO]. Notice that when locking and unlocking a Logo file, you must include the .LOGO suffix at the end of the file name. A simpler method of modifying a locked file would be to call the modified version by a new name (such as CHAMELEON.MOD in this case), thus avoiding the locking and unlocking of the original file.

The games on the Games and Answers Disk are locked to prevent accidental modifications or erasure. As stated earlier, the original disk should be copied and then stored safely away. Do not unlock the games on the original disk. If you choose to copy the Games and Answers Disk with the Logo commands READ and SAVE, the copied files will not be locked. If you choose this method, you will also need

to transfer all the files on the original disk whose names include the
.PICT suffix (see **READPICT** and **SAVEPICT**). If you choose to copy the
entire Games and Answers Disk with **COPYA** or a similar program,
the games on the copy will remain locked.

Suggestions for Modifications

Once the disk is copied, you may make modifications to the games.
Before modifying any game, be sure to remove the line that clears
memory at game's end (**GOODBYE**). Otherwise, modifications will be
lost if the game is played before being saved on disk.

Here is a list of possible modifications for each game. Investigate
making several of these modifications. The modifications suggested
here assume that the reader has worked through the text and has
acquired the necessary background to attempt these projects.

DARTGAME

1. Modify the game so that the dart (turtle) is set at any random
   location on the screen outside of the target rather than confining
   it to the bottom of the screen.

2. Change the shape, colors, and number of rings in the target. Save
   the new target under the name **TARGET**, since this is the picture
   automatically loaded by DARTGAME.

3. Create several new targets and save them in **PICT** files. The game
   could select a target randomly and read in that picture or ask
   the player to choose a target.

SKETCH

1. Many more features can be added to this program through modifications in the **CHECK** procedure. The user could change the
   background color by pressing a certain key (it may help to see
   how the pen colors are changed in **SKETCH** before trying this),
   and another key can be used to send the turtle to any point on
   the screen. When the appropriate key is pushed, the computer
   asks the user to enter new x- and y-coordinates for the turtle and
   then moves the turtle to that point before resuming animation.

2. The Shape Editor can be used to design the shape of a pen. When SKETCH is used, it can automatically load this shape in and use it instead of the turtle.

3. When the user wishes to store a picture, SKETCH stores that picture in a file called **STEADY.PICT**. It is possible instead for the computer to ask the user for the name of a file in which to store (and from which to read) the picture. Try to implement this modification and consider the advantages and disadvantages of both systems.

CHASE

1. If paddles are available, use a paddle instead of the keyboard to control the rabbit.

2. Have more than one fox chase the rabbit. It may also be interesting to place the fox and rabbit at random positions on the screen.

CHAMELEON

1. This game places only one fly at a time on the screen. Placing several flies on the screen at once will make the game more interesting. You will also have to address the issue of how to adjust the length of the chameleon's tongue for the various flies (it may help to check how the adjustable tongue works in the original version).

2. The Shape Editor can be used to create the shape of a chameleon that is loaded in automatically when the game is executed.

3. The chameleon does not have to travel along a straight line. The player could control the chameleon's path, or the chameleon could move along a predefined shape such as a circle, figure eight, or rectangle.

GOLF

1. Using the SKETCH program, you can create an attractive picture of a golf course that is automatically read in when the game begins.

2. A golf ball does not always travel along a straight line. Wind and terrain may influence its path. You may wish to warn the player of a gust of wind, both its direction and its magnitude (force), and have this gust of wind influence the path of the ball (you might first want to examine the LANDER game, where a similar thing is done with gravity and engine thrusts). Some knowledge of vector addition and trigonometry is required for this modification.

LANDER

1. There are only three flat spots, each with the same elevation, on which the rocket can land safely. You can create a more interesting terrain and save it in the PICT file TERRAIN. You will also need to modify the game to verify that the rocket has landed on the new terrain.

2. If paddles are available, the game can be modified so that one paddle controls the rotation (heading) of the rocket and the other paddle adjusts the thrust of the rocket's engine.

Using the Answers Portion of the Disk

The disk contains the solutions to odd-numbered problems in the book. Logo must be loaded in order to examine these solutions.

When cataloging the Games and Answers Disk, you will notice that after the games there are many other files that look something like this:

```
B 014 ONE.2.LOGO
B 003 ONE.3.LOGO
B 008 ONE.PROBLEMS.LOGO
B 011 TWO.1.LOGO
```

The file ONE.2.LOGO contains the solutions to the odd-numbered problems in section 2 of Chapter 1 (labeled 1-2 in the book). Similarly, ONE.3.LOGO contains the solutions to the odd-numbered problems in section 3 of Chapter 1. The file ONE.PROBLEMS.LOGO contains the solutions to odd-numbered problems in the Chapter 1 Problem Set. Remember that when reading in any Logo file we omit the .LOGO suffix.

The names of the procedures in these solution files are easy to remember. The name of the solution to problem 1 is **ONE**, the name of the solution to problem 3 is **THREE**, and so forth. If problem 5 has parts (a), (b), and (c), the solution procedures will be called **FIVE.A**, **FIVE.B**, and **FIVE.C**. If part (a) of problem 5 has four parts, the solution procedure will be called **FIVE.AI**, **FIVE.AII**, **FIVE.AIII**, and **FIVE.AIV**. If the solution to a problem is a procedure that does not require variables in its title line, typing the name of the problem (ONE, THREE, FIVE, and so on) will cause the procedure to be executed. If the solution requires variables in its title line, the solution procedure will print out a message such as TO SEE THE PROCEDURE, TYPE EDIT (procedure name). You can then edit (procedure name) to see how the procedure works and how many variables it has in its title line. Once you know how many variables are in the title line, you can execute (procedure name) with that number of inputs. If the problem requires a written answer rather than a procedure, the solution procedure, when run, will print out the written solution. For example, if problem 1 requires a written answer, then executing the **ONE** procedure will print out the answer.

Glossary

Logo Commands

This Appendix lists all the Logo commands used in this book, along with corresponding abbreviations (given in parentheses) and examples of their use when appropriate.

ALLOF   Takes two inputs that are either true or false and outputs TRUE if all are true and FALSE otherwise. It may take more inputs if parentheses are used. For example,

ALLOF (1+2=3) (3<0)
RESULT: FALSE
(ALLOF (1+2=3) (3>0) (0<−1))
RESULT: FALSE

ANYOF   Takes two inputs that are either true or false and outputs TRUE if any of the inputs are true and FALSE otherwise. It may take more inputs if parentheses are used. For example,

ANYOF (1+2=3) (3<0)
RESULT: TRUE
(ANYOF (1+2=3) (3<0) (0<−1))
RESULT: TRUE

ATAN   Takes two numeric inputs and outputs an angle whose tangent is the first input divided by the second input. The angle is expressed in degrees between 0 and 360. For example,

ATAN 1 2
RESULT: 26.5652

BACK (BK)   Takes one input. Moves the turtle backward the number of turtle units that are input. For example,

BK 40

(Moves the turtle backwards 40 units.)

BACKGROUND (BG)   Takes one input, which must be an integer between 0 and 6 inclusive. Sets the color of the monitor screen background. For example,

BG 5

(Causes the monitor screen background to be blue.)

BUTFIRST (BF)

Takes one input and outputs all but the first item of the input. (If the input is a word, the output is all but the first character of the word.) For example,

BUTFIRST "HOUSE
RESULT: OUSE

BF [GONE WITH THE WIND]
RESULT: [WITH THE WIND]

BUTLAST (BL)

Takes one input and outputs all but the last item of the input. (If the input is a word, the output is all but the last character of the word.) For example,

BUTLAST "HOUSE
RESULT: HOUS

BL [LITTLE GREEN HOUSE]
RESULT: [LITTLE GREEN]

CATALOG

Takes no inputs. Prints the names of the files on the disk in the disk drive.

CLEARINPUT

Takes no inputs. Clears the character buffer.

CLEARSCREEN (CS)

Takes no inputs. Clears the graphics screen without moving the turtle.

CONTINUE (CO)

Takes no inputs. Continues execution of a procedure after **PAUSE** or CTRL-Z is used.

COS

Takes one numeric input—an angle in degrees. Outputs the cosine of the angle. For example,

COS 60
RESULT: .5

CTRL

This is called the CONTROL key. Holding the CTRL key down while pressing another key allows entry of control characters. (See separate listing of control characters.)

CURSOR

Takes two inputs, column number and row number, and positions the cursor there. Column numbers range from 0 to 39 and row numbers range from 0 to 23. For example,

CURSOR 0 0
(Places the cursor at the upper left corner of the screen.)

CURSOR 10 20
(Places the cursor at column 10 and row 20.)

DRAW

Takes no inputs. Sends the turtle home with heading 0 and clears the graphics screen.

* EDIT (ED)

Takes one or no inputs. The input may be the name of a procedure or the qualifiers **ALL**, **NAMES**, **PRO-CEDURES**. If no input is specified, **EDIT** causes the computer to enter the editor with the last defined procedure or a blank screen if there are no procedures in the workspace. For example,

EDIT ALL
(Puts all currently defined procedures as well as **MAKE** statements in the editor.)

EDIT NAMES
(Puts all **MAKE** statements in the editor.)

EDIT PROCEDURES
(Puts all the currently defined procedures in the editor.)

In Terrapin Logo version 2.0, **EDIT (ED)** *can take a list of procedures as input, for example,* **ED [TRIANGLE SQUARE]**

END

Use only as a last line in a procedure, as a signal to the computer that there are no more instructions to be given in a procedure.

ELSE

Used in the conditional form
IF ---- THEN ---- ELSE ----. The instruction following ELSE is executed only if the hypothesis is false. For example,

TO BI :N
IF :N = 0 PRINT 1 ELSE PRINT 0
END

BI 0   BI 5
1   0

*ERASE (ER)

Takes a particular procedure name as input and erases the procedure from the workspace. The input may also be one of the qualifiers **ALL**, **NAMES**, or **PROCEDURES**. For example,

ERASE BOX
(Erases the procedure named **BOX** from the workspace.)

ERASE ALL
(Clears the workspace.)

ERASE NAMES
(Erases the names and associated values given by all the **MAKE** statements.)

ERASE PROCEDURES
(Erases all the currently defined procedures.)

In Terrapin Logo version 2.0 **ERASE (ER)** *can take a list of procedures as input, for example,*
ER [TRIANGLE SQUARE].

ERASEFILE

Takes one input. Erases the file with the input name from the disk. For example,

ERASEFILE "MONDAY

(Erases the file named **MONDAY** from the disk in the disk drive.)

ERASEPICT

Takes one input. Erases the picture with the input name from the disk. For example,

ERASEPICT "HOUSE

(Erases a picture saved under the name **HOUSE** from the disk in the disk drive.)

FIRST

Takes one input and outputs the first element of that input. (If the input is a word, then the output is the first character in the word.) For example,

FIRST "MINDSTORMS
RESULT: M

FIRST [LOGO IS FUN]
RESULT: LOGO

FORWARD (FD)

Takes one input. Moves the turtle forward (in the direction the turtle is facing) the number of turtle units that are input. For example,

FD 20

(Moves the turtle forward 20 units.)

FPUT

Takes two inputs, the second of which is a list, and outputs a list consisting of the first input followed by the items of the second input. For example,

FPUT "S [TOP]
RESULT: [S TOP]

FPUT [X Y] [Z W]
RESULT: [[X Y] Z W]

FULLSCREEN
(CTRL-F)

Takes no inputs. In the draw mode, gives a full graphics screen.

GOODBYE

Takes no inputs. Clears the entire workspace and restarts Logo.

HEADING

Takes no inputs. In the draw mode, outputs the turtle's heading in degrees.

HIDETURTLE (HT)

Takes no inputs. In the draw mode, causes the turtle to disappear.

HOME

Takes no inputs. Returns the turtle to the center of the screen and sets its heading to 0. If the pen is down, it leaves a track from the turtle's initial location to the home position.

IF	Takes two inputs. It is used in the conditional form IF ---- THEN ----. The first input (the hypothesis) must be either true or false. The second input (the conclusion) contains instructions that are carried out if and only if the first input is true. The use of THEN is optional.
IFFALSE (IFF)	Executes the instructions following **IFFALSE** if the condition tested by the **TEST** command is false. (See **TEST**.)
IFTRUE (IFT)	Executes the instructions following **IFTRUE** if the condition tested by **TEST** is true. (See **TEST**.)
INTEGER	Requires one numeric input. Outputs the integer obtained by discarding the decimal part of the input, if any. For example, INTEGER 13.6 RESULT: 13 INTEGER −13.6 RESULT: -13
LAST	Takes one input and outputs the last element of that input. (If the input is a word, the output is the last character in the word.) For example, LAST "ALPHABET RESULT: T LAST [LOGO IS FUN] RESULT: FUN
LEFT (LT)	Takes one input. Turns the turtle left from its present heading the number of degrees that are input. For example, LT 90 (Turns the turtle left 90 degrees.)
LIST	Takes two inputs (may take more if parentheses are used) and outputs a list of the inputs. For example, LIST "HELLO "THERE RESULT: [HELLO THERE] (LIST 1 2 [3]) RESULT: [1 2 [3]]
LIST?	Takes one input and outputs TRUE if its input is a list and FALSE otherwise. For example, LIST? LOGO POWER RESULT: TRUE LIST? 3 RESULT: FALSE

LPUT

Takes two inputs, the second of which is a list, and outputs a list consisting of the items of the second input followed by the first input. For example,

LPUT "D [ABC]
RESULT: [ABC D]
LPUT [X Y] [Z W]
RESULT: [Z W [X Y]]

MAKE

Takes two inputs. The first, preceded by a quotation mark, is the name of a new variable. The second is the value of a new variable. For example,

MAKE "PI 3.14
PR :PI
RESULT: 3.14

NODRAW (ND)

Takes no inputs. Exits the graphics mode, clears the screen, and places the cursor in the upper left corner.

NOT

Takes one input. Outputs FALSE if the input is true; outputs TRUE if the input is false. For example,

NOT 2>3   NOT 2=2
RESULT: TRUE   RESULT: FALSE

NOTRACE

Takes no inputs. Causes the computer to turn off **TRACE**. Like **TRACE**, it can be included in a procedure.

NOWRAP

Takes no inputs. Causes Logo to give an error message any time the turtle attempts to cross the boundaries of the screen.

NUMBER?

Takes one input and outputs TRUE if that input is a number; FALSE otherwise. For example,

NUMBER? 0/5   NUMBER? THREE
RESULT: TRUE   RESULT: FALSE

OUTPUT (OP)

Takes one input. Causes the current procedure to stop and output the result to the calling procedure.

PADDLE (0)

Takes no inputs. Outputs an integer value from 0 to 255 depending on the position of the first paddle.

PADDLE (1)

Takes no inputs. Outputs an integer value from 0 to 255 depending on the position of the second paddle.

PAUSE

Takes no inputs. Can be added to a procedure at a point where you want to stop its execution. Allows you to type command lines while the procedure is stopped. Execution of procedure can be continued by typing **CONTINUE (CO)** if no errors have occurred during the pause.

PENCOLOR (PC)	Takes one input, which must be an integer between 0 and 6 inclusive. Determines the color of the turtle tracks in the draw mode. For example, **PENCOLOR 5** (Sets the turtle's pencolor to blue.)
PENDOWN (PD)	Takes no inputs. In the draw mode, it sets the turtle so that it can leave a track.
PENUP (PU)	Takes no inputs. In the draw mode, it enables the turtle to move without leaving a track.
PRINT (PR)	Takes one input. (May take more if parentheses are used.) Prints them on the screen, separated by spaces, and moves the cursor to the next line. **PRINT (PR)** can take a list as inputs. For example, **PR "WE** WE **(PR "WE "ARE "LEARNING "LOGO)** WE ARE LEARNING LOGO **PR [WE ARE LEARNING LOGO]** WE ARE LEARNING LOGO
PRINT1	Takes one input. (May take more if parentheses are used.) Does not move the cursor to a new line after printing the input.
*PRINTOUT (PO)	Takes one input, which can be a procedure name or one of the qualifiers: **ALL**, **NAMES**, **PROCEDURES**, or **TITLES**. **PRINTOUT TITLES** is abbreviated **POTS**. If a procedure name is input, **PRINTOUT** prints out the text of the procedure. For example, **PRINTOUT POLY** (Prints out the text of the procedure names **POLY**.) **PRINTOUT ALL** (Prints out everything in the workspace.) **PRINTOUT NAMES** (Prints out the names and associated values by all the **MAKE** statements.) **PRINTOUT PROCEDURES** (Prints out the texts of all the currently defined procedures.) **PRINTOUT TITLES** (Prints out the titles of all procedures in the workspace.) *In Terrapin Logo version 2.0*, **PRINTOUT (PO)** *can take a list of procedures as input—for example,* **PO [TRIANGLE SQUARE]**.

QUOTIENT	Requires two number inputs. Rounds the inputs into integers if they are not integers already. Outputs the integer part of the result of dividing the first integer by the second. For example, **QUOTIENT 9 4** RESULT: 2 **QUOTIENT 9.2 4.9** RESULT: 1
RANDOM	Takes one input, a natural number n. Outputs an integer between 0 and n-1 inclusive.
RANDOMIZE	Takes no inputs. Randomizes the sequence that is generated by calls to **RANDOM**.
RC?	Takes no inputs. Outputs TRUE if the buffer is not empty and FALSE otherwise.
*READ	Takes a file name as input. Reads the file with the input name from the disk in the disk drive. For example, **READ "SEQUENCES** (Reads the file named **SEQUENCES** from the disk in the disk drive.) *In Terrapin Logo version 2.0, Apple Logo files can be read into Terrapin Logo using the **READ** primitive.*
READCHARACTER (RC)	Takes no inputs. Outputs the first character in the character buffer and waits for a character to be entered into the buffer if the buffer is empty.
READPICT	Takes one input. Reads the picture with the input name from the disk and displays it on the screen. For example, **READPICT "HOUSE** (Reads the picture whose name is HOUSE and displays it on the screen.)
REMAINDER	Requires two number inputs and rounds them to integers if necessary. If the inputs are positive, outputs the remainder obtained when the first integer is divided by the second. For example, **REMAINDER 13 7** RESULT: 6 **REMAINDER 13.8 7.2** RESULT: 0
REPEAT	Takes a number and a list as input. Executes the instructions in the list the designated number of times. For example, **REPEAT 4 [FD 100 RT 90]**

REQUEST (RQ)	Accepts an input that the user types and outputs it as a list.
RIGHT (RT)	Takes one input. Turns the turtle right from its present heading the number of degrees that are input. For example, RT 90 (Turns the turtle right 90 degrees.)
ROUND	Requires one numeric input. Outputs the integer nearest to its input. When ROUND is applied to a number with only 5 after the decimal point, as in 7.5, the result is the nearest integer greater than the number if the number is positive and the nearest integer less than the number if the number is negative. For example, ROUND 12.8 RESULT:　13 ROUND −12.5 RESULT:　−13
*SAVE	Takes one input. Saves the contents of the workspace on disk under the input name. For example, SAVE "FILE.1 (Saves the contents of the workspace on disk under the file named FILE.1.) *In Terrapin Logo version 2.0, SAVE can be used to save selected procedures from the workspace; for example, SAVE "POLYGONS [SQUARE TRIANGLE PENTAGON].
SAVEPICT	Takes one input. Saves the picture on the screen to the disk under the input name. For example, SAVEPICT "HOUSE (Saves on disk the picture on the screen in a file named HOUSE.)
SENTENCE (SE)	Takes two inputs (may take more if parentheses are used) and outputs all the inputs into a single list. For example, SE "GO "ON RESULT:　[GO ON] SE [HOW ARE] "YOU RESULT:　[HOW ARE YOU]
SETHEADING (SETH)	Takes one number input and rotates the turtle to point in the direction specified. For example, SETH 180 (Rotates the turtle until it has heading of 180, regardless of its initial heading.)

SETX	Takes one number input and moves the turtle horizontally to the point with that x-coordinate. Draws a trail if the pen is down.
SETXY	Takes two number inputs, **A** and **B**, and moves the turtle to the point with the given coordinates (A,B). Draws a trail if the pen is down. For example, **SETXY 70 40** (Moves the turtle to the point whose x-coordinate is 70 and whose y-coordinate is 40.)
SETY	Takes one number input and moves the turtle vertically to the point with that y-coordinate. Draws a trail if the pen is down.
SHOWTURTLE (ST)	Needs no input. Causes the turtle to reappear.
SIN	Takes one input as an angle in degrees and outputs the sine of the angle. For example, **SIN 30** RESULT: .5
SPLITSCREEN (CTRL-S)	Takes no inputs. In the draw mode, gives a mixed graphics and text display.
SQRT	Takes one positive number input and yields the square root of that input. For example, **SQRT 3** RESULT: 1.73205
STOP	Takes no inputs. Causes the current procedure to stop and returns control to the calling procedure.
TEST	Takes one input, a condition, and checks the condition for truth or falsity. Execution of subsequent lines depends upon the result of the test. For example, **TEST (SQRT 2)/2<(SQRT 3)/3** **IFTRUE PR "TRUE** **IFFALSE PR "FALSE** FALSE
TEXTSCREEN (CTRL-T)	Takes no input. In the draw mode, gives a full text screen.
TO	Takes the name of a procedure as input and causes Logo to enter the edit mode.
TOPLEVEL	Stops the current procedure and all calling procedures.
TOWARDS	Takes two number inputs, which are interpreted as x- and y-coordinates of a point, and outputs the heading from the turtle to that point. For example, **DRAW** **TOWARDS 0 (−10)** RESULT: 180

TRACE	Takes no inputs. Causes the computer to wait for a character to be typed before executing a procedure line. Any character except CTRL-G and CTRL-Z may be used to cause execution of the next line. TRACE can be included in a procedure before the line where you want tracing to begin.
WORD	Takes two word inputs (may take more if parentheses are used) and outputs one word composed of the inputs. For example, WORD "EN "GLAND RESULT: ENGLAND (WORD "MA "THE "MATICS) RESULT: MATHEMATICS
WORD?	Takes one input and outputs TRUE if that input is a word, FALSE otherwise. For example, WORD? "FXR RESULT: TRUE WORD? 5 RESULT: TRUE WORD? [FXR] RESULT: FALSE
WRAP	Takes no inputs. Causes the turtle to "wrap around" the screen when commands take the turtle off the screen.
XCOR	Takes no inputs. Outputs the turtle's current x-coordinate.
YCOR	Takes no inputs. Outputs the turtle's current y-coordinate.

Editing Commands

*ESC	This is called the ESCAPE key. It causes the character immediately to the left of the cursor to be rubbed out and then moves the cursor one space to the left. *On the Apple IIe and IIc with version 2.0 Terrapin Logo, the DELETE key acts like the ESC key.
→ or ←	These keys move the cursor one space right or left, respectively, without erasing any characters.
*REPT	This is called the REPEAT key. Holding the REPT key down and pressing any other key causes the

character generated by the other key to be transmitted as long as the two keys are held down.

The Apple IIe and IIc do not have a REPT key. Instead they have an automatic repeat feature that is activated by holding down the key to be repeated.

CTRL-A	Moves the cursor to the beginning of the current line.
CTRL-B	Scrolls the text backward (window moves up).
CTRL-C	Exits the editor and processes the edited text.
CTRL-D	Deletes the character over which the cursor is flashing.
CTRL-E	Moves the cursor to the end of the current line (E stands for "end").
CTRL-F	Scrolls the text forward.
CTRL-G	Exits the editor and does not process the text.
*CTRL-K	Deletes all the characters on the current line, beneath and to the right of the cursor (K stands for "kill").

In Terrapin Logo version 2.0, CTRL-X is used instead of CTRL-K to delete all the characters on a line.

CTRL-L	Scrolls the text so that the line containing the cursor is approximately on the center of the screen.
CTRL-N	Moves the cursor down one line (N stands for "next").
CTRL-O	Opens a new line at the position of the cursor (O stands for "open").
CTRL-P	Moves the cursor up one line (P stands for "previous").
CTRL-Y	In Terrapin Logo version 2.0, the most recently deleted line can be "yanked" back into the editor with CTRL-Y.

Non-Editing Control Characters

CTRL-F	In graphics mode, acts like **FULLSCREEN**—gives full graphics screen.
CTRL-G	Causes Logo to stop and waits for a new command. The message STOPPED! appears on the screen.
CTRL-P	Takes no inputs. In the draw or nodraw mode, in many cases it causes the previously typed line to be retyped. Type RETURN to execute the line.

CTRL-S	Takes no inputs. Acts like **SPLITSCREEN**. In the draw mode, it gives a mixed graphics and text display.
CTRL-T	Takes no inputs. Acts like **TEXTSCREEN**. In the draw mode, it gives a full text screen.
CTRL-W	Stops the screen from scrolling. Repeated typing of CTRL-W causes Logo to stop after printing the next line (or next list element). Typing another character will resume normal processing.
CTRL-Z	Causes a procedure to pause. Can be used while the procedure is running. Allows commands to be inserted. Execution of procedure can be continued by typing **CONTINUE (CO)**.

Shape Editor Commands

CTRL-C	Exits the editor and defines the shape.
CTRL-G	Exits the editor without defining the shape.
CTRL-N	Moves down and draws a segment if the pen is down.
CTRL-P	Moves up and draws a segment if the pen is down.
D	Puts the pen down.
SIZE	Takes a positive integer as input and changes the size of the current shape according to that number.
U	Puts the pen up.
1...9	Specifies **SIZE** in the Shape Editor; for example, typing 5 is equivalent to typing **SIZE 5**.

Error Messages

When a programming error occurs while a procedure is running, the execution of the procedure is halted and an error message is printed. Error messages may also appear in other situations. In this section of the glossary we list the most commonly encountered error messages and describe the reasons for their occurrence.

- THERE IS NO PROCEDURE NAMED . . .(name of procedure), IN LINE . . .(the line in which the error occurred.)
  AT LEVEL . . .(level number is given) OF . . .(the name of the procedure)

This occurs when a procedure is run and Logo does not recognize a name of a called procedure or it does not understand the directions and "thinks" that you called a procedure but it does not find its name in the workspace. For example, suppose the **FAN** and **SQUARE** procedures are defined and **FAN** is executed.

```
TO FAN
REPEAT 10 [SQUARE RT 36]
END
TO SQUARE
REPEAT 4 [FD 50 RT 90]
END
```

```
FAN
THERE IS NO PROCEDURE NAMED FD50, IN LINE
  REPEAT 4 [FD50 RT 90]
AT LEVEL 2 OF SQUARE
```

Here Logo "thinks" that FD50 is a name of a procedure (notice the lack of space between FD and 50.) Because no such procedure is found in the computer memory, Logo prints the error message. LEVEL 2 in the error message indicates that the error occurred in the called procedure (second procedure). This type of error message along with level numbers is discussed in more detail in Section 2-3.

• THERE IS NO PROCEDURE NAMED...

This occurs when Logo does not recognize the name of a procedure that the user tries to run. For example,

```
RIHT 90
THERE IS NO PROCEDURE NAMED RIHT
```

Here the user typed RIHT instead of RIGHT. Consequently Logo "thought" that RIHT was the name of a procedure.

• THERE IS NO NAME...

This occurs when the user refers to the value of a name, but there is no such name in the workspace. For example, assume the workspace is empty and the following is typed:

```
MAKE "M 3
PRINT :N
THERE IS NO NAME N
```

• ...(name of procedure) NEEDS MORE INPUTS

This happens when a procedure was called with fewer inputs than the number of variables in its title. For example,

```
TO RECT :W :L
REPEAT 2 [FD :W RT 90 FD :L RT 90]
END
```

```
RECT 50
RECT NEEDS MORE INPUTS
```

• MISSING INPUTS INSIDE ( )' S

Here Logo tells us that the procedure with insufficient inputs occurred within a parenthetical expression. For example,

```
TO AVE :X :Y
OUTPUT (:X + :Y)/2
END
```

(2 + AVE 5)/3
MISSING INPUTS INSIDE ( )' S

● YOU DON'T SAY WHAT TO DO WITH...

This message is given when a procedure generates some data but no instructions are given about what to do with the data. Usually the commands **PRINT** or **OUTPUT** should have been included but were omitted. For example,

TO POWER2 :X
:X*:X
END

POWER2 7
YOU DON'T SAY WHAT TO DO WITH 49, IN LINE
  :X*:X
AT LEVEL 1 OF POWER2

It is important to keep in mind that outside a procedure Logo will print RESULT rather than an error message when **PRINT** or **OUTPUT** is omitted. (In a procedure, whenever **OUTPUT** is used before the data to be generated, Logo displays the answer preceded by RESULT.) For example,

7*7
RESULT: 49

Users sometimes forget to include **OUTPUT** in recursive procedures. For example,

TO POWER :BASE :EXP
IF "EXP=0 OUTPUT 1
:BASE*(POWER :BASE :EXP-1)
END

POWER 3 4
YOU DON'T SAY WHAT TO DO WITH 3, IN LINE
  :BASE*(POWER :BASE :EXP-1)
AT LEVEL 4 OF POWER

One way to edit the **POWER** procedure so that it will work is to include **OUTPUT** at the beginning of the line :BASE*(POWER :BASE :EXP-1)

● ...(name of a procedure) DIDN'T OUTPUT

This occurs when the user attempts to use a value generated by a procedure but the procedure did not output any value. For example,

TO POW :X
PRINT :X*:X
END

FD POW 6
36
POW DIDN'T OUTPUT

Here the number 36 generated by POW 6 is printed on the screen but is not accessible to FD. To make the value accessible to FD, PRINT should be replaced by OUTPUT.

- NO STORAGE LEFT

This occurs when all the available storage has been used. For example, consider executing the POWER procedure mentioned earlier (and developed in Section 6-2) for large exponents, as in the following:

POWER 2 100
NO STORAGE LEFT! IN LINE
  OUTPUT :BASE*(POWER :BASE :EXP-1)
AT LEVEL 56 OF POWER

In this case, when POWER 2 100 is executed, all the available storage has been used by the time 55 procedures have been called; no storage is left to complete the computation.

- . . .(name of Logo primitive) DOESN'T LIKE (data) AS INPUT

This occurs when the user asks the computer to do an operation with data that the computer does not know how to handle. For example,

TO POW :X
PRINT :X*:X
END

POW "A
DOESN'T LIKE A AS INPUT, IN LINE
  PRINT :X*:X
AT LEVEL 1 OF POW

- . . .(name) IS A LOGO PRIMITIVE

This occurs when the user tries to use a Logo primitive as the name of a procedure.

- CAN'T DIVIDE BY ZERO

Occurs whenever there is an attempt to divide by 0 and an output is expected.

- NUMBER OUT OF RANGE

Occurs when an operation generates a number too small or too great for Logo to handle.

- TOO MUCH INSIDE PARENTHESES

This message is given when Logo doesn't "comprehend" the meaning of parentheses. For example,

PRINT 7*(9-8((8)
TOO MUCH INSIDE PARENTHESES

- TURTLE OUT OF BOUNDS

This occurs when Logo is in NOWRAP mode and the turtle is moved beyond the screen boundary.

- FILE NOT FOUND

Occurs when the user tries to read the name of a file not on the disk in the disk drive.

- THE DISK IS FULL

Occurs when the user tries to save a file but there is no more space on the disk.

- THE FILE IS LOCKED

This happens when the user tries to erase or make changes in a file that is locked. (See your Apple DOS manual for information on locking and unlocking files.)

- DISK ERROR

This error message occurs if the user forgets to put a disk in the disk drive or in case of some unidentified disk error.

- (name of Logo primitive) SHOULD BE USED ONLY INSIDE A PROCEDURE

This occurs if **OUTPUT** or **STOP** commands are used outside a procedure.

- END SHOULD BE USED ONLY IN THE EDITOR

This occurs if **END** is used in a procedure line other than the last statement. For example,

```
TO POLY :S :A
IF HEADING = 0 END
POLY :S :A
END

POLY 50 30
END SHOULD BE USED ONLY IN THE EDITOR
```

- THE DISK IS WRITE PROTECTED

Occurs when the user tries to save some work on a write-protected disk.

Select Bibliography

Books

Abelson, Harold. *Apple Logo*. New York: McGraw-Hill, 1982.

—————— . *Logo for the Apple II*. New York: McGraw-Hill, 1982.

—————— . *TI Logo*. New York: McGraw-Hill, 1982.

Abelson, Harold, and diSessa, Andrea. *Turtle Geometry: The Computer as a Medium for Exploring Mathematics*. Cambridge: MIT Press, 1981.

Allen, John, et al. *Thinking About [TLC] Logo*. New York: Holt, Rinehart and Winston, 1983.

Babbie, Earl. *Apple Logo for Teachers*. Belmont, CA: Wadsworth Publishing Company, 1984.

Bailey, Harold, et al. *Apple Logo: Activities for Exploring Turtle Graphics*. Bowie, MD: Brady Communications Company, 1984.

Bearden, Donna. *A Bit of Logo Magic*. Reston, VA: Reston Publishing Company, 1983.

—————— . *1, 2, 3, My Computer and Me: A Logo Funbook for Kids*. Reston, VA: Reston Publishing Company, 1983.

Bearden, Donna, et al. *The Turtle Sourcebook*. Reston, VA: Reston Publishing Company, 1983.

Bitter, Gary, and Watson, Nancy. *Apple Logo Primer*. Reston, VA: Reston Publishing Company, 1983.

—————— . *Commodore 64 Logo Primer*. Reston, VA: Reston Publishing Company, 1983.

—————— . *CyberLogo Primer*. Reston, VA: Reston Publishing Company, 1983.

Burnett, Dale. *Logo: An Introduction for Teachers*. Morris Plains, NJ: Creative Computing Press, 1982.

Conlan, Jim, and Inman, Don. *Sprites, a Turtle, and TI Logo*. Reston, VA: Reston Publishing Company, 1983.

Kwok, Annie, et al. *The Workbook for Learning Logo*. Montreal: Turtle Publishing, 1983.

Martin, Kathleen, and Bearden, Donna. *Polyspi—Inspi*. Irving, TX: Martin-Bearden, Inc., 1983.

——————— . *Primarily Logo.* Reston, VA: Reston Publishing Company, 1984.

——————— . *The Rule of 360.* Irving, TX: Martin-Bearden, Inc., 1983.

——————— . *The Turtle Goes to Kindergarten.* Irving, TX: Martin-Bearden, Inc., 1984.

Moore, Margaret. *Geometry Problems for Logo Discoveries.* Palo Alto, CA: Creative Publications, 1984.

——————— . *Logo Discoveries.* Palo Alto, CA: Creative Publications, 1984.

Muller, Jim. *Logo Discoveries,* Reston, VA: Reston Publishing Company, 1983.

Papert, Seymour. *Mindstorms: Computers, Children, and Powerful Ideas.* New York: Basic Books, 1980.

Ross, Peter. *Introducing Logo for the Texas Instruments 99/4A, Tandy Color Computer, and the Apple II Computer.* Menlo Park, CA: Addison-Wesley, 1983.

Rowley, Tom, and Leckrone, Ron. *The Big Trak Book: Your Computer on Wheels.* Reston, VA: Reston Publishing Company, 1983.

Sharp, Pamela. *Cyberlogo Turtle: A First Step in Computer Literacy.* Reston, VA: Reston Publishing Company, 1983.

——————— . *TURTLESTEPS: An Introduction to Apple Logo and Terrapin Logo.* Bowie, MD: Brady Communications Company, 1984.

——————— . *TURTLESTEPS: An Introduction to Atari Logo.* Bowie, MD: Brady Communications Company, 1984.

——————— . *TURTLESTEPS: An Introduction to IBM Logo and Dr. Logo.* Bowie, MD: Brady Communications Company, 1984.

Stranger, Donna, et al. *Learning Through Logo.* Pleasantville, NY: Sunburst Communications, 1983.

Thornburg, David. *Computer Art and Animation: A User's Guide to TI 99/4A Color Logo.* Meno Park, CA: Addison-Wesley, 1983.

——————— . *Discovering Apple Logo: An Invitation to the Art and Pattern of Nature.* Menlo Park, CA: Addison-Wesley, 1983.

Torgerson, Shirley. *Logo in the Classroom.* Eugene, OR: International Council for Computers in Education, 1984.

Watt, Dan. *Learning with Apple Logo.* New York: McGraw-Hill, 1983.

——————— . *Learning with Atari Logo.* New York: McGraw-Hill, 1983.

——————— . *Learning with Commodore Logo.* New York: McGraw-Hill, 1983.

——————— . *Learning with Logo.* New York: McGraw-Hill, 1983.

Articles

Abbott, Hilton. "Three Key Logo." *Classroom Computer News,* May/June, 1983.

Abelson, Harold. "A Beginner's Guide to Logo." *Byte*, August, 1982.

Adams, Roe. "The New Shell Game." *Softalk*, July, 1982.

Anderson, Judy, et al. "In-Service Workshop, Part VI, Programming in Logo." *Electronic Learning*, March, 1984.

Bamberger, Jeanne. "Logo Music." *Byte*, August, 1982.

Bandelier, Nellie. "TI Logo and First Graders—A Winning Combination." *The Computing Teacher*, November, 1983.

Barnes, B.J., and Hill, Shirley. "Should Young Children Work with Microcomputers—Logo before Lego™?" *The Computing Teacher*, May, 1983.

Bearden, Donna. "Optical Illusions—A Challenge in Problem Solving." *The Computing Teacher*, December 1983/January, 1984.

Bearden, Donna, and Muller, Jim. "Logo Talks Back." *inCider*, September, 1983.

_____ . "Turtle Graphics: On and Off the Screen." *Classroom Computer News*, April, 1983.

Bies, Richard. "Vectors in Logo: Of Stars and Sprites." *99'er Home Computer Magazine*, February, 1983.

Billstein, Rick. "Learning Logo and Liking It." *The Computing Teacher*, November, 1983.

_____ . "Turtle Geography." *Classroom Computer Learning*, October, 1983.

Billstein, Rick, and Moore, Margaret L. "Recursion, Recursion." *The Computing Teacher*, December, 1983/January, 1984.

Birch, Louisa. "The Turtle's Corner." *Classroom Computer News*, April, 1983.

Bull, Glen. "Microworlds: Design of a Language." *The Computing Teacher*, November, 1983.

Burrowes, Sharon. "Some Logo Drawing Ideas." *The Computing Teacher*, April, 1983.

Bussey, Jim. "Logo: A Language for Everyone." *Commodore: The Microcomputer Magazine*, April/May, 1983.

Cannara, A.B. "Toward a Human Computer Language." *Creative Computing*, May, 1975.

Carlin, James B. "The Turtle and the Children at Center State." *Childhood Education*, November/December, 1981.

Carter, Ricky. "The Complete Guide to Logo." *Classroom Computer News*, April, 1983.

_____ . "Logo and the Great Debate." *Kilobaud Microcomputing*, September, 1981.

_____ . "Turtle Topics: Drawing Polygons." *Classroom Computer News*, April, 1983.

Chace, Susan. "Technology: New Language Eases Writing of Microcomputer Programs." *Wall Street Journal,* August 27, 1982.

Chumley, James. "The Turtle as Tutor." *PCjr Magazine,* April, 1984.

Clarke, Valerie. "Children's Perception of Logo." *COM3 Magazine,* August, 1983.

Clements, Douglas H. "Supporting Young Children's Logo Programming." *The Computing Teacher,* December, 1983/January, 1984.

Cron, Mary. "Trouble In Logoland." *Teaching, Learning, Computing,* December, 1983.

diSessa, Andrea A., and White, Barbara Y. "Learning Physics from a Dynaturtle." *Byte,* August, 1982.

Dyrli, Odvard E. "Logo, a Language that Empowers Children." *Learning,* October, 1983.

Euchner, C. "Debate Grows on Logo's Effect on Children's Reasoning Skills." *Education Week,* November 23, 1983.

Eyster, Richard H. "Seymour Papert and the Logo Universe." *Creative Computing,* December, 1981.

Fagan, Edward. "Writing/Reading: Logo's Syntonic Learning." *The Computing Teacher,* April, 1983.

Feurzeig, Wallace, and Lukas, George. "Logo—A Programming Language for Teaching Mathematics." *Educational Technology,* March, 1972.

Friedland, Edward I., and Friedland, Mark. "The Future of Logo." *TurtleTalk,* Winter, 1984.

Goldenberg, E. Paul. "Logo—A Cultural Glossary." *Byte,* August, 1982.

Goldberg, Kenneth P. "Different Versions of Logo." *Family Computing Magazine,* February, 1984.

Goodman, Danny. "Logo: A Language for Children of All Ages." *PC Magazine,* December, 1982.

Goodman, William. "Logo Goes to Camp." *Info Age,* November, 1982.

Gorman, Henry, Jr. "The Basic Issue and the Tortoise's Retort." *99'er Home Computer Magazine,* May, 1983.

—————. "Lamplighter Project." *Byte,* August, 1982.

Grant, June, and Semmes, P. "A Rationale for Logo for Hearing Impaired Preschoolers." *American Annals of the Deaf,* Vol. 128, No. 5, 1983.

Harris, Ross J. "An A-Mazing Logo Experiment." *Hands On!,* Summer, 1983.

Harvey, Brian. "Why Logo?" *Byte,* August, 1982.

Hawkins, J., et al. "Microcomputers in Schools: Impact on the Social Life of Elementary Classrooms." *Journal of Applied Developmental Psychology,* Vol. 3, 1982.

Hayes, Brian. "Computer Recreations: Turning Turtle Gives One a View of Geometry from the Inside Out." *Scientific American,* February, 1983.

Jewson, Jan, and Pea, Roy D. "Logo Research at Bank Street College." *Byte*, August, 1982.

Kelman, Peter. "Journey Through Mathland: An Interview with Seymour Papert." *Classroom Computer News*, March/April, 1981.

—————— . "Seymour, Has Your Dream Come True?" *Classroom Computer News*, April, 1983.

Kildall, Gary, and Thornburg, David. "Digital Research's DR Logo." *Byte*, June, 1983.

Kramer, Sharon. "Word Processing in a Logo Environment." *Electronic Learning*, March, 1984.

Lamster, Jane, and Lamster, Hal. "Logo: A Language for Grown-ups, Too." *PC Magazine*, May 15, 1984.

Lough, Tom. "A Cure for Recursion." *The Computing Teacher*, December, 1983/January, 1984.

—————— . "Exploring New Horizons with Logo: How One School Is Charting the Course. Part II." *Electronic Learning*, April, 1983.

—————— . "WATERCROSS: A Logo Exploration." *The Computing Teacher*, November, 1983.

—————— . "Where Is Logo?" *The Computing Teacher*, December, 1983/January, 1984.

Lough, Tom, and Tipps, Steve. "Is There Logo After Turtle Graphics?" *Classroom Computer News*, April, 1983.

Lowd, Beth. "Hints on Introducing Logo in the Classroom." *Classroom Computer News*, March, 1983.

Mace, Scott. "Papert Keynotes Computer Faire." *Infoworld*, March, 1982.

—————— . "Where Is Logo Taking Our Kids?" *Infoworld*, January, 1984.

Markoff, John. "Logo Overturns Old Computer Education Models." *Infoworld*, December, 1981.

—————— . "Logo Fever: The Computer Language Every School Is Catching." *Arithmetic Teacher*, September, 1983.

Martin, Kathleen, et al. " Turtle Graphics On and Off the Computer." *The Computing Teacher*, November, 1983.

Martin, Kathleen, and Berner, Andrew. "Teaching Turtles." *The Computing Teacher*, November, 1983.

McCauley, Jim. "Kepler." *The Computing Teacher*, December, 1983/January, 1984.

McLeod, J. "Take the Turtle to School: A Child's View of Programming." *Classroom Computer Learning*, November/December, 1983.

McLees, Jock. "Where Do Turtles Come From?" *Kilobaud Microcomputing*, March, 1982.

Min-Chih, Earl. "Logo for the IBM PC, Part 1: Waterloo Logo." *TurtleTalk*, Winter, 1984.

Moore, Margaret L. "A Recursion Excursion with a Surprising Discovery." *The Computing Teacher*, December, 1983/January, 1984.

Moore, Mary Jo. "The Art of Teaching Logo, or When and When Not to Bother the Learner." *Hands On!*, Spring, 1983.

————— . "The Art of Teaching Logo." *Classroom Computer News*, April, 1983.

Moursund, David. "Logo Frightens Me." *The Computing Teacher*, December, 1983/January, 1984.

Menconi, Dave, and Richards, Ted. "Logo vs. BASIC: Which Language Is Best?" *Atari Connection*, Fall, 1983.

Muller, Jim. "Dumping the Turtle." *The Computing Teacher*, December, 1983/January, 1984.

————— . "The Friendly Languages." *Creative Computing*, October, 1981.

————— . "Logo, for the Imagination." *Infoworld*, March, 1982.

————— . "The Million Dollar Smile." *The Computing Teacher*, February, 1983.

————— . "No Threshold, No Ceiling . . . Really!" *The Computing Teacher*, December, 1983/January, 1984.

————— . "What Can the Computer and the YPLA Do for Handicapped Children?" *The Computing Teacher*, November, 1983.

Nelson, Harold. "Learning with Logo." *onComputing*, Summer, 1981.

————— . "Logo for Personal Computers." *Byte*, June, 1981.

————— . "Logo: Not Just for Kids." *Microcomputing*, March, 1982.

Nelson, Harold, and Friedman, Rich. "Seymour Papert: Spearheading the Computer Revolution." *onComputing*, Summer, 1981.

Olds, Henry F., Jr. "Through a New Looking Glass." *Kilobaud Microcomputing*, September, 1981.

————— . "The Year of the Turtle." *Classroom Computer News*, April, 1983.

Pantiel, Mindy, and Peterson, Becky. "Learning Logo Is a Family Affair." *Family Computing Magazine*, February, 1984.

Papert, Seymour. "And a Little Child Shall Lead Them." *Instructional Innovator*, February, 1982.

————— . "Computers and Computer Cultures." *Creative Computing*, March, 1981.

————— . "Micros Becoming a Social Force." *Infoworld*, April, 1982.

————— . "New Cultures from New Technologies." *Byte*, September, 1981.

————— . "Society Will Balk, but the Future May Demand a Computer for Each Child." *Electronic Education*, September, 1981.

Raleigh, Lisa. "Logo Isn't Just for Kids Anymore." *ISO World*, November 14, 1983.

Raskin, B. "Logo for the Reluctant Learner—Me." *Learning*, October, 1983.

Riordon, Tim. "Creating a Logo Environment." *The Computing Teacher*, November, 1983.

—————— . "Helping Students with Recursion: Teaching Strategies. Part I: Introducing Recursion with Non-Computer Recursive Experiences." *The Computing Teacher*, December, 1983/January, 1984.

—————— . "Helping Students with Recursion: Teaching Strategies. Part II: Moving to the Computer." *The Computing Teacher*, February, 1984.

—————— . "Helping Students with Recursion: Teaching Strategies. Part III: Teaching Students about Embedded Recursion." *The Computing Teacher*, March, 1984.

Rosch, Winn L. "Logo: The Advanced Course." *PCjr Magazine*, April, 1984.

Rousseau, J., and Smith, S. "Whither Goes the Turtle?" *Kilobaud Microcomputing*, September, 1981.

Russell, Susan Jo. "Had We but World Enough and Time: Logo in Special Education." *Classroom Computer Learning*, October, 1983.

Sandberg-Diment, Eric. "Logo, the Friendliest Language." *Science Digest*, November, 1983.

Solomon, Cynthia. "Introducing Logo to Children." *Byte*, August, 1982.

Stavely, Tony. "List Processing in Logo." *The Computing Teacher*, December, 1982.

Strausberg, Robin. "Helping the Girls Catch Up." *Teaching, Learning, Computing*, March, 1984.

Steffin, Sherwin A. "A Challenge to Seymour Papert." *Educational Computer*, July/August, 1982.

—————— . "The Instructional Applicability of Logo." *Classroom Computer News*, April, 1983.

Stone, Greg. "Of Cats and Turtles in Mathland." *inCider*, June, 1983.

—————— . "Solving Problems with Logo." *inCider*, April, 1983.

—————— . "Solving Problems with Logo, Part II." *inCider*, May, 1983.

Streibel, M. "The Educational Utility of Logo." *School Science and Mathematics*, October, 1983.

Sullivan, Nick. "The Man Behind Logo." *Family Computing Magazine*, February, 1984.

Swaine, Michael. "Young People Race to the Future on the Shoulders of Turtles." *Infoworld*, November, 1981.

Sweetnam, G.K. "Turtle Talk (Logo for Children)." *Science Digest*, November, 1982.

Swett, Sheila. "Logo Offspring: A Look at Modified Versions of Logo and Turtle Graphics Programs." *Electronic Learning*, May/June, 1983.

Todd, Nancy. "Hello Logo." *Educational Computer*, March/April, 1983.

Torgerson, Shirley. "Classroom Management for Logo." *The Computing Teacher*, December, 1983/January, 1984.

Torgerson, Shirley, et al. "Logo in the Classroom, Session 1." *The Computing Teacher*, December, 1983/January, 1984.

Upitis, Rena. "Logo and the Primary-Junior Pupil: One Student's First Encounter." *The Computing Teacher*, November, 1983.

_____ . "Turtle Talk." *The Computing Teacher*, November, 1983.

Vidya, S. "Using Logo to Stimulate Children's Fantasy." *Educational Technology*, December, 1983.

Voderberg, Hank. "Use Logo Graphics in Your BASIC Program." *The Computing Teacher*, March, 1984.

Watt, Dan. "A Comparison of the Problem Solving Styles of Two Students Learning Logo: A Computer Language for Children." *Creative Computing*, December, 1979.

_____ . "Learning with Logo." *Classroom Computer News*, April, 1984.

_____ . "Logo: What Makes it Exciting?" *Popular Computing*, September, 1982.

_____ . "Logo in the Schools." *Byte*, August, 1982.

_____ . "Should Children Be Computer Programmers?" *Popular Computing*, September, 1982.

_____ . "Teaching Turtles: Logo as an Environment for Learning." *Popular Computing*, July, 1982.

Watt, Molly. "Logo Building Blocks." *inCider*, January, 1984.

_____ . "De-Bug Collection." *inCider*, February, 1984.

_____ . "Logo: Where's the Pony?" *inCider*, March, 1984.

_____ . "What Is Logo?" *Creative Computing*, October, 1982.

Weinreb, William. "Problem Solving with Logo: Using Turtle Graphics to Redraw a Design." *Byte*, November, 1982.

Weir, Sylvia. "Logo: A Learning Environment for the Severely Handicapped." *Journal of Special Education Technology*, Winter, 1982.

_____ . "Logo and the Exceptional Child." *Kilobaud Microcomputing*, May, 1981.

Weir, Sylvia, et al. "Logo: An Approach to Educating Disabled Children." *Byte*, September, 1982.

Weir, Sylvia, and Watt, Dan. "Logo: A Computer Environment for Learning Disabled Students." *The Computing Teacher*, January, 1981.

Wierzbicki, Barbara. "The Success of Logo Hinges on Teacher Training." *Infoworld*, January, 1984.

Williams, Gregg. "Logo for the Apple II, the TI-99/4A, and the TRS-80 Color Computer." *Byte*, August, 1982.

Periodicals

Logo Periodicals

DR. Logo Newsletter. Digital Research, P.O. Box 579, Pacific Grove, CA 93950.

FOLKlore. P.O. Box 22094, San Francisco, CA 94122.

Logo and Educational Computing Journal. 1320 Stony Brook Road, Stony Brook, NY 11790.

Logophile. College of Education, MacArthur Hall, Queen's University, Kingston, Ontario, Canada K7L 3N6.

Logos, British Logo User Group. 33 Croft Gardens, Old Dalby, Melton Mowbray, Leicestershire LE14 3LE, England.

The National Logo Exchange Newsletter. P.O. Box 5341, Charlottesville, VA 22905.

Polyspiral. Boston Computer Society, Three Center Plaza, Boston, MA 02108.

TI Source and Logo News. Microcomputer Corporation, 34 Maple Avenue, Armonk, NY 10504.

Turtle News. Young People's Logo Association, P.O. Box 855067, Richardson, TX 75085.

TurtleTalk. 955 Greenwood Boulevard, Issaquah, WA 98027.

Periodicals with Regular Logo Features

Closing the Gap: Microcomputers for the Handicapped. P.O. Box 68, Henderson, MN 56014. Logo column by Griff Wigley.

COMPUTE! P.O. Box 5406, Greensboro, NC 27403. Logo column, "Friends of the Turtle," by David Thornburg.

The Computing Teacher. University of Oregon, 1787 Agate Street, Eugene, OR 97403. Logo column, "The Logo Center," by Kathleen Martin and Tim Riordon.

Creative Computing. P.O. Box 789-M, Morristown, NJ 07960. Logo column, "Logo Ideas," by Robert Lawler.

Hands On! Technical Education Research Centers, 8 Eliot Street, Cambridge, MA 02138. Logo column by various staff members.

Home Computer Magazine. 1500 Valley River Drive, Suite 250, Eugene, OR 97401. "Logo Times," a section of short Logo articles, edited by Robert Ackerman.

Softalk. 7250 Laurel Canyon Boulevard, North Hollywood, CA 91602. Logo column, "The Voice of the Turtle," by Donna Bearden.

Teaching and Computers. Scholastic, Inc., 730 Broadway, New York, NY 10017. Logo column, "Logo Notebook," by Tom Lough and Steve Tipps.

Index

Abelson, Harold, 2, 3, 401, 402
absolute value, 201
algorithm, 288
Al-Khowarizmi, 288
ALLOF, 203, 208, 384
angle, obtuse, 107
animation, 303
ANYOF, 198, 208, 384
arc, 111
arrow keys, 13, 394
ATAN, 283, 384

BACK (BK), 16, 25, 384
BACKGROUND (BG), 117, 121, 384
backup copy, 74
BF (see BUTFIRST)
BG (see BACKGROUND)
BK (see BACK)
BL (see BUTLAST)
booting, 11
brackets, 12
bugs, 2
BUTFIRST (BF), 336, 341, 345, 385
BUTLAST (BL), 336, 341, 345, 385

Cartesian coordinate system, 179
CATALOG, 71, 76, 385
CHAMELEON, 378, 381
CHAR 7, 230
character buffer, 305
CHASE, 377, 381
circumference, 113
CLEARINPUT, 308, 313, 385
CLEARSCREEN (CS), 20, 26, 385
Closed Path Theorem, 105
CO (see CONTINUE)
color, 117
command lines, length of, 43
composite, 257
COPYA, 374, 380
conclusion, 135
congruent, 104
CONTINUE (CO), 98, 99, 385
CONTROL (CTRL), 13
COS, 283, 385
crash, 15
CS (see CLEARSCREEN)
CTRL, 385
CTRL-A, 45, 56, 395

CTRL-B, 53, 55, 56, 395
CTRL-C, 41, 318, 321, 395, 396
CTRL-D, 13, 395
CTRL-E, 45, 56, 395
CTRL-F, 53, 55, 56, 395; see also
    FULLSCREEN
CTRL-G, 24, 26, 318, 321, 395, 396
CTRL-K, 45, 56, 395
CTRL-L, 53, 56, 395
CTRL-N, 45, 56, 318, 321, 395, 396
CTRL-O, 45, 56, 395
CTRL-P, 23, 26, 45, 56, 318, 321, 395, 396
CTRL-RESET, 15
CTRL-S (see SPLITSCREEN)
CTRL-T (see TEXTSCREEN)
CTRL-W, 54, 55, 56, 396
CTRL-X, 56
CTRL-Y, 15, 395
CTRL-Z, 99, 385, 396
cursor, 11
CURSOR, 338, 341, 385

D, 318, 321, 396
DARTGAME, 376, 380
debugging, 2
decimal,
    repeating, 246
    terminating, 246
DELETE, 13
difference, 254
diSessa, Andrea, 2, 3, 401, 404
distance formula, 184
DRAW, 15, 25, 387
draw mode, 15

ED (see EDIT)
EDIT (ED), 45, 385
ED ALL (see EDIT ALL)
EDIT ALL, 52, 55, 386
edit mode, 40
EDIT NAMES, 386
EDIT PROCEDURES, 386
editor, 40
ELSE, 136, 140, 386
empty list, 344
END, 41, 43, 386
ER (see ERASE)
ERASE (ER), 54, 55, 56, 386
ER ALL (see ERASE ALL)

ERASE ALL (ER ALL), 55, 56, 386
ERASEFILE, 75, 76, 387
ERASEPICT, 75, 76, 387
ERASE NAMES, 386
ERASE PROCEDURES, 386
Error messages, 396-400
ESC, 13, 394
Euclidean Algorithm, 277
exponential notation, 239

FD (see FORWARD)
Fibonacci sequence, 363
file, 71
   locked, 380
FIRST, 336, 341, 345, 387
FORWARD (FD), 16, 25, 387
FPUT, 346, 348, 387
FULLSCREEN (CTRL-F), 20, 26, 387,
   395
fullscreen mode, 15

GOLF, 378, 381
GOODBYE, 10 14, 56, 387

heading, 15
HEADING, 18, 25, 387
HIDETURTLE (HT), 16, 25, 387
home, 15
HOME, 20, 26, 387
HT (see HIDETURTLE)
hypothesis, 135

IF, 135, 140, 388
IFF (see IFFALSE)
IFFALSE (IFF), 164, 166, 388
IFT (see IFTRUE)
IFTRUE (IFT), 164, 166, 388
initialize, 70
INITSHAPES, 319
input, 12
INTEGER, 237, 239, 388

LANDER, 378, 382
LAST, 336, 341, 345, 388
LCM (see least common multiple)
least common multiple (LCM), 260
LEFT (LT), 16, 25, 388
level number, 66
line segment, 184
LISP, 1
LIST, 344, 346, 348, 388
LIST?, 344, 348, 388
list processing, 331

Logo, 1
Logo Shape Editor, 317
LPUT, 346, 348, 389
LT (see LEFT)

MAKE, 145, 151, 389
memory, 10
   permanent, 70
microworld, 5
mode,
   draw, 15
   edit, 40
   fullscreen, 15
   nodraw, 11
   splitscreen, 15
multiple, 260

ND (see NODRAW)
N-factorial, 251
NODRAW (ND), 14, 25, 389
nodraw mode, 11
NOT, 166, 389
NOTRACE, 97, 99, 389
NOWRAP, 21, 26, 389
NUMBER?, 333, 341, 389
number,
   negative, 31
   rational, 276
   real, 236

operation,
   addition, 30
   division, 30
   multiplication, 30
   subtraction, 30
OP (see OUTPUT)
origin, 180
OUTPUT (OP), 189, 195, 389

PADDLE(0), 326, 389
PADDLE(1), 326, 389
palindrome, 338
Papert, Seymour, 1, 402, 406
PAUSE, 98, 99, 385, 390
PC (see PENCOLOR)
PD (see PENDOWN)
PENCOLOR (PC), 117, 121, 390
PENDOWN (PD), 16, 25
PENUP (PU), 16, 25
perimeter, 113
Piaget, Jean, 1
PO (see PRINTOUT)
PO ALL (see PRINTOUT ALL)

polygon,
  concave, 103
  convex, 102
  regular, 105
position, 15
POTS (see PRINTOUT TITLES)
primitive, 2
PR (see PRINT)
prime, 245
PRINT (PR), 11, 14, 31, 390
PRINT1, 248, 250, 335, 390
PRINTOUT (PO), 53, 54, 56, 390
PRINTOUT ALL (PO ALL), 54, 55, 56, 390
PRINTOUT NAMES, 390
PRINTOUT PROCEDURES, 390
PRINTOUT TITLES (POTS), 53, 55, 56, 390
procedure, 3, 39
  recursive, 131
programming, top-down, 62
prompt, 11
PU (see PENUP)
Pythagorean Theorem, 185

queue, 305
quotes,
  double, 331
  single, 336
QUOTIENT, 236, 239, 391

RANDOM, 118, 121, 263, 391
RANDOMIZE, 119, 121, 391
ratio, 254
RC (see READCHARACTER)
RC?, 307, 313, 391
READ, 73, 76, 391
READCHARACTER (RC), 306, 313, 391
READPICT, 75, 76, 391
recursion, 4, 131
  embedded, 162
  tail-end, 132
regular tessellation, 217
relatively prime, 276
REMAINDER, 236, 239, 391
REPEAT, 23, 26, 391
REPEAT key, 13, 395
repetend, 246
REPT (see REPEAT key)
REQUEST (RQ), 348, 392
RESET, 15
RETURN, 12
RIGHT (RT), 16, 25, 392
ROUND, 237, 239, 392
RT (see RIGHT)

SAVE, 73, 76, 392
SAVEPICT, 75, 76, 392
SE (see SENTENCE)
SENTENCE (SE), 347, 348, 392
sequence,
  arithmetic, 254
  Fibonacci, 255
  geometric, 254
SETH (see SETHEADING)
SETHEADING (SETH), 188, 195, 392
SETX, 180, 195, 393
SETXY, 182, 195, 393
SETY, 180, 195, 393
SHOWTURTLE (ST), 16, 25, 393
similar, 271
simplest form, 245
simulation, 287
SIN, 283, 393
SKETCH, 376, 380
software, 10
SPLITSCREEN (CTRL-S), 20, 26, 393, 396
splitscreen mode, 15
SQRT, 186, 195, 393
ST (see SHOWTURTLE)
STOP, 135, 140, 393

telescoping model, 160, 161
tessellate, 179
TEST, 164, 166, 393
TEXTSCREEN (CTRL-T), 20, 26, 393, 396
THEN, 135, 140, 388
TO, 40, 393
TOPLEVEL, 216, 225, 393
Total Turtle Trip Theorem, 105
TOWARDS, 187, 195, 393
TRACE, 96, 99, 394
triangle, equilateral, 46
turtle, 2, 15
Turtle Geometry, 2
turtle graphics, 2, 11

U, 318, 321
Utilities disk, 71

variables, 88
  global, 151
  local, 95

Walter, Grey, 2
word, 149, 331
  empty, 333

WORD, 333, 341, 394
WORD?, 333, 341, 394
workspace, 41
WRAP, 21, 26, 394

XCOR, 186, 195, 394

YCOR, 186, 195, 394

Index of Procedures

ABS, 202
ADD, 189
ADD1, 189
ADD2, 189
ADJECTIVE, 362
ADVERB, 362
ANIMATE, 304, 309, 311, 314, 315
ARTICLE, 362
ASA, 200
ASEQ, 255
AVERAGE, 241, 242
AVSQ, 241, 242

BE.BUG1, 300, 325
BE.BUG2, 300, 325
BE.BUG3, 301, 325
BE.BUG4, 301, 325
BE.BUG5, 326
BE.THE.FOX, 296
BE.THE.HARE, 296
BOAT, 65
BODY, 64
BOTTOM, 66
BOUNCE?, 230
BOUNDARY, 228
BUBBLES, 267
BUTTERFLY, 72

CHASE, 295
CHECK, 259, 304, 308, 309, 314
CHECKHEAD, 202
CHECKSIDE, 208
CHIMNEY, 80
CIR, 267
CIRCLE, 109

CIRCLE1, 194
CIRCLE2, 195
CLOSER?, 289
COMPARE, 315, 316
COMPUTE, 236
CORSQUARE, 189
COUNT, 359
CSQUARE, 119

DIAMOND, 44
DISTANCE, 190, 289
DISTANCE.ORIGIN, 311
DISTANCE2, 186
DOOR, 80
DOTTED, 43
DOWN, 158
DOWN1, 162

ELL, 95, 98
EXPERIMENT, 265

FCIRCLE, 111
FIB, 257
FIBONACCI, 364, 365
FILLCIR, 121
FILLRECT, 182
FRAME, 60, 79

GPOLY, 157

HEX, 52
HEXAGON, 223
HEXSTRIP, 224
HOUSE, 66, 81, 90, 92
HOUSE1, 97

INSPI, 155
INTERACT, 300, 325

L.ANTENNA, 72
LARC, 112
LCM, 261
LCM1, 261
LENGTH, 358

MAKESHAPE, 317
MESSAGE, 316
METRIC.HEIGHT, 238
MFACT, 350
MOTOR, 64
MOVE, 93, 229

NESTEDSQ, 280
NESTSQUARES, 91
NEWPOLY, 156
NEWPOLY1, 157
NEWTOWER, 151
NOUN, 362
NUM, 266

OFF.TRACK, 311

PAL, 339
PCIRCLE, 192
PENT, 52, 54
PENTAGON, 171
PICK, 359
PICKRANDOM, 361
PILE, 165
PLUS, 40, 41, 45
POLY, 132, 144, 270
POLYGON, 106
POLYHALT, 146
POLYROLL, 148
POLYSPI, 134, 154
POLYSPIRAL, 154
POLYSTOP, 144, 146
POWER, 244
POWER2, 241, 242
PRIME, 259
PROCEDURE1, 159
PROCEDURE2, 159
PROCEDURE3, 159
PROCESS, 253
PROLL, 148

RACK, 165
RAINBOW, 119
RANDOMCOORDINATE, 315
RANDOM.WALK, 266

R.ANTENNA, 72
RARC, 111
RCIRCLE, 114, 191
READKEY, 307, 314
RECTANGLE, 93
REPETEND1, 249
REVERSE, 339
ROLL, 165
ROOF, 79
ROW, 93
RVARC, 126

SANDH, 126
SAS, 198
SAVESHAPES, 318
SEARCH, 291
SEGMENT, 184, 353
SEMICIRCLE, 111
SEGSLOPE, 354
SENTENCE1, 361
SET, 268
SETSHAPE, 319
SETTURTLE, 229
SETUP, 213, 317
SETUP.M, 65
SETUP.W, 65
SHAPE, 164
SHAPE1, 166
SIZE, 136, 319, 396
SIZE1, 137
SLOPE, 351, 352
SPINPENT, 171
SQ., 66
SQUARE, 44, 80, 87, 89, 219
SQUAREBOUNCE, 230
SQUARESTRIP, 219
SQUARE2POINTS, 190
SSS, 206
STAR, 107, 210
STARSTRIP, 216
STARTUP, 362
STARTUP1, 292
STARTUP2, 296
STARTUP3, 302
STARTUP4, 309, 310, 321
STARTUP5, 315
STARTUP6, 323, 324
SUB, 158
SUN, 120
SWING, 60
SWING.SET, 61

TOSSES, 265
TOWER, 139, 371